STANDARDIZED
:   DEVELOPMENT
:   OF
:   COMPUTER
:   SOFTWARE

STANDARDIZED
: **DEVELOPMENT**
: **OF**
: **COMPUTER**
: **SOFTWARE**

Robert C. Tausworthe

Jet Propulsion Laboratory
California Institute of Technology
Pasadena, California

PRENTICE-HALL, Inc., Englewood Cliffs, New Jersey 07632

Published in 1977 by Prentice-Hall, Inc., Englewood Cliffs, New Jersey 07632

Printed in the United States of America

10   9   8   7   6   5   4   3   2   1

ISBN: 0-13-842195-1

PRENTICE-HALL INTERNATIONAL, INC., *London*
PRENTICE-HALL OF AUSTRALIA PTY. LIMITED, *Sydney*
PRENTICE-HALL OF CANADA, PTD., *Toronto*
PRENTICE-HALL OF INDIA PRIVATE LIMITED, *New Delhi*
PRENTICE-HALL OF JAPAN, INC., *Tokyo*
PRENTICE-HALL OF SOUTHEAST ASIA PTE. LTD., *Singapore*
WHITEHALL BOOKS LIMITED, *Wellington, New Zealand*

PREFACE

This monograph started as a set of rules given piecemeal as standards to a team developing a conversational, incrementally-compiled, machine-independent version of the Dartmouth BASIC language for the Jet Propulsion Laboratory, called MBASIC. (Originally, "M" stood for "management-oriented", indicating its intended set of users; however, its great flexibility and ease of use has since won over many scientific and engineering users as well.) The first draft was a mere collection of the first sketchy set of rules, along with some background material on structured programming.

As the design progressed, the emphasis expanded from the design of a language processor to a project developing software methodology using the MBASIC development as a testbed activity. New rules were supplied as necessary and old ones had to be revised or discarded. Some of the ones that sounded so good when first imposed had effects just opposite to what was desired. The MBASIC design and documentation standards underwent several complete iterations, each under new rules to calibrate their effectiveness. The working drafts of this monograph were in constant revision to maintain a current set of standards for the project.

Further expansions of the working drafts were made to include much tutorial material, since I used portions of the text as lecture topics for graduate-level computer science classes at West Coast University and for seminars in software standards at the Jet Propulsion Laboratory. Interactions with the students and professional programmers with widely different backgrounds proved to be very enlightening.

I realize that some who have already "learned programming" may find fault with what they read here. I hope their objections are mostly with how the rules impact their personal programming style. Style is a reflection of a programmer's personal programming *habits* and his own *preferences* in the way he does things. If the rules given here don't work, that is another matter.

What I have attempted to do is to merge individual disciplines and good practices into a methodology that neither destroys personal style nor reduces motivation and involvement. The given set of rules is the base for a consistent and effective methodology; but there may be other equally effective and consistent methodologies. I do not allege to profess the *only* way toward improved software development—just one that works.

The monograph does not reflect, nor is it meant to reflect, exact standards or practices now in effect at JPL; however, much of the material has formed the basis for Deep Space Network software guidelines and standard practices currently in effect.

Several individuals at the Jet Propulsion Laboratory have reviewed the drafts and many have provided rules, suggestions, and other material. I have expected such criticism, and welcomed constructive material by any who cared to supply it. I have tried to be open to all correct, potentially worthwhile ways to improve the development of software and to build these into a uniform coordinated methodology for programming, a set of rules universally sound.

I offer one apology at the outset—for my literary style. About half-way through writing this monograph, I was suddenly surprised to learn that I often referred to software development personnel in the masculine. Lest I be accused of male chauvinism, let me attempt to defend myself by explaining that the references appear thus because I tended to place myself in the roles of these individuals. In writing, I also tended to be addressing myself, rather than any envisioned reader or actual software development person. By the time I realized I might be taken to task for this by distaff readers, the style was set and writing was too far along— another case where a software error was discovered too late to change the product without having major schedule and economic impact!

I would like particularly to acknowledge the aid given to me in the form of encouragement, ideas, criticisms, reviews, questions, and informative discussions by Walter K. Victor, Mahlon Easterling, Robert Holzman, James Layland, Robert Chamberlain, Edward Posner, Daniel Preska, Richard Morris, and Henry Kleine of the Jet Propulsion Laboratory, and Daniel Lewis, Frank Bracher, John MacMillan, Richard Jaffee, and Howard Mayberry of National Information Systems, Inc. Also, I want to express my appreciation to Margaret Seymour for typing the many drafts and to Shozo Murakami for editorial assistance on this final version.

Finally, I wish to thank those who have attended the many seminars and classes given from this work during its various stages of completion; many insights into the secrets of software engineering across a broad programmer base occurred to me as the result of these classroom discussions.

Robert C. Tausworthe

CONTENTS

STANDARDIZED
:   DEVELOPMENT
:   OF
:   COMPUTER
:   SOFTWARE

I. INTRODUCTION

A computer system is a rigid, dispassionate machine; it is designed and built to react in definite, microscopically precise ways to programmed commands. The program it executes comprises a large collection of atomic instructions organized into macroscopic algorithms and computational procedures in performance of a desired task. The differences between a hoped-for behavior and the actual are evidences of *human failures* to instruct the computer properly. Nevertheless, such failures are referred to as "errors in the program" or "bugs", and justly so—the servant has executed but cannot comprehend any reasoning behind the instructions given it. Moreover, it has constrained the human capacity to communicate in doing even this much, as it has required instructions in its own programming language, rather than in more human terms.

Computer programs have thus, from the very first been subject to error—missteps in coding committed by the programmer—and then not discovered until after the program's operation can be examined and seen to be in error. The cause of such errors may then be either obvious, very elusive, or somewhere in between. In any case, the diagnosis comes *after the fact*, as the computer proceeds at such a pace as to make concurrent diagnoses out of the question. Once diagnosed, any subsequent (trial) corrections must be rerun to validate the proper response, at extra expense. The human proclivity to err in programming is probably the singularly most prominent, overriding factor against producing economical, reliable software.

Because the computer lacks judgement itself and responds to direction totally ignorant of the task to be done, programmers attempt to build in some measure of quasi-judgement by instructing the device to perform certain tests on input and to check for known or probable processing anomalies. They may instruct the computer, based on such information, to take some less abrasive action than complete failure. Such programming practices are often called "user forgiving", "error insensitivity", or "defensive". Regardless of the terminology, such practices are attempts to establish the proper master/servant relationship, whereby the machine adapts to the human, rather than vice-versa.

R. Holzman, a colleague at JPL, once remarked (1972) "When you can tell a computer, 'Oh, *you* know what I mean!'—and it *does*—then that's a computer language!" The industry, of course, may never attain that goal of man/machine communication, but it is reaching. In its reaching, it has made several significant progressions to define methods, procedures, and standards for use by programmers to reduce the number and severity of their "program errors".

Among the first significant developments were the inventions of higher-level languages, language processors, and the provisions for programmers to annotate their programs with some form of rationale for their own benefit. In addition, novice programmers learned to draw flowcharts, as a prelude to coding, as a means of developing their skill, and as a method for designing the program procedure—the algorithm scoping the task. But programmers still made errors, at about the same rate per instruction as they had previously. The only difference was that as many errors did not reach the run-time stage, and each instruction did more in a higher-level language. Still more higher-level languages have been developed; until today, there are probably as many programming languages as there are natural languages.

At some point, programmers, or their supervisors, or their customers, recognized that, even though a program might be working, no one could understand *how* it was working well enough to make changes without introducing a lot of side-effect errors, or how *well* it was working enough to assess the programming quality. So the idea, "document what you have coded so I can understand it", sprang up. Managerial seminars developed methods to cajole and coerce [1,2] designers, programmers, coders, *et al.*, to document. The necessity to document [3] was evident to all who had to read and maintain the software, but dreaded by the documentor. Flowcharting was a nuisance and rarely matched the code, regardless which was produced first. Annotations of the code were in a similar state, as were narrative descriptions. Since the computer cannot execute a flowchart, narrative, or annotation anyway (only the code), and the human was just as likely to err in describing his code as he was in coding it, other systems emerged: self-documenting code, automatic flowcharting, standardized documentation formats, etc. Computer technology was beginning to evolve into an engineering discipline.

1.1 THE NEED FOR SOFTWARE STANDARDS

Years ago, the cost of computing was largely in machine costs; now the larger portion is paid to people developing, using, and maintaining programs. In fact, the trend in computing costs is the complete dominance of manpower costs over machine costs.

Software is big business; the indirect costs caused by failures to meet schedule or performance requirements often exceed the costs of the software itself, because software development always seems to be on the "critical path" of a system development. Boehm [4] suggested the following prescription for software headaches:

a. Get software off the critical path in system development.

b. Increase software productivity.

c. Improve software management.

d. Get an earlier start.

e. Make software responsive to actual user needs.

f. Increase software reliability.

The present monograph is an attempt to provide *formal disciplines* for increasing the probability of securing software that is characterized by high degrees of initial correctness, readability, and maintainability, and to promote *practices* that aid in the consistent and orderly development of a total software system within schedule and budgetary constraints. These disciplines and practices are set forth as a set of rules to be applied during software development to eliminate (this is the goal)—or at least to drastically reduce—the time spent debugging the code, to increase understandability among those who come in contact with it—especially managers, who must often make decisions relative to competing resources (such as budget, schedule, execution speed, memory size, etc.)—and to facilitate operation and alteration of the program as the requirements or program environment evolves.

To be effective, I recognize that a set of standards must not be *imposed* so much as *adopted*. But once a set is adopted, its rules should be enforced. Needless to say, some of the rules I give are broad and, therefore, open to interpretation. I have tried to make these as specific as I could without destroying their general applicability. But some vagueness may yet remain.

One may question whether the strict adherence to definition, design, production, testing, and documentation rules hamper programmer creativity or decrease his motivation and involvement; this has not, in my experience, turned out to be the case. Programming methodology tends to be rather scantily taught in computer-science courses in the universities. What methodology a programmer possesses he may have had to learn largely for himself, tutored by his own coding, discovered osmotically from reading programs others have written, or found through discussion with his peers. Programmers, as any problem-solvers, generally *welcome* a workable, well-disciplined approach to problem solving, so they do not have to re-invent the wheel, so they know what is expected of them and how they will be judged on their performance, so they know what level of reporting is required, and so they can really get into the design and make a clean, good, well-operating system.

Good standards enforce themselves. Once the programmer recognizes that his own performance is improved by standardized methods, he is its foremost proponent. When he suddenly realizes that he is capable of understanding a program written by someone else, he is convinced forever. I have personally seen instances where experienced programmers have at first rebelled at the entire concept, but once forced, they recognized the benefits derived, assisted in further development, and helped enforce standards in their own organizations.

The reports from industry are equally encouraging. Although productivity indices tend to be highly variable across wide ranges of applications and across software development personnel, nevertheless, analysis of quantitative data [5] indicates that the standards forming the basis of this monograph generally produce better than 50% improvement in overall project productivity. This overall productivity figure includes analysis, design, testing, management, support, and documentation, in addition to coding and debugging. Moreover, the figures in support of this improvement have been computed in terms of delivered code—the incidental effort spent in developing code used to support the production and code, which later had to be replaced, have not been counted.

1.2 SOFTWARE DEVELOPMENT

At the outset of a programming project, there are only a problem (program requirement) and a programming language in which the solution to that problem is to be stated. In between, there is the gap to be bridged by the development process.

The actual creative process which goes on in a program designer's mind is certainly not well understood. It probably rambles from broad concept to details and completeness, and, perhaps on occasion, from detail to the broader concept.

When writing a paper or preparing a talk, one first jots down notes, then an outline of the material to be covered. After the outline is expanded by way of a few iterations, the narrative is written. Many revisions are usually necessary if the paper or speech is to be of any significance.

A piece of software probably should not be much different in the way it is created. Successive refinements and revisions of a program are going to be necessary if it is to be of high quality.

Moreover, the revision process in software development is unavoidable. People cannot think of everything, in the right order, correctly, in one pass (Figure 1-1). One can hope, however, that there are procedures that tend to let the creative process take a natural course, but yet minimize the probability that, at some advanced stage of development, one must "throw out the whole thing and start all over from scratch."

One of the most costly ways to develop software is to begin the production phase before the program definition and design have reached an adequate state of completion. A small change in the program definition, for example, can avalanche down through the work done, resulting in suboptimal design, patched programs and code, introduction of undesirable side effects, and excessive debugging time.

The pressure of a schedule and the awareness that a great deal of coding has to be done cause many managers to let the design or coding begin, anyway, just to get started on a job that is obviously huge. Hence, the process of design is begun throughout the system at the very bottom before the design has been properly thought out and precisely defined at the top. A classical "bottom-up" design emerges, leading to difficulty in integrating the resulting components in a system.

Yet cooperative interaction between the definition, design, and production activities associated with developing a program can be mutually beneficial when properly interfaced. The proper interface in this

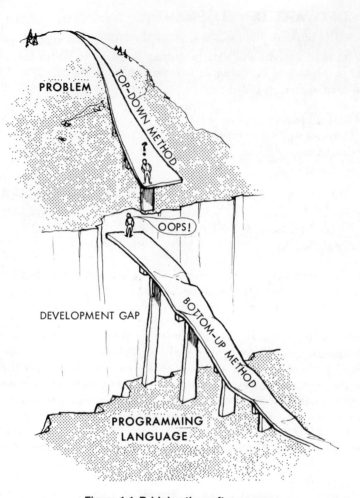

Figure 1-1. Bridging the software gap

context is an organization of the tasks to permit revisions and refinements without requiring extensive rework.

The procedures of this monograph have evolved from the belief that successive refinement of a concept by *adding* more and more detail is a less costly, more certain discipline than refinement by succesive *alterations* of the original concept.

One principle by which program concepts evolve in a natural, structured way emerged from Dijkstra's work in the THE Multiprogramming System [6]. He conceived that a program could be organized into hierarchic levels of support. The principle, known as *levels of abstraction* (see Sec. 2.5), formed the basis for what has become known since as *structured programming*, the subject of Chapter 5. The augmentation of that same basic method into a uniform discipline for software development is the substance of this monograph.

1.3 ORIENTATION

This work, while getting down to a very fundamental tutorial level in many areas, is not aimed at being a course in programming fundamentals. I realize that one could have no better success in impressing a set of rules on programmers than to get at them during their very earliest experiences in machine computation, teaching them the method before their biases begin to prevail. However, my aim is to provide people who must cope with the development of large programs an organized methodology for accomplishing their tasks. Many such people obviously may have already had software experience.

Neither do I want to get into the area of the complexity of computation, although I recognize that software designers need to be aware that there are limits of computability. But I believe that the extent to which a human being is capable of producing a correct program is primarily limited by his mental capacity to comprehend and retain, rather than by computational limits. The intricacy with which the various parts of a program interact, the sheer number of such interactions, the organization and methodology which produces the program, and the clarity, completeness, and information-retrievability of the working documentation which holds the rationale for those parts of the program already written and the intentions for those that will follow, are all important factors.

This work, then, addresses these factors by structuring the ways in which programs may interact, by organizing the development of the software into workable tasks, and by providing enhancements to mental retention by means of clear, worthwhile documentation. The methods given are not 100% foolproof, nothing ever is. The procedures and standards are meant to be *aids* toward increasing the *probability* of earlier, less expensive success than one would otherwise achieve.

The rules given here are based on mathematical theorems and program-organization methods intended to motivate programmer concentration, help avoid errors of carelessness, and display the design process as a set of procedures that split the development process into increasingly more detailed program specifications, with checks and balances. The methodology represents programming as a top-down, modular, structured, hierarchic function-to-algorithmic-realization synthesis. Besides design rules, there are rules for the function, level, content, and format of documentation, rules for the management of software projects, rules for how progress is to be monitored and evaluated, and rules for defining and assessing program correctness and quality.

The rules are meant to provide a precise, disciplined framework for achieving consistency, compatibility, correctness and control of complexity in the software definition, design, documentation, and implementation. The rules are oriented toward that middle ground between pure, extreme theory and pure, extreme practice, and are directed toward obtaining a quality-controlled product under economic and schedule considerations.

Because of its content and orientation, this monograph could have merely been titled "Software Engineering". Engineering, to me, in any context means solving problems with given constraints in an organized, responsible, professional way, and that is certainly the intended orientation of this work. Anything less than engineering is tinkering, however grandiose. Those involved in the software tasks that I shall be describing later are truly *engineers*: software *design* engineers, software *implementation* engineers, software *quality-assurance* engineers, and so on. The idea is to adapt good engineering practices to the development of software.

Most of what the reader will find in the coming chapters is not new. Many, in fact, will claim they have been using some of the principles for years. What I have tried to do is take individual good ideas and bind them all together into a uniform, coordinated discipline of ideas that are still good when combined.

The monograph focuses primarily on software development standards within, or for, technically-oriented organizations, although many, if not all, of the rules and methods apply to other orientations as well.

II. FUNDAMENTAL PRINCIPLES AND CONCEPTS

As I stated in the first chapter, the degree to which concepts in this monograph are "fundamental" is based on my intended audience: those who have some experience in software development and are looking for methods to enhance their effectiveness. The purpose of this chapter, then, is to present basic principles for software development and to define some commonly used terms and concepts the way I mean to use them. I do this, not to be picky about existing definitions, or even rigorously precise in the ones I give, but to be as clear as possible in exposing the material to come.

By and large I have used terms that agree with or generalize the ANSI standard vocabulary definitions [7] for information processing. In some cases, however, I have restricted the ANSI definitions to a narrower or slightly different context.

9

2.1 SYSTEMS, PROGRAMS, AND PROCESSORS

First, let me define what will be meant in this monograph by references to such general terms as "system," "program," and "processor;" all of which could be, and many times have been, used interchangeably.

A *software system* is an organized collection of procedures united by regulated interaction to accomplish a specific set of functions. The software system consists of two basic subsystems: the *operating subsystem* and the *application subsystem*. The operating subsystem (often called the operating system, or *executive*) consists of a number of parts that interface the applications subsystem to the computer resources, such as input/output (I/O) media, storage media, supervision and execution management, etc. The application subsystem is that part of the computer software performing the body of user-oriented functions.

A *program*—more correctly, a *computer program*—is a series of instructions or statements, in a form acceptable to a computer, prepared to achieve a certain result; i.e., to perform a certain function within a subsystem. From time to time, I will refer to a program as a system, to emphasize its characteristics as a functional unit and to de-emphasize its sequential nature.

In software, a *processor* usually refers to a computer program that includes the compiling, assembling, translating and related functions for a specific programming language, such as a COBOL processor, a FORTRAN processor, etc. The term is sometimes used in a looser context to refer to programs that process any set of data. In hardware, the term is synonymous with *data processor*, a device capable of performing the execution of a systematic sequence of operations on data, such as the Central Processing Unit (or CPU).

A *multiprocessor* is a computer that employs two or more processing units (CPUs, I/O channels, etc.) under integrated control. By *multiprocessing*, I shall refer to the (perhaps simultaneous) execution of separate sequences of actions by such multiple hardware processors. I shall say that a single processor is *multiprogrammed* if it executes two or more programs or program modules by interleaving them in time. It is even possible for a multiprocessor to be multiprogrammed, in which case, several programs share each of several processors. Both multiprocessing and multiprogramming are capable of concurrent execution of programs, and I shall refer to both as *concurrent processing*.

2.1.1 Parts of a Program

Identifiable subportions of a program also fitting the "program" definition will be referred to as *modules*. A *routine* is an ordered set of instructions (a *module*) that may have some general or frequent use. In this monograph, the words routine and *subroutine* will be used interchangeably, and will always refer to modules that, when called, return after execution to their point of call. The term *subprogram*, on the other hand, will always refer to a module that invariably is only invoked at one point in the program.

Subprograms and subroutines are modular subdivisions of a program having specific *interfaces* or *connections* to other parts of a program. The interface of a module is defined as the set of assumptions that the surrounding program makes about that module. Modules have control interfaces via their entry and exit points, data interfaces via arguments or shared data structures (some of which may be control data), and interfaces that provide services between modules.

An *operation* is defined as a finite-time execution performing a time-independent function based on its input. By this definition, every non-real-time program, as well as each instruction within that program, can be viewed as an operation. A sequence of operations performed one at a time constitute a *process*; two processes are then said to be *concurrent* if their operations can either overlap or interleave arbitrarily in time. Two concurrent processes are said to be *parallel* when operations in the processes occur simultaneously (within a predefined time-divisibility convention), shown in Figure 2-1.

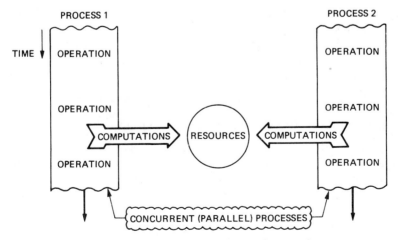

Figure 2-1. Operations, processes, computations, and resources

The results of processes are *computations* applied to *resources*. The term "resource" is an abstraction for any set of system features, such as CPUs, storage, files, magnetic tapes, printers, etc. The condition of the entire set of resources is the computer *state*; that part of a computer's storage accessed by a program is its *data space*.

Computations are characterized by *accuracy*, which means the degree to which it is free from error—the degree to which it conforms to truth or to a rule. Numeric accuracy contrasts with *precision*, which represents the degree of discrimination with which a quantity is stated. A three-digit numeral discriminates among 1000 possibilities and, therefore, is less precise than a four-digit numeral, which discriminates among 10,000 possibilities. Nevertheless, a properly computed three-place numeral might be more accurate than an improperly computed four-place numeral.

A prescribed set of well-defined rules or processes for the solution of a problem in a finite number of steps is an *algorithm*. Algorithms have a stated *function*; i.e., a specific purpose, or characteristic action. An algorithm is also generally expected to be effective. This definition means that all of the operations to be performed in the algorithm must be sufficiently basic and definite so that they can, in principle, be done exactly and in a finite length of time by a human using a pencil and paper. For an algorithm to be useful, it is not sufficient that the number of steps merely be finite; computers have their limits. The number must be *reasonable*.

A *program mode* (short for mode of operation) is a way of operating a program to perform a certain subset of the functions that the entire program can perform. The subset of functions is usually data-coupled, rather than control coupled. However, the set of functions is usually selected by control data. For example, language processors usually consist of "compile" and "runtime" modes (and perhaps some transition modes between these two) that pass the compiled program as data between the two. Often the modes of operation will be shown graphically in a *mode diagram*, which displays the various program modes and the permissible transitions between modes, annotated to show the events causing the transition.

2.1.2 Procedural Representation of a Program

A *flowchart* is a graphical representation for the definition, analysis, or solution of a problem. Symbols are used to represent operations, data, flow, equipment, etc., and are annotated to describe the function of each symbol. As we shall encounter the term herein, a flowchart will generally refer to a drawing describing the logic and sequence of operations in a program (subprogram, routine, etc.) and drawn to conform to ANSI Standards [8], which are summarized in Appendix B. However, this definition does not exclude pidgin English or the program code from being referred to as a "flowchart," given suitable interpretations of the terms "symbols," "operations," etc. Proper indentations of the lines of pidgin English or code and a limited program logic structure can, in fact, provide a very graphic display of the program function, as will be shown later in Chapter 7.

2.1.3 A Word on Program Syntactic Notation

In such program-related expressions to come as DO *f* THEN *g*, IF *c* THEN *f* ELSE *g*, etc., the italicized letters will stand for definite types of text that can occupy those positions in the constructions. For example, *f* and *g* above represent arbitrary program functions, while *c* represents an arbitrary test condition. The italics thus identify which parts of an expression are variable within the syntax of the construction. The unitalicized capitals, however, DO, IF, THEN, etc., are not; they designate specific syntactic literals, to be interpreted as they stand.

I shall thus designate hereafter all qualities to be identified as syntactic variables as italicized characters. Hence, if I am discussing a procedure, such as SEND(*message, device*), for example, then I shall mean that *message* and *device* are to be replaced by non-variables in actual usage, as perhaps, SEND("HELLO", PRINTER). Italicized characters thus represent variables in the meta-language I use to describe a program, not the variables in the program itself.

In the example, LET *variable* = *expression*, which describes the format of an assignment statement in BASIC, the name of a program variable, such as A1, is to be substituted for the syntactic variable, *variable*, and an actual expression, such as (3+8*5)/2, is to replace the syntactic variable, *expression*. If a decision box on a flowchart is labeled *d*, then an actual condition to be decided is to be substituted. If I show that a subprogram is actuated by *event*, then an actual event, such as FILE ERROR, replaces *event* in practice.

2.2 STRUCTURES

Perhaps the most overused word in this monograph is "structure". I use it in many ways for many different concepts—information, data, and storage structures; structural design; structured programming; and so on.

The concept of *structure* may pertain to the manner or form in which something is constructed, or it may pertain to the actual system being constructed. Descriptions of structure focus primarily on the interrelations of the various parts of a system, as dominated by the general character or function of the whole. Defining the "structure" of a problem can be described as a process of identifying, analyzing, and selecting among alternatives within design categories.

In software development there are topological alternatives (control logic and data structures), clocking alternatives (sequential, concurrent, parallel, real-time), protocol alternatives (interface disciplines with the operating system or other programs), connectivity alternatives (accessibility and security of programs and data), and resource allocation alternatives (fixed, dynamic), to name a few. Selection among major alternatives defines the *architectural framework* of the program (another word for structure).

Some of the things which influence a program's structure are its envisioned capability (utility, efficiency, cost, accuracy, throughput rate, etc.), its use needs (maintenance and support requirements, use constraints, etc.), and its implementation criteria (short-term vs long-haul solution, real vs virtual memory, etc.).

2.2.1 Program Control Structure

The statements in a programming language primarily affecting the logical sequencing of operations in a program are called *control statements*. Examples of control statements are jumps, conditional branches, subroutine calls, interrupt arming, etc. The *control flow* of a program is a general concept referring to the time-ordering relationships among the various operations comprising the program. The *control structure* of a program is then the topological format of this control flow.

There are several ways that one may describe different aspects of importance in a program's control structure, depending on the needs of communication. One such way has already been mentioned, namely the program flowchart. A flowchart, such as that appearing in Figure 2-2, characterizes the control structure by showing its *procedural* steps (i.e., its algorithm), in execution sequence. Whenever the fundamental topological structures, which one may be permitted to use in programming, are limited to a set of very basic forms, then I will call it a *structured program*. Structured programs are discussed more fully in Chapters 5 and 6.

Another way to illustrate some of the control structure of a program is to depict the program as a directed graph, such as that shown in Figure 2-3, in which each node represents a given function to be computed, and the edges connect that function to each of the first-order subfunctions called upon to perform the given function. The maximal connected subgraph emanating from a given node thus represents the entire set of subfunctions necessary to compute the node function; for this reason, this subgraph is called the *scope of control* of the given function. More discussion on the use of such program graphs is to be found in Chapters 4 and 5.

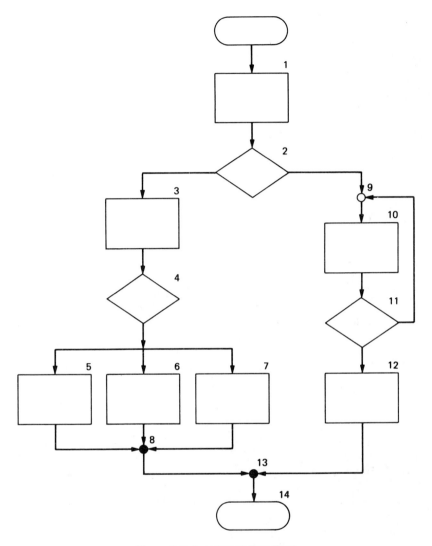

Figure 2-2. A program flowchart

2.2.2 Information, Data, and Storage Structures

A program operates on data. An *information structure* is a representation of the elements of a problem or of an applicable solution procedure for the problem; a *data structure* is a representation of the ordering and accessibility relationships among data items, without regard to storage or implementation considerations; and a *storage structure* is a representation of the logical accessibility between data items as stored in a computer [9].

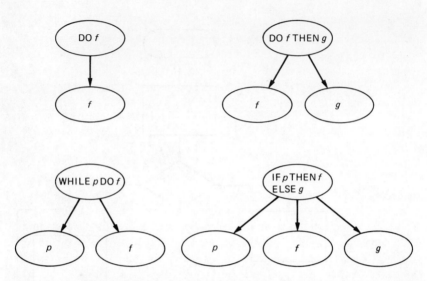

Figure 2-3. Representation of a program as a graph in which nodes represent functions and edges represent control connections (each of *p*, *f*, and *g* may have further expansion)

As an example, in the problem

$$\begin{bmatrix} 2 & 1 & 3 \\ 4 & 5 & 6 \\ -1 & 0 & 3 \end{bmatrix} \begin{bmatrix} x \\ y \\ z \end{bmatrix} = \begin{bmatrix} 1 \\ -1 \\ 0 \end{bmatrix}$$

the matrix and the two vectors are information structures. When we agree to represent these in our problem as the matrix A[I,J], I,J = 1,2,3 and vectors X = (X[1], X[2], X[3]) and B = (B[1], B[2], B[3]), then A, B, and X become our data structures; and when we represent these in computer memory, as for example

$location\ (A[I,J]) = location\ (A[1,1]) + J-1 + 3*(I-1)$

then this becomes the storage structure.

A data structure is generally specified as a set of data items (variables or constants), each *typed*: a) by a *range of values* (such as logical, integer, real, complex, double precision, string, or an enumerated set of values), and b) by a *connectivity* of items within the structure (such as those implicit in a linear list, stack, queue, deque, orthogonal array, tree, ring, or graph). The simplest example of a data structure is a single integer-valued variable. A variable used to influence the control logic of a program is called a *flag*.

The ease with which data structures can be used often depends on the handling capability of the programming language to accommodate that structure. For example, FORTRAN only accommodates integer, real, and complex data types, in simple or matrix-array data structures. It is certainly *possible* in FORTRAN to create and manipulate a queue of string records as a data structure; but it is not as easy as it is in PL/1, where string variables and linked-list data structures are included in the language repertoire.

A data structure also possesses another attribute having to do with when and where it is accessed in the program. This is called its *scope of activity* (or merely, its *scope*). The scope of a structure extends from the earliest point in a subprogram where information appears in that structure, until the latest point that the structure is needed, either by the current module or by another interfacing subsequent module. A data structure is said to be *active* whenever the program is executing within the scope of that structure. The scope need not be continuous. For example, an index variable for an iteration is only active during the iteration, and may be reused by other parts of a program once the iteration has been completed.

2.3 SOFTWARE DEVELOPMENT

That part of a software project up to the delivery of a working program for operation by organizations and individuals other than those involved in this evolution, I shall refer to as the *software development* period. It begins with the flash in someone's mind that a computer shall do an envisioned task and ends when the program is "operational".

Several mutually interacting activities during this period can be identified (Figure 2-4). First, a customer organization establishes a *requirement* with certain resources (manpower, schedule, dollars) allocated to provide the needed service. When the requirement is given, it generally only contains a sketch or outline of the tasks that a computer will be called upon to perform, the expected results, and some of the problem-related constraints.

The function of this requirement is to characterize the program, its environment, and needed resources in that amount of detail which justifies to a conscientious, informed management the commitment of such resources. It also forms the basis for the program functional requirement or statement-of-work specification to come. Additionally, the requirement may contain, besides the resource estimate and justification for its expenditure, some reasonable evidence that the estimate is accurate, within certain bounds.

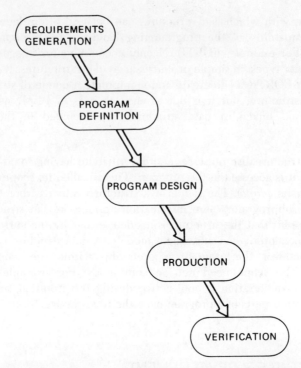

**Figure 2-4. Software development activities and principal
flow of these activities in a top-down development**

The second activity in the software development process is the precise *definition* or *functional specification* of the program behavior. This activity is perhaps the most difficult in the whole development process, as there is almost invariably a trichotomy between what the customer *thinks* he wants, what he *really* wants (this is particularly true of the non-programming customer), and what he can *actually have* within his resource constraints. In the end, the definition should contain enough detail to permit the program to be designed without ambiguity as to its external (black box) transfer function: specification of I/O media and formats, input-to-output transformations, interactions with users, interactions with other programs, response to errors and other contingencies, and response to system failure. *Any* operating program that meets these detailed specifications may be said to be *correct.*

The level of detail provided in a program definition, however, will rarely be such that any two correct programs independently derived from that definition will be *interchangeable.* Such detail would undoubtedly be too costly to develop. Moreover, human fallibility will almost assuredly produce vagaries, omissions, and contradictions in such detailed specifications.

The third development activity one can identify is that of *design*. Design is an alternative-feasibility-study discipline. It bridges the gap between the program definition and the program code. It is the process that analyzes the external black-box definition of the program behavior and translates it into functioning and efficient abstractions of internal machine structures (data configurations, algorithms, etc.).

It sets forth program and system restrictions, policies and protocols. The end product of this activity is a number of documented abstractions that represent the eventual system in a characteristic way. For example, flowcharts are an abstraction of the function and control logic of the program to be produced. Other abstractions have to do with data flow, the management of system resources, policies to prevent system deadlocks, inter-program data interfaces, and so forth.

The fourth activity is program *production*. It consists of coding, checkout, and integrating the program into the system that forms its environment. It implements the design abstractions, organizing the physical resources of a system to perform according to the program specification. *Checkout* here refers to the testing of a program, or part of a program, by the programmers themselves. In Chapter 9, I discuss checkout disciplines for *correctness testing*.

The final activity to be identified as a development task is *verification*. Software verification is that aspect of development asserting that the program response falls within acceptable limits of functionally specified behavior. It testifies that design and production activities conform to program requirements and project standards; it generates test procedures and conducts tests to evaluate the program behavior; it identifies all anomalies for corrective action; and it ultimately certifies that the program is ready for user operation.

2.4 HIERARCHIES

A *hierarchy* is a structure by which classes of objects are ranked according to some subordinating principle. Pictorially, a hierarchy can be represented by a tree-graph, as shown in Figure 2-5. A specially denoted object (represented as the *root* node of the tree) heads the hierarchy, and other objects (represented by the other nodes) are ranked by order (indicated by lines between nodes) into *levels* of subordination. The *level number* of an object within the hierarchy is its degree of subordination. Each object (node) occupies a well-defined place within the hierarchy.

Hierarchy can be applied to software development in many ways: to structure concept refinements in problem definition; to structure programs

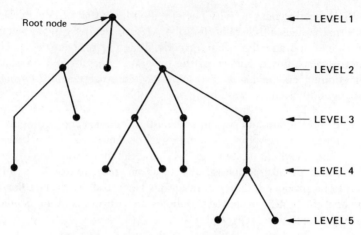

Figure 2-5. Graphical representation of a hierarchy

into modules, submodules, sub-sub-modules, etc.; to structure data by refinement of attributes; to structure tests to avoid repetitive testing of the same specification; and to structure documentation for reference and cross-reference. I shall begin, in the next chapter, to develop methods to establish how hierarchies of program elements can aid in software development.

2.5 CONCEPT HIERARCHIES

Dijkstra's work [6] involving levels of abstraction permitted him to formulate the solution of a problem in terms of concepts capable of being implemented (and interpreted) in many ways, but which were perhaps not yet fully understood at a particular stage of the development. Later stages then provided refinements to each concept until the program was entirely complete.

Alternately, the levels of abstraction could proceed from specific concepts, which may be combined into broader, more general concepts, until the most general (level-1) concept results.

In *top-down methodology*, the hierarchy of development tasks proceeds from a job represented by a node at level n, upon completion, to jobs represented by its subordinate nodes at level $n+1$. By such methodology, one need never lose sight of the original assumptions which appeared at level 1. In *bottom-up methodology*, the opposite precedence of tasks results; one never loses sight of the actual capability being built up.

Neither methodology is entirely satisfactory, because, as stated earlier, people just can't do intricate thinking tasks correctly in one pass, start to finish.

The potential risk, doing a strict top-down development, is that there may be no way to ensure that operations at one level in the hierarchy are supportable by some abstract resource provided (later) at subordinate levels.

The sense that I shall give to an *abstraction* in this work is that it is a mechanism for hierarchic refinement by which it is possible, at a particular stage of development, to express relevant details and to defer non-relevant details for later refinement. Such abstractions apply to concepts during problem definition, as well as to the considerations of physical resources during program design and to the manipulations of computer structures in program execution.

The purpose of using an abstraction as a program development discipline is threefold: first, it somewhat matches our tendency to solve problems by outlining broad concepts, which may then successively be refined or generalized; second, it tends to permit detail to be added or generalizations made without requiring global revisions of the previously outlined concepts; and third, because such global revisions tend to be minimized, the various development activities (specification, design, coding, testing) can take place in concert rather than in series, thus speeding up the development process.

I don't mean to imply that there aren't going to be times when development reaches a point where a serious conceptual error is detected, rather than an error in the detail within a concept, which will necessitate a major program revision. (An acquaintance of mine refers to this situation, labeled "Oops!" in Figure 1-1, as "#*%/+@!", an expression familiar to all who read the Sunday funnies.) The seriousness, in such cases, will naturally depend on how much the development effort has to be backed up to correct the concept, and how profusely the changed concept creates side effects in the work already done.

The way abstractions are formulated also greatly influences the extent and likelihood that a program will need major revision during the development process. A proper discipline for abstraction can therefore be a great asset toward timely program delivery.

An abstract resource may be characterized, according to Hoare [10], by three sets of hierarchies:

The *representation* of an abstract resource is the set of symbols that one may substitute for the physical aspects of a problem either in a concept or in its computer implementation. For example, a certain set of data may be represented in one abstraction by a queue whose name only is of importance at the first hierarchic level. Deeper levels in the hierarchy detail other attributes of the representation, such as queue dimension, location in memory, element-addressing method, etc.

Manipulations must be defined to provide the transformation rules for representations, as a means of predicting the effect of similar manipulations on the physical resources. In the queue example above, operations INSERT and FETCH, which access elements based only on the queue name (its level-1 representation) can be defined.

Axiomatization is the generation of statements concerning the physical properties of the problem and the extent to which they are shared by their representations, in virtue of which, manipulation of the representation by a computer program will yield results that can successfully be applied back to the physical aspects of the problem. Axioms provide the assumptions on which the computer program is based, stating the necessary properties that must be possessed by a resource representation.

The extent to which an abstraction leads to a successful program is dependent on three conditions. First, the axioms must adequately and accurately describe the problem. Second, the axioms must correctly describe the behavior of the program; and third, the choice of the representation and its manipulations must yield acceptable performance merits, such as cost to run the program, time to process a certain volume of data, etc.

2.5.1 Semantic Refinement

Many rules for writing technical specifications of any ilk also apply to those specifying computer programs. However, the more complex a function is, the more important a highly structured approach becomes. The basic elements to be preserved are an understanding of the function to be served and the mechanisms available to carry out the job.

Semantic refinement is a method for hierarchic abstraction of *meaning.* The definition of a concept or function takes the form of a tree in which the level-1 node is a broad, perhaps vague (yet unambiguous) statement of the concept or function to be defined. The next level in the hierarchy is composed of a set of nodes, each corresponding to a vague, incomplete component of the level-1 statement. Each of these nodes supplies a more detailed explanation for that component of its parent node. This hierarchy continues until the definition reaches a point where the entire meaning is clear.

This technique can serve as a very useful method for stating program requirements and specifications, as well as some of the program design concepts, which will follow. The meaning given to "meaning" as the subordinating relationship of the hierarchy need not be made rigid, so long as deeper levels in the hierarchy provide useful information. However, it is worth pointing out that, if the set of final, terminal nodes in the hierarchy are statements in a precise, well-defined language (a problem definition language), and if each terminal set of nodes emanating from a given node provides the exact definition for the given node (i.e., no vague component remains unrefined), then there is no opportunity for misunderstanding the requirement.

Meaning can be refined not only by language explanations, but by the presentation of mathematical algorithms or graphical material, as well. All these furnish detail relative to the semantic content of the entity being defined.

As an example of the technique, let me proceed, with the aid of Webster [11], to define "opossum." Obviously, anybody who has seen one knows what one is, so the definition could well, for that person, end right there. Otherwise, the creature can be defined by a set of attributes that characterize it completely for an intended application.

Webster offers the following explanation: "Any of a family ... of American marsupials, chiefly nocturnal, largely arboreal, and almost omnivorous." (Regrettably, this beautiful definition does not appear in a later version of the lexicon.) For a more detailed description, one may look up "marsupial," "nocturnal," "arboreal," and "omnivorous," arranging the information as shown in Figure 2-6, and, in turn, look up any new words that are not clear.

The reader may well appreciate that circular definitions must be avoided, that refinements should get simpler at each succeeding level, that logical constructions should be sound, that the process should ultimately terminate, and that the hierarchy reveals everything *intended* to be revealed. Hopefully, the hierarchy reveals everything that will be *needed*— that is, that the definition will be *complete* enough for the intended application.

However, no amount of descriptive detailing produces an actual opossum, only a representation. The extent to which we can treat the representation (our abstraction) as the actual animal is limited. Care must be taken to orient the abstraction to the application at hand.

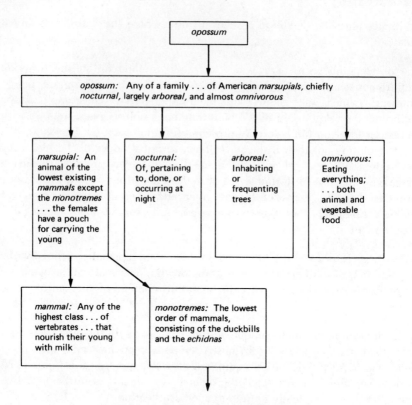

Figure 2-6. Semantic refinement of "opossum"

As a perhaps more relevant example, a top-level program requirement may read

> *read data*
>
> *process data*
>
> *print report*

At the time this requirement is formulated, the precise character of the concepts *"read," "data," "process,"* and *"print"* may be undefined. But anyone reading the requirement can understand the fundamental job to be done. Details at further levels will answer the questions "what does *data* mean?" and "how is *data* to be *processed?*"

In hierarchic refinements of sentences in the imperative mood, nouns to be explained at deeper levels tend to correspond to resources whose physical characteristics need to be tied down. As with *"data"* in the requirement above, one may detail "what kind?", "where from?", "what is its format?", "what is its nature?"; in defining its nature, one may further detail "are there errors in it?", "what probability of error?", "how can errors be detected?", "what is to be done if an error is detected?", etc. As the latter questions show, the physical characteristics of a noun can often lead to definitions in terms of tests, or criteria to be met.

Adjectives or other modifiers applied at one level to nouns from a preceding level act to limit the scope of definition to special attributes (what kind of *data*? *Test* data!). The entire noun phrase may then become an indivisible concept insofar as further refinement goes.

Verbs in the imperative mood direct that an action be taken. Explaining that action at succeeding levels is tantamount to providing an algorithm in successive detail. Adverbs and other modifiers act to define the scope or to provide some of the inner-workings of the algorithm.

It is not necessary for a semantic refinement to be purely lexical, as in the "opossum" case, applying meaning to concepts on a word or phrase basis (Figure 2-7a). On the contrary, an entire concept at one level may be refined at the next, as alluded to in Figure 2-7 (b and c). For example *"read data"* may expand to *"read data from terminal and read data from file"* at the next level, and may refine at the next to *"read control data from the user operations terminal"* and *"read personnel capabilities data from file specified by input at user operations terminal."*

The refinement of an algorithm may, in turn, be an extended algorithm that includes the algorithm at the previous level (Figure 2-7b), or it may be an entirely new algorithm that performs a similar function more efficiently, or with wider applicability, etc. (Figure 2-7c). Of the three methods of refinement depicted, one may ask which of the methods will be least susceptible to redefinition and revision of initial concepts; which will require the least work when an initial concept is changed; and which method will allow the creative process to flow in its most efficient way.

I think it is rather obvious that if an entire concept changes at one hierarchic level, there is going to be serious undoing of any concurrent efforts based on the earlier concept. For this reason, I do not recommend developing software abstractions by the replacement method of refinement.

2.5.2 Example: Skills Inventory

The following example depicts a hierarchically refined program (partial design) using levels of abstraction. The representations, manipulations, and axioms at each stage are explicitly defined. Only the first upper levels of the hierarchic refinement process are given.

Problem: An organization having 1000 employees wishes to make a skills inventory of its personnel. The organization has determined that about 800

(a) DETAILED SUBCONCEPTS

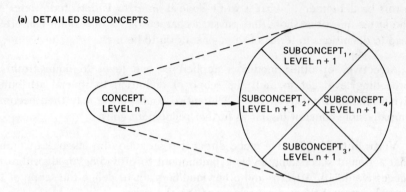

(b) EXPANSION OF CONCEPT

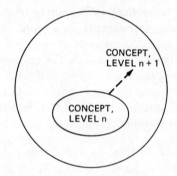

(c) REPLACEMENT WITH DIFFERENT CONCEPT

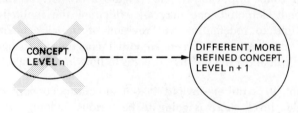

Figure 2-7. Semantic refinement hierarchies

basic skills will be utilized within the company, but that no employee possesses more than 8 of these basic skills. It has, therefore, issued a questionnaire requesting the return of an IBM card from each employee with his employee number and a list of his skills by code number. The company then intends to generate a computer listing containing each employee with a given skill designated.

Analysis: The information structure of the problem consists of an employee identification (represented by a number), and a corresponding set of skills (each also represented by a set of code numbers), for each employee. The manipulations that seem necessary on the structure are the conversion of identification numbers to names and skills, the collection of employee names for each skill present in the company, and the listing of such information on a line printer or some other device. For convenience to the reader, a requirement may occur to have the listings to appear in sorted form, by skill code and by employee name.

The first-level data structures I have chosen to represent the information are as follows (see Figure 2-8): ENAME, a structure to hold 1000 Employee NAMEs as character strings; SKILL, a structure to hold 800 SKILL titles as character strings; INCARD, a structure to hold the INput CARD numbers (up to 9 of them) in integer format; and LINKS, a structure to hold up to $8 \times 1000 = 8000$ name-skill relationships (LINKS).

The manipulations on these structures needed (at level 1) are: input from the card into INCARD, copying from INCARD into LINKS, translation of links to employee names and skill titles, sorting the links by employee name and skill code, and printing the sorted information. Axioms required at level 1 are that employees and skills can be represented by their numbers 1-1000 and 1-800, respectively; that ENAME and SKILL contain but representations of strings that faithfully reproduce names and titles when output; that INCARD and LINKS contain bit patterns corresponding to integers in the programming language; that the elements of ENAME(Ei) and SKILL(Sj) access the name of employee numbered Ei and the title of skill Sj, respectively; that LINKS(Sj,k) produces the kth employee found to have

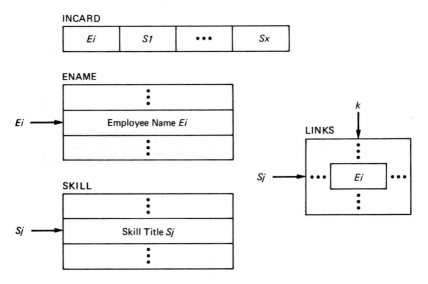

Figure 2-8. Level-1 data structure definition for skills inventory

skill *Sj*; that sorting by the internal representations are lexicographic on output; and that sorting internal integers also sorts their external representations.

Most of these axioms are usually taken for granted and left unstated. But for illustrative purposes, it is useful to write them down, to see that such correspondences of internal program behavior and external interpretation are present, even if implicit.

The second level data structures, expanded versions of the previous definition level, are shown in Figure 2-9. ENAME consists of two parts, a pointer array EPTR and an array of employee names, arranged such that EPTR (*Ei*) locates the string name of employee *Ei*. Similarly, SKILL possesses a pointer array SPTR that locates the string skill titles, and LINKS has a pointer array LPTR that links each skill number *Sj* to the linked list of identifiers for employees avowed to possess that skill.

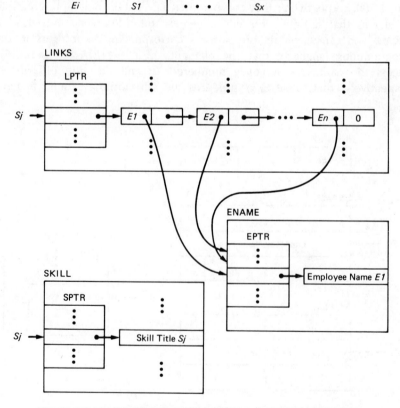

Figure 2-9. Level-2 data structure definitions for skills inventory

Manipulations for level-2 structures include list handling by following pointers, such as locating from an Sj on an INCARD the Ek-links in LINKS and then inserting an Ei-token into the chain. Other list handling manipulations needed are the ability to scan LINKS along pointers into ENAME and SKILL during printing.

Axioms for level 2 are that strings begin in data substructures addressable by pointers (important in systems that are not byte addressable), that zero is not a valid pointer, and so forth.

Storage structures are something else again. The placement of LINKS in core, for example, may not need to have an explicit array LPTR, because the first Ei-token for each Sj can take the place of the pointer in the top 800 locations of LINKS, as shown in Figure 2-10. Similarly, EPTR and SPTR may not be required if the programming language has string data types.

The reasons for deciding on the data structures shown are a process of design. I shall delay giving such rationale until Chapter 4, which treats design in more detail. The structures for this example, the reader may later note, are very similar (as is the problem) to the example given in paragraph 4.6.1, Card Cross-References (Chapter 4). Consequently, the rationale for the structures shown here is essentially the same as that given in the later example.

2.6 THE TOP-DOWN PRINCIPLE

The fundamental, guiding principle throughout this work is tenacious adherence to the top-down procedure of software development. By this is meant that the program proceeds from the program requirements to functional specification, to design, to coding, to verification and testing, and

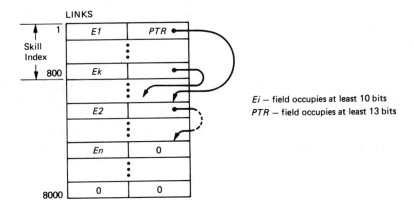

Figure 2-10. The storage structure for LINKS

finally, to operations. It means that the resulting design itself is readable from the top down and organized in a highly structured, modular, hierarchic way which decomposes and partitions each program subfunction into a sequence of simpler functional subspecifications, each producing yet simpler subspecifications to handle, until finally, the level of programming language instructions or statements is reached. It means that coding and then testing and verification of the design follow as each phase of the design is accomplished. It means that programming projects are managed from the top down—from allocation of resources to utilization of resources—in a way assuring management visibility into and understanding of the end product. It means that the design-team skills are ordered with high design capability at the top, leading to special skills at the bottom.

To minimize the risk mentioned earlier, that operations at one level in the hierarchy are supportable by resources at subsequently defined levels, I envision that those engaged in providing the top-down development must be very well trained in dealing with the characteristics of the program environment. In this way there can be reasonable assurance that the development gap will be bridged effectively, with minimal redesign.

The reason for strict enforcement of the top-down principle is that it forces a complete requirement to be stated prior to its accomplishment. Properly done, unrequired actions never appear in the finished product.

But, as a replacement, it requires a high level of discipline on the part of its adherents. Those involved must learn to *think* top-down. They must learn to think of *function* before *algorithm*. They must learn to describe functions functionally and accurately. They must learn to *prove* or *assess* that a program at any given stage in the design is correct, within its functional specification. They must learn that programs *can* be written with logical and interface precision. In the end, there is evidence [12] that a psychological reinforcement—a vital ingredient in self-discipline—emerges.

As Mills [12] points out, once a programmer *knows* what is in his mind is correct, then getting it programmed precisely, checking details, etc., is all that is required for the program to work. On the other hand, if he only thinks that what he has in mind is *probably* all right, but is subconsciously counting on debugging and integration runs to iron out logic and interface errors, then the entire process suffers in small ways to torment him later. Only 14 concatenations of subprograms that are probably 95% correct reduce the overall program probable correctness to 49%. An increase to 99% probable correctness—a small 4%—in each subprogram brings the overall probable correctness up to 87%—*a 38% difference!*

Another reason for tenuously propounding the top-down method is that the bottom-up approach has classically been typified by programmers who spend more time debugging code than they do writing it. According to Boehm [4], programmers usually spend under 20% of their total effort in coding and auditing, with the other 80% about evenly split in design and debugging. They are apt to spend great amounts of time in redesign (and then more debugging) due to faulty logic or faulty communication with other programmers. In short, it is the thinking errors even more than the coding errors, which hold the productivity of programming to such low levels.

In the top-down approach, the program designer proceeds to define the problem as a "black box" imbedded in an environment composed of a subset of available resources. This environment, with its attributes, exerts external influences on the developing system independent of and, hopefully, not contrary to the problem constraints to which the developing program *must conform* before it can respond to the *internal* demands of the problem.

The top-down approach also leads to structured programs [12] in which major programs can be broken into smaller subprograms through a combination of code and the design of subprogram "stubs" which are referenced or called by that code. By designing the program that calls the stubs before the stubs themselves are developed, the functional role of the called programs can be defined completely, so that no interface problems need be encountered later.

Coding, verification, and testing can begin immediately with dummy stubs to test the control logic and interfaces of the calling module. These test stubs can check for the presence of data to be passed, its format, its range, etc., and can also return prearranged test-case data.

This approach also satisfies the need on the part of programmers to *get running*. However, it is not the subroutines and the like that get written first—it is the encompassing code, always executed and checked before the next hierarchic level of executable code is created, checked, and integrated into the program. "Checking" in this top-down hierarchy means validated to the point of verifying the syntactic structure of the code and making a correctness assessment of the program. I shall have more to say on testing in a later chapter.

One should note that the top-down discipline may elicit some *bottom-up response* as a natural unavoidable by-product. For instance, when coding top-down in a very low-level language, dummy stubs used for checkout may be called to print trace information as evidence of the program's execution sequence. But then there must be provided a bottom-level support function, PRINT, that may not even be a part of the final program. Also, some critical low-level interrupt-handling routines must be programmed early to assure timing feasibility for an entire program.

I do not consider this effort at variance with the top-down approach. Design has preceded coding, and the requirements for the stubs were established first, before any functions within the stubs were coded.

Some developers may choose, and some problems may require, an other than top-down approach. Some, for example, may adopt a "hardest-out" philosophy — one in which the program development begins with the design of the most difficult, policy-setting decisions known to be within the system, and evolving upward to meet requirements, and downwards, to the code. Such a philosophy has many adherents and many virtues. The chief asset of such a design methodology is probably that it proceeds along lines of greatest feasibility.

However, as a formal discipline, I know of no way to instruct a would-be adherent to isolate the "hardest" nut to crack, without resorting to a top-down structurized design sketch, such as I discuss in Chapter 4. Once the hardest portion of the program is identified, that portion can be defined as a high-priority phase for further top-down design evolution. Therefore, even the "hardest-out" approach can be made to fit into the top-down *design* philosophy, even if not the top-down *coding* discipline. Such deviations from true top-down development are accommodated by the "look-ahead" design principle discussed in Section 4.2.2 of Chapter 4.

The look-ahead principle is a pre-implementation design technique that "breadboards" potentially upcoming problem areas for feasibility, before the risk of incorporating that design into the program is too great for catastrophic recovery.

2.7 THE CONCURRENT DOCUMENTATION PRINCIPLE

The second principle guiding this work is that the definition, design, coding, and verification phases of development cannot be regarded as complete until the documentation is complete and certified by some form of correctness audit. This view, which reflects the importance and place of documentation, is taken because good documentation is inextricably bound up in each facet of the project, from conception, to design, to coding, testing, etc., and because the formalization enforces a discipline, creating a program methodology.

But documentation for documentation's sake is not necessarily any good at all. Documentation is part of a software development, inseparable from the analytical, design, programming, coding, and testing phases, and must be integrated into these activities. To be effective, documentation has to have *purpose, content,* and *clarity.*

Just as the top-down procedure requires a special form of training, programmers must also learn *what* "good" documentation consists of, *how* to provide it, and how to *use* it to enhance the project. To do this, it is important that they understand the function of good documentation.

2.7.1 Documentation Goals

Until coding begins, documentation *is* the specification and *is* the design [13]. If documentation is bad, the design is bad. After all, the rationale of a program is for humans, not the computing system. The goal of documentation is *communication.* During the project, documentation serves as a working vehicle to prevent distortion of ideas, promote project control, record design-phase decisions, permit orderly subsystem development, and make the system visible, both in its capabilities, as well as its limitations. When the project is complete, it records the history of development, serves as a tutorial guide to system operation, demonstrates that the program works, and provides a means for maintenance and evaluation of obsolete or amendable portions of the system.

To fulfill these goals, the documentation must describe the program elements not only so that the design analysis and programming functions are exhibited clearly, but also so that management has visibility into the technical, budgetary, and schedule implications of system changes. It must contain a system description that a user can understand—function of the system, rules for use, domain of input, algorithms and procedures that turn input into output, etc. It must tell how the program is to be operated—the system environment, how much storage is used, how fast the program runs, how to load and start or restart after failure, how to keep the program maintained, etc.

That's a tall order, right? And, moreover, all this *content* has to be organized for *clarity.* Some clarity is a natural consequence of the way the content is presented—its *format.* But format can't do it all; creativity and aptness in expression has to come from the documentor.

I have often been presented with two versions of a program, one "structured", and the other "unstructured". To the naked eye, both versions are often equally obscure. It is insufficient to present only the end-product and then to expect a beholder to perceive its significance by inspection, or even after deep meditation. Instead, the beholder must also be able to see at least part of the programming thought processes that went into that end product, starting with the original, highly abstracted motivations, and proceeding to the final program via a clearly presented sequence of clear refinements.

The understandability of the product remains basically a matter of style; some programmers have good style, others do not. Good programming style is not automatically introduced by the rules of structured programming, any more than good English prose style is guaranteed by following the ten famous rules listed in Strunk and White [14]—though these rules can go a long way toward influencing programmers or writers in the direction of good style, by establishing a mental atmosphere conducive to it.

2.7.2 Amount of Documentation

Several problems always exist when a project insists that a program be documented. Probably the most serious are the sins of omission—the cases where something that will be needed later has been left out. Then there are the cases where the documentation does not serve a useful purpose because it does not match the running program. Another frequent form of misdocumentation is irrelevant or redundant *over*documentation, which serves only to drive up development costs.

Conceptually, if an ensemble of development projects were commissioned at varying documentation-level requirements, the plot of the attendant program costs would appear as in Figure 2-11. With no documentation provided—not even annotations in the code or mnemonic variable names—one can readily agree that the complexity of developing a large program poses a nearly impossible barrier, so that costs (dollars, manpower, schedule) would be astronomical. But the costs start to drop as the developers are permitted to write down some of their ideas for later reference. This type of documentation is an *aid*; it reduces errors in thinking (and remembering), so produces a more reliable program in a shorter time.

At some point, as more and more documentation is required, over-documentation sets in, making the costs again rise. That is, *having* documentation can enhance the development process, but *producing* it takes time and runs up the cost. Undoubtedly an optimum exists somewhere in between.

Maintenance software costs probably take a similar shape and results. If program documentation is too thin, the maintainer cannot understand the program. He thus requires a longer time to effect repairs or other changes; he is very apt to introduce undesirable side effects, as well. Provided with

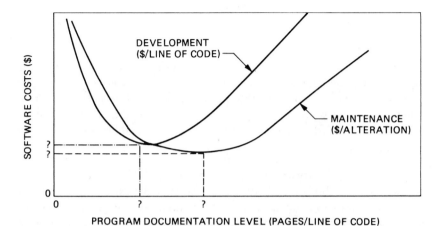

PROGRAM DOCUMENTATION LEVEL (PAGES/LINE OF CODE)

Figure 2-11. Program costs versus documentation level

too much documentation, he spends too much time reading irrelevant data, and then has problems maintaining uniformity when changes are made, catching all the changes to be made in redundant statements.

The optimum level of documentation depends on several factors. When the costs involved cover the developmental phase only—by a fixed-man team—then a low level of documentation suffices. But when there is the possibility that design team personnel can change during the project, or when later maintainability of the program is stated as a documentation requirement, then a higher level is needed. Then too, if humans must draft flowcharts, type narrative, and then maintain these in an error-free condition, there is quite a different cost associated with documentation than when automatic documentation facilities are available.

2.7.3 Types of Documentation

Although the *level* may vary from project to project in rather a subjective way, I shall not leave the question of the documentation *content* to subjective interpretation. I shall produce, as Appendices to this monograph, detailed tables of contents for each of the most important documents to be produced, along with detailed instructions as to what each entry must include. Later chapters will provide disciplines for creating and limiting the entries.

These outlines provide useful baselines from which actual project documentation guidelines can be drawn. In producing the outlines, I have tried to include documentation requirements for every pertinent aspect of the developing program. In forming them, I have extracted, merged, rearranged, and reoriented outlines from several sources [1,15–20] into what I believe is a uniform, coordinated approach to useful software documentation.

I have failed so far to mention what is perhaps the best news about concurrent documentation to the one who must document the program development. It is probably the most natural and easiest technique, because things are written down *as* they occur during the creative process, rather than afterward, when some of the ideas may have been forgotten.

Figure 2-12 depicts a model, or conceptual set of documents that may be produced during a software development. Many of the documents shown may not need to be formal, but may, in fact, only exist in the form of memoranda or even conversations. Which among these actually become formal documents, which remain memoranda and which remain scratchings on the backs of envelopes, are largely the prerogative of project management; but some may also be specified as a requirement for delivery by the customer or operations organization.

The figure shows four organizations, each having its own piece of the documentation pie; any two (or all) of these may, in actuality, be the same organization. Because of this possibility, the need for some of the documents shown may disappear (such as the implementation agreement when originator and implementor are the same). The major flows of information may also differ from case to case.

The model shown depicts things getting started in a Software Justification, by which management is appraised of the needs and costs of a software development. Upon approval, User Requirements and other considerations coalesce into a Functional Requirement; while planning information collects into an Acquisition Plan, which tells how the required capability will be achieved (outside contract, in-house implementation, etc.). The requirements activity then culminates in a Software Requirements Document (SRD). More about this document appears in Chapters 3 and 11 and Appendix C.

The implementing organization, upon receipt of requirements, enters into an analysis of organizational matters to determine such things as whether it can do the job at all, whether it can make a profit, how much of the job it is willing to take on, how much it will bid, whether it has the manpower available, and so on. Based on this Organizational Feasibility Study, it then enters into an Agreement with the requester, detailing what will actually be provided, when, and for how much.

Once agreement has been reached, the implementor is shown to produce a Software Design Definition (SDD). This document is a translation of the

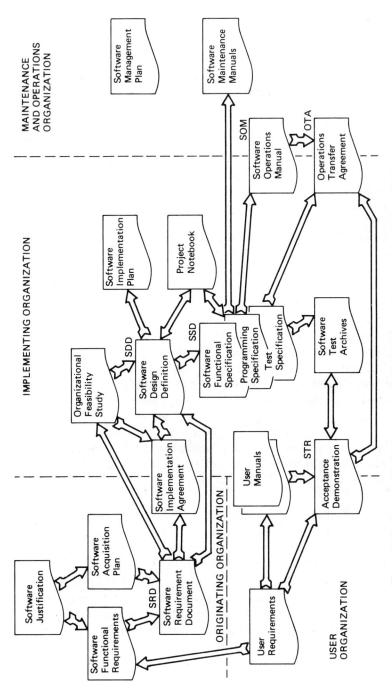

Figure 2-12. A conceptual set of documents which may be generated in a software project

37

requirements embodied in the SRD into a conceptual or architectural design of the program; its purpose is to determine the scope of the work, to refine the original cost and schedule estimates, to formulate the design base at the highest levels of abstraction, and to initiate team selection, work planning, and coordination activities. (A candidate outline for the SDD appears in Appendix D.) The actual detailed work plan appears as a separate Software Implementation Plan.

The main body of the program development work culminates in the Software Specification Document (SSD), shown to be comprised of three subspecifications: 1) The Software Functional Specification (SFS), or the program definition; 2) the Programming (Design) Specification (PS), or merely the program design, and 3) the Software Test Specification (STS). The first of these is the product of the Program Definition Activity; the second, the Program Design Activity; and the third, a mutual product of both the Design and Production Activities. I address the program definition process in the next chapter, the program design in Chapter 4, and testing in Chapter 9. An outline for the SSD appears in Appendix E.

User Requirements and the Software Functional Specification (i.e., the program definition) form the basis for writing User Manuals, a task I have shown as taking place in concert by the user and implementor. User instruction manuals (see Appendix F) concern themselves with instructing the person who must use the program. The contents include just what data to input, how to format and prepare it, how to get it into the system, when and how the output will be received, what that output will say, and perhaps, even how that output is to be interpreted. User Requirements and User Manuals are then the primary source materials used to formulate an appropriate Acceptance Demonstration.

The results of all development tests and acceptance tests are deposited in the project Test Archives (not, as is all too often the case, the waste basket). In addition, a Software Test Report (STR) may be warranted (see Appendix J) to summarize the material in the archives.

As in all good engineering practice, the project progress, design decisions, analyses, etc., are recorded in a Project Notebook (Appendix H). More about the Project Notebook appears in Chapter 10.

If the *user* of the program is not also the *operator* of the program, there will also be a Software Operations Manual (Appendix I), which contains instructions telling how to set up and run the program, where to send the results, how to respond to any promptings for command or data input, and the like.

The Operations Transfer Agreement represents the final delivery of the completed, accepted software package into the maintenance and operation organization. This organization is also shown to have its own Software Management Plan and Software Maintenance Manuals.

It is mandatory, in the interests of project unity, that the project manager define, at the outset, which of these (or other equivalent) documents are to be produced, and in what detail (see Chapter 16 for standard levels of detail). The greatest and most painstaking effort of all should be directed toward producing documentation having the highest impact on project success (including later operations). The documentation that survives the development phase and that will be of high use in later operations should certainly rate a high priority among candidates for that receiving the most effort. High-cost, low-use documentation should be avoided by proper project organization and management.

2.8. SUMMARY

The salient concepts I have tried to introduce in this chapter have to do with hierarchic representations of program specification, data structures, etc., from the topmost, most generalized abstractions, downward to the bottommost, most detailed considerations. I have identified a certain set of activities and interfaces contributing to the end product, and have indicated the role documentation must play, if that end product is to be a success.

In forthcoming chapters, I shall extend these concepts in much more detail. Most of the exposed practices are based on the application of proven and effective standard engineering practices, combined with the concepts and theorems of structured programming, along with its consequent enabling of top-down methods.

Problems for Chapter 2

2-1 Take a short (one or two page) program listing of your choice and with
a set of colored pens draw lines to show the scope of each variable in the
program. Does the scope of any variable depend on the program
execution path? Do any variables possess scopes of activity that are
entirely conditioned?

2-2 Develop 3 story outlines based on the (root) theme "boy meets girl", as
a top-down concept hierarchy using each of the semantic refinement
techniques of Figure 2-7 down to about 4 levels. Compare the plots.
Change one of the concepts (nodes) at level 2 and alter it to a new one,
then recomplete the plot. Compare again each of the three. Which
refinement technique caused the least rework to complete?

2-3 Develop a two- or three-level abstraction hierarchy of data structures
needed to model some particular characteristic of a waiting line at an
airport terminal ticket counter. Identify the representation, manipulations, and axioms needed at each level. Develop both the problem details
(requirements) and solution details (data structure plus access functions
and operations) in level-by-level concurrency, from the top down.

2-4 Let a program with E lines of executable code have D of these, at
random, documented in the form of comments attached to the code. If a
line is fully documented, assume it takes a time T_R to read and
understand (i.e., to absorb the meaning); if a line is undocumented,
assume it takes time T_C to recreate the rationale. Further, assume that
the level of documentation, when it appears, is q, that the amount of
time to read it and comprehend what is there is T_Rq, and that the extra
time needed to create the rest of the rationale is $(1-q)T_C$, where $0 \le q \le$
1. Assume the time to recreate the rationale if none was given takes the
form $T_C(1-dq)^k$ for some k, where $d = D/E$ (this model states that a time
T_C is needed if no documentation, or worthless documentation is
provided, and that no time is required if the code is fully and adequately
documented). Discuss this model and solve for d and q which minimize
the time to read and understand the program. Compare with Figure
2-11.

III. SPECIFICATION OF PROGRAM BEHAVIOR

I identified two activities in the last chapter concerning the definition of program function: requirements and functional specification. It is my view that these two, in their combined content, should be detailed to that level which permits software design or production activities to make arbitrary (but identified and approved) decisions without jeopardizing program functioning. For example, if a functional specification states that the program, upon detecting an error, shall "print an appropriate diagnostic error message on the user's terminal," then I would expect that any message deemed "appropriate" by the program designer or coder would suffice. If the specifier has a different idea of what "appropriate" means, let him so state.

I have alluded to certain beneficial reinforcements that can occur when requirements, definition, design, and production are permitted to take place concurrently on an interacting, cooperating basis. I have also alluded to disasters that can result when this concurrency is improperly structured.

Dijkstra's levels of abstraction seem particularly appropriate in this context. A functional definition developed to a given hierarchic level permits a programmer to proceed immediately with the design, so long as he does not assume specifications beyond this level. In fact, the design process can be used as a tool to verify that the functional specifications at a particular stage are supportable in the design (thereby reducing the risk in top-down development). Unsupportable concepts are nipped in the bud, reducing the amount of revision which would undoubtedly be warranted had the fault been detected at a later time. Side effects are likewise reduced.

3.1 SOFTWARE REQUIREMENTS

The concept of a "software requirement", as the term is often used, sometimes conjures up rather a fuzzy mixture of customer goals, program definition, and even program design. I shall try to be more explicit here, however, by differentiating between two types of requirements, and between software requirements and the program definition.

The foremost characteristic of a requirement is that it primarily addresses the *needs* of the customer (or user) organization. Such requirements are levied in furtherance of the customer's goals, such as to lower production costs, provide a more reliable service, better the organization's capability to compete with other organizations, respond to operational missions, and so forth. These are the requirements *for* the software; they form the *justification* to purchase or develop an automated data processing capability.

The second characteristic of a requirement is that it establishes the set of interfaces and performance criteria on which the justification is based and to which the development that is to follow must conform. These criteria address the needs *of* the software. Such requirements, for example, specify how the user expects to interact with the data, to cause runs to be executed, etc. Some requirements will be highly technical in nature, specifying that certain existing interfaces be observed, certain functions be performed, certain accuracies be achieved, certain services be provided, and perhaps, certain mathematical algorithms be implemented. Other requirements may be more non-technical, such as for development in accordance with certain cost or schedule guidelines, or documentation in accordance with a company standard, etc.

Many of the problems that traditionally arise in software developments are traceable to ill-conceived, poorly specified, misdirected sets of software requirements [21]. Some of these problems are due to a mismatch between the levels of expertise of the originators and the developers; the mismatch then manifests itself as a communication barrier between the two. Other problems arise when customers attempt to define their requirements in terms that properly are prerogatives of development. Other problems, needless to say, arise in redirected efforts, changes in requirements during the development phase, oversights, and so on.

It is important that requirements *be* requirements, not constraints, definitions, or design specifications. That is, those items listed as requirements should state restrictions or expectations relating to organizational goals, user (or operational) environment, or the accomplishment of the assigned mission. Functional requirements should be stated in the form of mathematical transformations, data processing modes, desired options, output criteria, input characteristics, etc., only up to the customer/user/operator interface. This interface may contain quite a lot of technical detail in some cases, but nevertheless, it is important that requirements concentrate on the program *needs*, not on the *program* that responds to those needs.

For example, if FORTRAN is prescribed as the *required* coding language for a project, then one must be able to assume that it is *really* a requirement, and that no other language (which is readily available, conscientiously maintained, or within the expertise of the developers or operational crew) is acceptable because the use of another language is inconsistent with the customer/user/operator interface, or else cannot perform the intended function.

Often, the justification of a software development is based on an assumed model, which relates how the requirer envisions the program to provide its service. He has, perhaps, based costs, schedules, and other plans on this model. But just how much of this planning model should carry over into true program requirements depends on many factors.

Useful guidelines for identifying requirements are:

a. If the requiring organization is attempting to establish a need beyond its expertise to describe, then that need is probably not a requirement, but properly, a part of the program definition or design.

b. If the developing organization is attempting to respond to an overly restrictive requirement when equivalent *or simpler* measures seem adequate, then again that requirement is probably artificial, and should be investigated more thoroughly.

c. If the developing organization *must* define program responses for which there must surely have been a requirement, but yet none was provided, nor was such expressed as a development prerogative, then probably the software requirements are incomplete, and new requirements must be generated, approved, and appended.

3.2 IMPLIED REQUIREMENTS

Whenever a customer organization is capable of defining its goals in terms of software requirements, then there is probably little difficulty in providing the proper tradeoffs and justifications for development. But often, software goals are so non-technical in nature or implied by system considerations that fiscal and schedule estimates cannot be made without extensive consultation by software specialists. In some organizations, the software specialists may even be given the job of establishing requirements for their software to achieve a particular set of system goals.

For example, a spacecraft project office may simply require that "spacecraft ranging data be provided at one-minute intervals over a 5-hour pass, accurate, in the mean-square sense, to one meter". Ranging data, let us suppose, can be extracted and processed in a real-time minicomputer that forms one part of the spacecraft-tracking ground instrumentation system. Since a computer program must then be developed to accumulate and process such data (a fact immaterial to the users of the data), the developing organization finds itself charged with costing, scheduling, planning, and justifying a software development project in response to the spacecraft-project-imposed requirement. The development project justifies its requirements *for* the software as a response to the spacecraft project *dicta*, but must establish the requirements *of* the software as a set of things needed to do the ranging function and to provide the proper user interface characteristics.

As long as such a developer orients his specifications toward the needs or goals of the customer/user/operator, such specifications still state requirements.

In such a situation, the developers have a strong tendency to *define* the program's characteristics, rather than state requirements. My guideline here is the following: *A statement that appears the same in the Software Requirements Document as it does in the Software Definition Document may not be truly stating a requirement, to which the definition is supposed to respond, but rather a program definition.* One may expect rife counter examples to this guideline, but it is still worthwhile to check. For example, the requirement "decode telemetry stream input using the Viterbi algorithm", although quite definitive, is very likely a program requirement, as it implies something about how the telemetry data was encoded at the source; the program definition has no alternative than to respond as required.

3.3 CREATING THE SOFTWARE REQUIREMENT

The justification of a software requirement, created to obtain management approval to proceed in a software development project, is apt to vary greatly among user organizations. One can, however, establish two phases in the creation of the requirement (Figure 3-1). One is the *planning phase* wherein non-technical (or low-level technical), highly interdisciplinary interactions (among users, system analysts, managers) determine feasibility, establish firm objectives, estimate costs, and provide orientation for the development project. This phase establishes the requirements *for* the software. Shaw and Atkins [22] estimate as much as 25% of the total development effort may go into this phase.

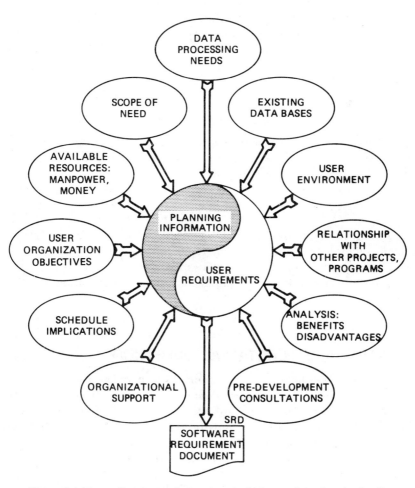

Figure 3-1. The software requirement and what goes into developing it

The other phase, which Shaw and Atkins estimate at perhaps another 25% of the total development effort, may be termed the *user requirements phase*. This effort covers input, information flow, output, documentation or display, environmental, computer-resource, program acceptance, and operational support requirements. Information provided in this phase is again largely non-technical (in the context of program development), oriented towards establishing output criteria, prescribing the program functional capabilities, and scoping the program-embedding environment. This phase establishes the requirements of the software.

Requirements are *definite* only to the extent they are *visible* in documentation. The output of the requirements activity is, therefore, a Software Requirements Document (SRD) satisfying the following criteria:

a. It must be adequate to identify the objectives of the program, its environment, the configuration needed for its operation, the resources required for its support, and the advantages and disadvantages in the service it provides, as related to the customer organization.

b. It must be adequate to permit the remaining developmental activities to proceed under a reasonable assurance that a major revision to the requirements will not be necessary.

c. It must be adequate for review and approval by management on the basis of its conceptual feasibility in accordance with the other criteria above. It must contain manpower, schedules, and development-cost estimates, as well as reasonably accurate variances for these estimates, at least for the next phase of activity.

A candidate outline for the SRD appears as Appendix C. It organizes planning information and user requirements into a hierarchic structure suitable for semantic refinement. Topics may be detailed to whatever level is needed to characterize the requirement. Rules for completing the SRD appear in Chapter 11.

3.4 SOFTWARE FUNCTIONAL DEFINITION

Up to this point, the software development activity has been largely non-technical. During the software definition activity, the analysis and documentation effort move toward the middle level of technical depth (Figure 3-2). Output of this activity will ultimately be a Software Functional Specification (SFS) containing technical material (as opposed to the conceptual layouts developed in the SRD) relative to input/output definitions (data base definitions, data base formats, I/O device handling, etc.), processing functions (decision tables, mathematical algorithms on information structures), definitions of technical constraints (such as execution time, storage limitations, etc.), and stipulation of control functions. In the end, the SFS characterizes the program to be written as a "black-box" response. However, some aspects of a computer program differentiate it from other black boxes and serve to make writing a definition unique. Depending on the specific situation, the SFS could contain material stipulating the utilization of certain logical algorithms; but generally, these are left as prerogatives of the design and production activities.

It is important that the definition concentrate on telling *what* the program is going to do. Descriptions of the environment, various conditions

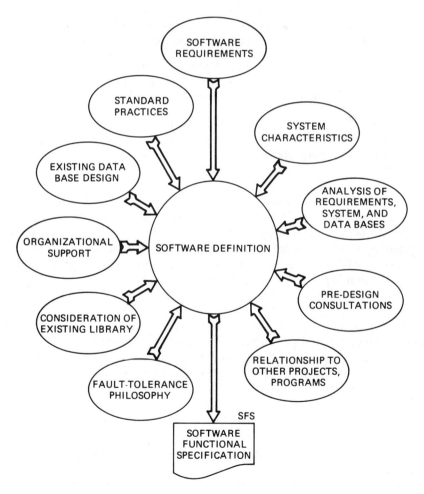

Figure 3-2. The software definition and what goes into it

to be met, and similar passive elements can obscure the main issues, if introduced at the wrong points.

The Software Functional Specification (SFS), when complete, satisfies the following criterion:

> It defines the meaning of program correctness; any program meeting the technical and documentation specifications will be deemed a satisfactory deliverable.

During the completion process, each phase of the SFS satisfies the following criteria:

a. It is sufficient to initiate the development of user manuals as a separate activity, parallel to (but coordinating with) any concurrent program development activities (design and production).

b. It is adequate for continuing the program definition and development activities (design and production) with reasonable assurance that major revisions will not be necessary.

c. It is reviewable by project and user personnel on the basis of its technical feasibility and accuracy, in accordance with the SRD and the other criteria above.

Appendix E gives a candidate outline for the SFS as a part of the overall Software Specification Document (SSD), which is arranged for hierarchic statement of program and documentation specifications. As was the case in Appendix C, the outline is very detailed and suitable for semantic refinement of both technical and non-technical program sub-specifications. Rules for completing the SFS appear in Chapter 11.

The generation of user and maintenance manuals could rightly be considered an integral part of a software development effort, and may well appear among the tasks of the development team in many cases. Moreover, the costs of developing such documentation must certainly be allocated, accounted for, and managed as effectively as any other development resource. Regrettably, however, I have not been able to organize these manuals into the same sort of detailed uniform treatment given to the rest of the development documentation. Their content, format, and level depend so heavily on the intended audience and the program function. I do, however, give some guidelines for their content (Chapter 16) and for their role and interaction with the other parts of the development effort (Chapters 10 and 15). Suggested outlines appear in Appendices F and K.

3.5 INTERACTION BETWEEN REQUIREMENTS AND DEFINITION ACTIVITIES

Requirements are primarily set by the customer organization, and definitions, by the implementing organization. These need not necessarily be distinct, but in the general case, they are. Such requirements are generally levied by persons with a different expertise than those who must respond to those requirements. But it is important that those setting requirements and those defining functional specifications *agree* to the feasibility of the technical task and the accuracy of manpower and budgetary estimates.

What a program is supposed to do is sometimes subject to wide interpretation, even after a previous initial agreement. It is important, therefore, that the customer remain involved with the remainder of the development, especially during program specification activity (Figure 3-3).

When a program is thus being developed, with concurrent interaction among requirements and definition (also definition and design), it is necessary to interpret the SRD and SFS criteria stated earlier as being true in a hierarchical sense. For example, in the SFS, the criterion by which program correctness is to be judged should be interpreted to apply only to that part of the definition stated so far, at the current hierarchical level. Before the design effort acts upon it, there should have been concurrence that the current level of definition agrees with the (perhaps also partially developed) software requirement.

The need for proper requirement and definition hierarchies to enable this interactive process to continue successfully is evident. Semantic refinement by way of detailed subconcepts (see Figure 2-7a) is ideal in this respect, as it allows the detailing of a requirement at level n + 1, based on a requirement at level n, to take place concurrently with the writing of a

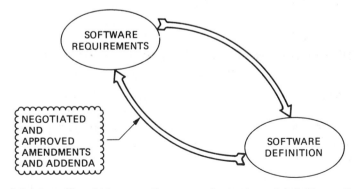

Figure 3-3. Interactions between software requirements and definition activities

definition in response to the level-n requirement, while design is working
on a program to satisfy the previous working-level definition (see Figure
3-4).

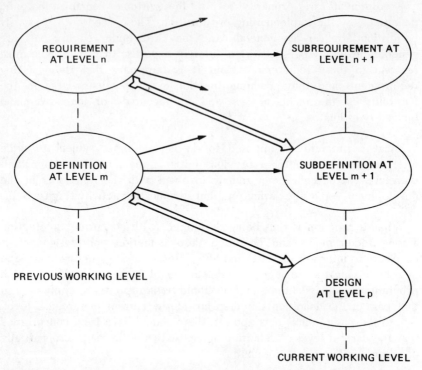

**Figure 3-4. Top-down precedence in requirement, definition, and design activities
at concurrent working levels (unterminated arrows point to other detailed
subconcepts not shown on this diagram; wide arrows show information flow)**

Detailed rules for encouraging and administering the cooperating
interaction of disciplines will be given in Chapter 10, Project Organization
and Management.

3.6 INFORMATION-FLOW DIAGRAMS

A similar diagram, flowcharts, have traditionally been an important
design and production aid because they display how control is passed from
program module to program module during execution. There is a tendency,
therefore, for those doing program definition to also try to use flowcharts to
describe what they intend a program to do. However, specifying the
control logic for a program so early in the development tends to obscure
what the program should do functionally in favor of ways a machine can
sequence its operations. Control logic is really the province of *design*,

whereas *definition* should precede it. Control-logic flowcharts, therefore, during definition may be premature.

Information-flow diagrams, on the other hand, can be a tremendous aid in specifying and clearly illustrating the necessary data routing and transformation procedures which operate on the *information structures* (see Section 2.2) of a program. Hardware design engineers have been using the equivalent of information-flow diagrams for years—they call them *block-diagrams.* They have an edge, however, because the blocks in their diagrams represent identifiable, real modules to be built. Whereas modules on information-flow graphs may merely be abstractions that serve to identify the *problem* and describe it in enough detail so that the design process can *solve* that problem unambiguously.

Nevertheless, programs can be defined in terms of modular, hierarchically-refined definition units characterizing the program response in a way that can be audited against the design for consistency. These units can be graphically displayed using information-flow diagrams. As an example, consider the chart shown in Figure 3-5, which depicts a generalized data processing problem. The information flows from a *read* unit, to a *process* unit, and finally to a *print* unit. In the program to be written, the actual order of reading, processing, and printing is likely to be intermixed. Hence, a flowchart at this stage obscures *what* is taking place with a lot of detail as to *how* it is being done, or how the flow of control is passed, or how the program is to be organized into execution modules.

At the next level, the *read* unit expands to a chart, such as that in Figure 3-6, showing the various data sources and *information structures* (not data structures) holding the data. The example shows that the data to be processed emanates from a data tape, while the printing format information comes from a control-data file. Additional information detailing both these inputs may appear at a next level of definition. The information at each level occupies certain structures assigned for communication with and reference by other definition units.

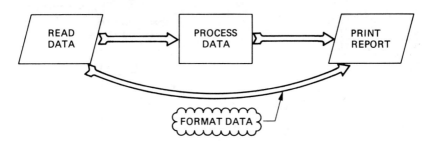

Figure 3-5. A data processing program information-flow diagram

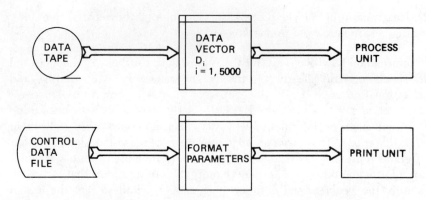

Figure 3-6. Expansion of the *read* unit of Figure 3-5

The data processing unit has its expansion depicted in Figure 3-7, which identifies a data-decoding function composed of a synchronization unit and a decomutation unit. Data output to the print unit are characterized at this level only by the information structure labels A and B, to be detailed at later levels.

Similar (data flow) diagrams are shown in the next chapter to be useful in the early parts of the design activity. As I have represented the two, definition and design take place in an integrated fashion, anyway. The difference between the two types of diagrams is that, in definition, information flow is concerned with communicating the program function, whereas, in design, the diagrams identify the *connectivity* between the executable program modules and data structures they access.

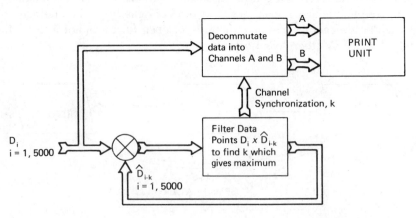

Figure 3-7. The process unit information flow diagram for Figure 3-5

3.7 SUMMARY

In this chapter I have formulated the technique of hierarchic refinement as a tool for *defining* program behavior without *designing* the program. I have given criteria for the documents to be developed, and I have indicated how the developmental activities all dovetail together in hierarchic unity. More specific rules for writing program definitions appear in Chapter 11.

Problems for Chapter 3

3-1 Establish a detailed software requirement for an opinion-poll company to automate its statistical data-reduction operations. State justification for expenditures based on company goals and current modes of operation. Sketch plans for acquiring and operating the automated capability. State technical requirements and criteria for accepting the program for operations. Develop this material into a set of view-graph slides suitable for presentation to a review board.

3-2 Define the external characteristics of the program in problem 3-1 in hierarchic levels of detail. Was it necessary to augment, change, or otherwise refine the customer requirements in doing so? Was it necessary to design any of the internal aspects of the program in doing so?

3-3 Structure the requirements of problem 3-1, the definitions of problem 3-2, and aspects of the internal program design discovered in problem 3-2 into hierarchic levels of detail such that requirements at level n are responded to by definitions at levels greater than or equal to n, and internal design aspects at still logically subordinate levels.

3-4 Specify, for the software to be developed in problem 3-1 above, which documents among those discussed in Section 2.7.3 are to be made formal and which are to be informal. Discuss the general level of detail for each document as it relates to this particular project and identify what is to become of each document at the termination of the development phase. Identify any other documents to be produced, along with their corresponding levels of detail and final destination.

IV. PROGRAM DESIGN

Even if there is very little hope of ever completely characterizing the "optimal design process", much progress in this direction can be made by adopting formal disciplines that encourage the identification of goals, problem constraints, design parameters, and solution alternatives. Design requires creativity, ingenuity, and innovation, and, for this reason, cannot be made a rigorously formal procedure. However, a sound approach methodology towards problem solving and a base of schooling and experience in software technology turns what otherwise would be an art, masterable by only a privileged few, into an engineering discipline that can be learned by many.

This chapter, then, coordinates several worthwhile programming tools and methodologies into a formalized rationale for software design. Included are: top-down development, look-ahead analysis, program modularization, structured control flow, and hierarchic levels of definition.

4.1 DESIGN CONSIDERATIONS

The typical software development project goal is to "produce a program, maximizing its *quality*, but subject to budgetary and schedule constraints". *Quality*, however, can be judged according to several, perhaps competing, criteria [23], among which are:

- Reliability (characterized by the number of bugs in a program)
- Maintainability (indicated by the ease in fixing bugs)
- Modifiability (measured by the cost of altering the program)
- Generality (characterized by the functional scope of the program)
- Usability (indicated by ease of use)
- Performance (characterized by running efficiency)

Design is a process that generates a link between a problem and its solution. As I shall use the term in this chapter, it generates the link between the program functional definition and the internal program code. Even programs "created on the coding pad", without a formal design phase, have nevertheless, required some design effort. The *quality* of a program is a direct reflection on the *quality* of its design. It therefore behooves the programmer to consider the design aspects very carefully and very deliberately.

The basic elements required to design a good program are an understanding of the function to be served and the mechanisms available to carry out the job. The design must then be conveyed clearly and unambiguously to the programmer along with any special rules for added clarity.

Not every first idea is a best one, and for this reason, there is usually an iteration process involved in coming up with a good design. Moreover, iteration and reworking a program rationale at design-time is the proper place for that iteration and rework, rather than later, when there may be a large investment in documentation and code.

The techniques discussed in this chapter help to make the investment during development less sensitive to premature design decisions. However, these are not replacements for design aptitude, but tools which serve to guide that aptitude through an otherwise uncharted region.

4.1.1 Characterization of the Design Process

Because it requires creativity, design is a difficult process to pin down definitively. Basically, however, its input is a problem and its output is a specification; in the present context, the output is a specification for how the coding is to take place.

As I shall be dealing with it, this process is that activity defining program data structures and logical algorithms in response to, and conforming with, the software functional definition. It consists of describing the program organization, data manipulations, I/O procedures, and the like, carried to a level of detail that will serve as the working basis for programming and operational implementation. This activity defines the modular breakdown of the entire program, thereby specifying work units for coding.

I have represented the design process in Figure 4-1 as being composed of (at least) two components and a number of considerations affecting the result. One part of design is non-procedural; that is, the allocation of program resources and definition of data structures. This part will then be accessed and manipulated by the second part, the procedure, or algorithms.

4.1.2 Design Requisites

The first requisite for a designer is technical skill. The aptitude of an individual for design is measurable to some degree by his ability to:

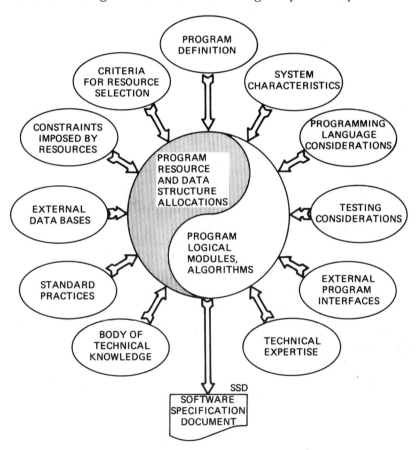

Figure 4-1. Considerations making up the program design

- Analyze problems

- Identify constraints and potential solutions

- Make trade-offs, choose alternatives, and render judgements

- Draw on background of technology, methods, and tools

He must know the fundamental principles of problem solving, and he must be capable of applying these to the problem at hand. He must be thoroughly conversant with the theory and practice of his trade, and he must be capable of identifying all potentially useful alternate approaches. Finally, he must be capable of making sound and responsible tradeoff judgements among these. In short, he must be a *professional.*

The need for a well-organized approach and well-structured documenta-tion, with inputs and outputs clearly defined and logically arranged, is fundamental. The product of a design *is* documentation. No amount of rote nor helpful hints will eliminate the need for painstaking care and use of techniques which allow the designers to keep track of all the program intricacies.

Full use of graphic and narrative material lends clarity to the design. Some things which contribute particularly well are data-base and data-structure design tables, logical flow diagrams, data-connection diagrams, decision logic tables, mathematical formulas, and perhaps even Boolean algebraic expressions.

4.1.3 Humans vs Tools in Problem Solving

Problems pertaining to the design of software systems may perhaps be categorized with regard to the required degree of comprehension required by the designer at any one stage of the solution. Small problems fit into the designer's head all at once, without segmentation in any form. Large problems, however, require segmentation into pieces which can fit into a single comprehension span before solution is feasible. Because human experience and intelligence is variable, the differentiation between which things are comprehensible as a unit, and which are not, is very subjective.

Moreover, small problems can usually be solved and implemented in a variety of ways, seemingly without undue difficulty; whereas, larger problems may require laborious study before they can, by abstraction, be made to resemble smaller problems, or can be dissected into a number of smaller subproblems that when taken together, solve the original problem. To convert large, incomprehensible problems concerning a great number of details into small, comprehensible subproblems with relatively few details means that the lines of dissection must be chosen to modularize the original problem into subproblems that contain only those details which are relevant and conceal those details which are not relevant. This systematic selective hiding of design details is what makes solution of a large problem possible.

The following design rules and restrictions are intended to guide the dissection of a large problem into comprehensible subproblems, not only for the designer, but also for his supervisors, managers, and any future readers. The use of top-down methods, hierarchic decomposition, levels of abstraction, structured control flow, semantic refinement, use of graphic and descriptive material, etc., are very effective, each in its own way. However, it is not the set of tools that solves a problem, it is the human that uses the tools. Part of the acumen of a good designer is the ability to match the right tool to the right problem.

Regrettably, then, this work will not be able to provide all designers with every tool they will need to solve problems, nor, once solved, to express their solutions in the most effective manner. However, it will provide a standard that can be applied in the absence of better methods.

4.2 TOP-DOWN PROGRAM DEVELOPMENT

The theme of this monograph is (I say again) top-down, modular, hierarchic, structured development of software. In keeping with the idea that cooperative interaction among development activities is beneficial, the design procedures I give permit the design to be checked concurrently by coding and testing through hierarchic levels from the top down.

In doing a structured, modular, hierarchic design, one starts with an end-to-end overall description (definition) of the program and analyzes it into a number of component parts according to a set of decomposition rules. In terms of flowcharts, one starts with a single box that represents the entire program at the top hierarchic level, and expands that box into a flowchart at the next level, which displays the component subfunctions as a structured algorithm, in keeping with certain flowchart-topology rules. Each of the subfunctions is given a precise, end-to-end subspecification, to be expanded into its own flowchart at the next design level, and so on, until such a level is reached that the collection of final subspecifications can be coded directly, without functional ambiguity. Figure 4-2 illustrates this hierarchic tree structure of the program modules.

I shall discuss permissible flowchart topologies (structures) and how they enhance the design process in the next two chapters. In the remainder of this chapter, let me show how the modular, hierarchic breakdown of program functions into subfunctions works to great advantage in the top-down development of programs.

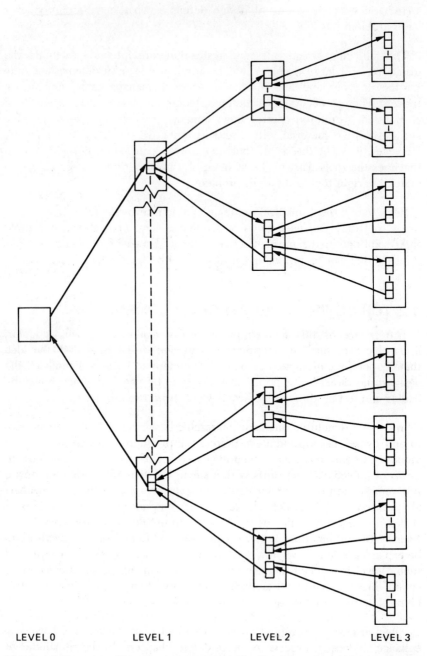

LEVEL 0   LEVEL 1   LEVEL 2   LEVEL 3

Figure 4-2. Decomposition of a program specification into a hierarchy of modular subfunctions

4.2.1 Hierarchic Decomposition

Hierarchic decomposition [12,24,25] identifies the programming process as a step-by-step expansion of mathematical functions into structures of logical connectives and subfunctions, carried out until the derived subfunctions can be directly realized in the programming language being used. The documentation of the program supplies the tool for assessing correctness of these expansions.

The documentation—that is, the design, for documentation *is* the design at this stage—is purely for the benefit of humans, not the computing system. The computer executes whatever instructions it receives. Hierarchic decomposition will channel documentation detail into functional levels, so that humans can comprehend the program at each level by regarding the next lower level as a functional subunit.

The technique thus provides a way to control program complexity in a disciplined, systematic way. With complexity under control, the possibility for producing a correct design is greatly enhanced.

Such a design, moreover, is suitable for coding immediately; those subfunctions that permit can be translated directly into the chosen programming language. Those which require detailing at the next hierarchic level can be programmed as blocks of temporary code or dummy "stubs", as Mills [12] calls them—simple procedures that merely supply or test interfaces for the algorithm at the current level. Furthermore, the program can then be run and tested, within the capability of the dummy stubs. Once there is verification that the program works with the dummy stubs as it should, the dummy stubs can be replaced using later-level designs for their intended subfunctions.

Of course, the dummy stubs cannot provide a full interface to the rest of the program for all possible inputs without being the full code for that stub. Rather, it is intended to work for one or more special test cases, to check the operation of that part of the program already designed and coded. Any errors detected can be corrected immediately, before they have a chance to penetrate further into the design.

Mills' correctness theorem in the next chapter states that (if flowchart topologies are structured as he prescribes) if the program at a given hierarchic level is known to be correct, then it will still be correct after all of the stubs are replaced. In principle then, using dummy stubs permits checking the entire design (and coding) for correctness from the top down, and, in practice, greatly reduces the amount of checking needed to achieve a given level of confidence in the program. The concurrency of design, coding, and testing provides checks and balances; when the design is complete, coding is not far behind, and the program is very likely to be correct.

The flowchart topologies, or logical connectivity of the subfunctions, to be studied in the next chapters, are structures which permit programs to be even more readily readable, understood, coded, and tested, and then maintained and modified. Control branching is entirely standardized so that the flowchart, accompanying narrative, and resultant code can be read from top to bottom without having to trace the branching logic in an intricate, convoluted way.

Thus, the design ultimately manifests itself as documentation that is readable from the top down, page by page, level by level.

4.2.2 Look-Ahead Design

The top-down method manifests itself in a series of hierarchies, not just one. So far, I have talked principally about developing the program control-logic hierarchy from the top down, in execution sequence. But the reader should not confuse this hierarchy with the top-down concept-development hierarchy by which the fundamental bases for the program emerge. One must realize that the mental abstractions needed to solve problems are quite different than the control- logic abstractions which result in flowcharts, code, or other equivalents of program procedure.

For example, in solving a concurrent processing problem, one of the top-level considerations affecting the whole design might be concerned with the feasibility and efficiency of certain resource arbitration algorithms. Thus, primitive functions REQUEST and RELEASE might be closely scrutinized early to determine that these key design elements are feasible and have certain envisioned (or discovered) properties.

Viewed with respect to the control-logic development hierarchy, however, these functions may appear as bottom-level modules. What were top-level considerations in the concept department are represented in the program tree by relatively bottom-level stubs.

The apparent misalignment of these two hierarchics does not mean that the top-down method should be abandoned. Instead, there needs to be an accommodation made in the development discipline to permit these hierarchics to interact in the most effective manner.

In bridging the software gap (Figure 1-1), there is always the risk, as in any systems design, of running up against an unsupportable specification made somewhere earlier in the design. This risk is true whether the procedure is top down, bottom up, or inside out. Concurrent coding and testing tend to minimize the chances of having an incorrect or inconsistent design up to a given point, but they do not negate the risk that the program might actually fail to connect the problem to the programming language.

This type of risk is not exclusive to programming design, but occurs everywhere that conceptual system specifications are to be connected to the real-world. It can be averted by resorting to a technique that can be called a "look- ahead" design, or a "baseline" design, or a "preliminary" design. What the designer actually does, according to M. Easterling in an internal JPL memorandum, is to "sketch out the key details of the remaining work to assure that what he is doing at present will be proper when reviewed in retrospect, at a later stage in the design". (See Figure 4-3.)

In the present context, the top-down design hierarchy with concurrent documentation is intended to provide a logical and orderly way for the various development team members to work together, to guard against mistakes, and to produce the needed documentation directly in the process. The team interactions and individual progress milestones can take place in a supervised, formalized discipline, as will be discussed in Chapter 10.

A complete look-ahead design may well precede the formal detailed design, to form the "architecture" or basis for estimating costs, schedule milestones, and the work task breakdown structure for later activity. During this architectural phase, detailed correctness of the algorithms is not as important as the development of a sound foundation for the later formal, detailed design. The look-ahead notes can include flowchart sketches, worked out algorithms, data structure preliminaries, and narrative descriptions of things to come. Only when the designer has assured himself that what he is formally obliged to produce at the current level is correct,

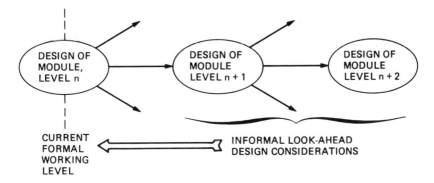

Figure 4-3. Logical precedence and flow of information in a look-ahead design

does he submit it into the body of project-controlled design documentation at that point. Then, and only then, is it coded and tested.

There are potential problems, however, that a project manager must avert in look-ahead efforts. Foremost, he must maintain adequate visibility into look-ahead activity, and avoid the ceaseless "tinkering" that sometimes has a tendency to occur.

4.2.3 Designing for Correctness

A correct program is one that performs according to its definition. In a correct, top-down design, the functionally specified behavior is considered paramount at each level of the development.

But while the program design may be correct at each succeeding level, deep into the program, the program still may not perhaps bridge the gap all the way to realization. An impase may occur at a certain level in which the function specified is not implementable. The design problem is to find the *correct* bridge that spans the *whole* gap. There may be many; in fact, that is far more likely to be the case than there being only one.

The end product of the design activity is a software specification, which can then be implemented into code. To avoid errors of omission in the design, I have provided a detailed outline (see Appendix E) for the Program Specification (PS). This PS, on completion, can be joined with the Software Functional Specification (SFS) and Software Test Specification (STS) to form the Software Specification Document (SSD). The SSD and code listings become the major portions of the program development documentation. During development, the SSD is the design document; afterward, it is the "as built" specification, satisfying the following criteria:

a. It is adequate to permit concurrent coding and checkout using dummy stubs at the completion of project-imposed design milestones.

b. It is adequate, upon completion of these milestones, for continuing the design to later milestones.

c. It satisfies the program requirements set forth in the Software Requirements Document (SRD) and conforms to design and documentation rules and standards in a reviewable, demonstratable way.

d. It is adequate for use as a later maintenance document.

e. It is adequate for use as a design-control agent within the development project.

In summary, the top-down approach keeps the design correct at each stage of the development, and look-ahead helps to make the bridge reach the other side of the gap. Concurrent documentation provides a way of writing the ideas down in the sequence they are generated and needed. The SSD outline (Appendix E)·helps avoid errors of omission. Concurrent coding and then testing validate the design. Everything coordinates and cooperates in the development process, so that when the design is finished, there is only a short step to program delivery, complete with documentation. That's the idea, anyway. But to make it work, I'll need to be much more specific about how things are carried out and coordinated, from top to bottom.

4.3 PROGRAM ALLOCATIONS

Allocation of data structures and other program resources need to be integrated with the procedural design. But this allocation as well as design of such resources cannot usually be separated from the algorithms and procedures that involve those resources. In fact, certain algorithms, by their nature, require certain structures. For example, an algorithm that creates and then consumes data on a first-in-first-out basis needs a queue; a last-in-first-out algorithm, a stack. If procedures are to be developed in hierarchic levels of subfunctions, then the corresponding resources need a corresponding design hierarchy.

4.3.1 Data Structures

Data structures to be used in a program are particularly well suited [10] to being designed in the "levels of abstraction" imposed by the hierarchic modular decomposition of the program specifications. Recall that top-layer considerations are concerned with the problem, and that deeper layers traverse the span to programming language. The specification hierarchy for a data structure will thus begin with one fitting the needs of the problem, and wind up with detail at the programming language level.

This technique permits one to concentrate on relevant features of the situation and to postpone for later consideration those factors believed to be less relevant. By this process, one decides to concentrate on properties shared by objects or situations by subordinating the differences between them.

For example, suppose, in the upper layers of a design, that one may recognize the need for a "stack" to hold certain data in a module. No more information is supplied at that level, not even the name, because no other interfaces appear. However, at some eventual hierarchic detailing of the module (Figure 4-4), the name will become important, as well as perhaps functions which fetch and store data in that stack. Upon expansion of those functions, more detail is needed about the stack, such as its size, and the pointer to its top element. Eventually, the entire detail of the stack, down to the bit-by-bit machine configuration will be specified. Figures 4-4 and 4-5 show alternatives for the stack level-3 design.

Thus, the process of hierarchic decomposition of the program into subprograms generates a hierarchic composition of the data structure definition. Only the details needed at a given level will have been supplied (although the designer is free to "look ahead" in data-structure design, just as he is in module design). And just as it is important to document the program logical algorithms—perhaps as narrative and flowcharts—it is

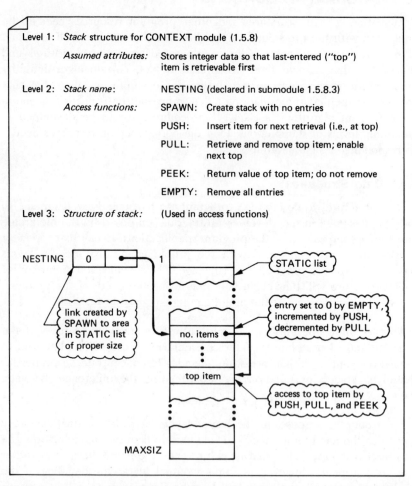

Figure 4-4. A simplified data structure design hierarchy for the stack structure first referenced in a module named CONTEXT (only the first three levels of definition are shown)

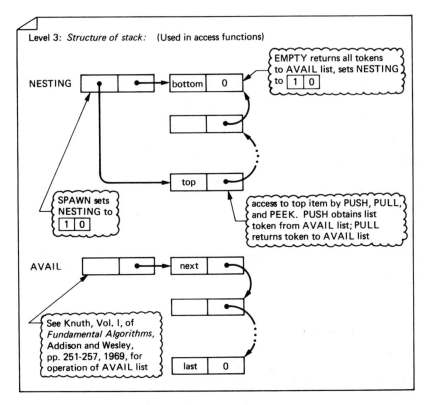

Figure 4-5. An alternate level-3 design for the stack structure NESTING of Figure 4-4 (note that levels 1 and 2 remain unchanged, as is the remainder of the design using the stack)

likewise important to keep the data structure definitions current in some documented form.

For this reason, the SSD (Appendix E) contains a Data Structure Definition Table, and I give specific rules for the format and content of the table entries in Chapter 12, Program Design Standards.

The process of abstraction hinges on finding generalized representations (or a set of symbols) to stand for objects or situations, a set of operations to manipulate the representations, and a set of rules to relate how the objects or situations in the real world react, based on similar actions on the representations.

I have not revealed how one goes about deciding which data structure to use in any given situation, any more than I have stated how one chooses procedures to solve a given problem. A programmer must still have the professional skill required for his trade. Data structuring by abstractions will, however, organize the approach.

As a starting point, one should probably begin with the most abstract concepts of the information structure of a problem and its envisioned method of solution. Then using stepwise refinements of both the procedure and information contents, one creates increasingly more concrete representations of the informational elements as data structures, accessed by certain operations in certain ways. One should concentrate primarily at each level with *what* is being done, rather than *how* it is to be done (which will be defined in later abstractions). It is proper to use look-ahead-design checks for feasibility; however, only design items approved at the formal current working level (Figure 4-3) may be used as interfaces for later design or coding.

At each level of abstraction, it is useful to study the needs of the problem, that is, to discover all the relevant aspects of the information elements, such as:

● Source

● Amount of information

● Types and other attributes of data elements (such as units)

● Relationships among data elements

● Decomposition of elements into subelements

● Operations to be performed on elements

● Access frequency to elements and response time required

● Accuracy, privacy, lifetime

Then, one may more rationally invent representations of data structures (or refinements of previously defined structures) and functions to accommodate the abstraction (see Figure 4-5). It is important to assess the correctness of the representation; i.e., to assure oneself that the defined functions on the invented representation correspond to intended operations on the actual information (in the real world).

For this assessment, in a conceptual sense, data items can be viewed as nodes, and relationships among items, as interconnecting lines, on a "data graph". In fact, it is often useful to display such a graph as a design aid—it tends to keep the data structure definition simple and documentable. The disjoint connected subgraphs can become separate data structures, since there are no cross-relationships among the disjoint items. Levels of abstraction can furthermore designate certain nodes of the graph as entities for later refinement into subgraphs, in many cases.

Once the structure is graphed, then one must decide whether the links between data nodes are to be realized as actual connections (pointers) within the data structure, or whether such links are programmed into the access functions. This decision primarily concerns whether data is structure-linked or access-linked, whether it is unpacked or packed, whether it is a direct or indirect representation, and whether the program is structure-driven or program-driven.

For example, a compiler may be built around rather simple algorithms that analyze each input string by following the set of language grammar rules stored off in some table, in comparison to algorithms that access no such table of rules, but have the grammar coded directly into the procedure. Which method is used depends on an analysis of each situation against the criteria and guidelines for program quality established at the outset.

These guidelines need to state both high-level and low-level policies for making design tradeoffs. Some of the things needed, for example, are an enumeration of the basic data types available in the programming language to be used (integer, floating point, string, etc.), and the facilities for building more complex types from these (automatic list generation, etc.). There also needs to be a guideline for the degree of data packing to save space, as opposed to the lack of packing to save access time. If packing saves both time and space, it may be necessary also to consider whether packing also causes the program to be more complicated or to require extra expense (e.g., garbage collection). In some cases such as that illustrated in Figure 4-6, one may decide to support two types of representations of the same general structure.

To make some needed judgements, it may be necessary to carry sample look-ahead efforts all the way from the top, down to the programming language level, and perhaps back up again, to learn about access times, storage, and other things. These items could seriously impact the data structuring and module functions if discovered after formal top-down coding has begun.

4.3.2 Resource Allocation and Access Hierarchies

Data structures are just one example of computer resources in which the top-down design process induces an increasingly more detailed definition hierarchy upon its constituents. The hierarchy describes the resource in *levels of access*. At the top, the only access was through the vague notion of the structure, or perhaps the type of structure. At the next level, the name could be used, etc. At some point in this hierarchy, the level of access becomes definite enough that hard program interfaces can be made.

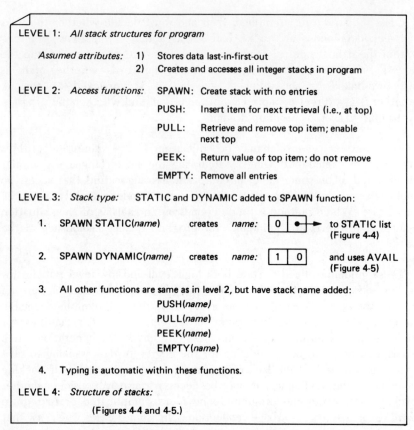

LEVEL 1: *All stack structures for program*

    Assumed attributes: 1) Stores data last-in-first-out

                      2) Creates and accesses all integer stacks in program

LEVEL 2: *Access functions:* SPAWN: Create stack with no entries

                               PUSH: Insert item for next retrieval (i.e., at top)

                               PULL: Retrieve and remove top item; enable
next top

                               PEEK: Return value of top item; do not remove

                               EMPTY: Remove all entries

LEVEL 3: *Stack type:*   STATIC and DYNAMIC added to SPAWN function:

    1. SPAWN STATIC(*name*)   creates   *name:*   0 ●→ to STATIC list
(Figure 4-4)

    2. SPAWN DYNAMIC(*name)*   creates   *name:*   1 | 0   and uses AVAIL
(Figure 4-5)

    3. All other functions are same as in level 2, but have stack name added:

                                   PUSH(*name)*

                                   PULL(*name)*

                                   PEEK(*name)*

                                   EMPTY(*name)*

    4. Typing is automatic within these functions.

LEVEL 4: *Structure of stacks:*

            (Figures 4-4 and 4-5.)

**Figure 4-6. An alternate definition hierarchy for declaring and accessing all
program stacks, both in static and dynamic lists**

It finally proceeds down to the level in which the individual computer
components are accessible.

As an example, let us suppose that data from a given last-in first-out
(LIFO) stack may be accessed at some level of the design via functions
PUSH, PULL, PEEK, etc., as illustrated in Figure 4-7. Then all accesses to the
stack in the rest of the program can be made only via this level of access,
except for those *inside* the access functions themselves which then have a
deeper, more detailed level of access to the data structure. In this case, the
access functions PUSH, PULL, PEEK are inextricable parts of the data structure
abstraction. The functions *own* the structure at that access level.

The concept may be extended; suppose functions PUSH(*stack*), PULL
(*stack*), etc., represent a level of access for a set of LIFO structures any of
whose names can then be substituted for the syntactic variable *stack* above.

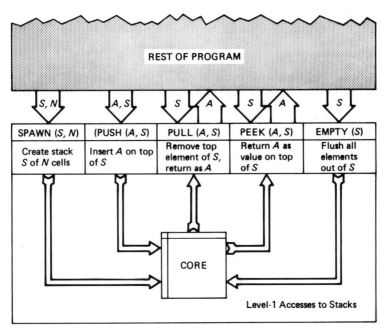

Figure 4-7. The top level of access to the STACK set of data structures

Again, the access functions own the set of stacks exclusively at that level of access, in the sense that modules outside PUSH and PULL wishing to access a stack *must* access that stack only through these functions.

The general idea here is that resources may be characterized by their levels of access as well as by the services they perform. A *level of access* for a set of resources is defined as an interface through which all accesses to any constituent part of a resource must pass, except for those at deeper levels within the hierarchy.

Levels of access can provide a conceptual framework for achieving a clear and logical design for a system. At the lowest level are the access functions for individual resource units such as arithmetic registers, memory cells, file elements, etc. File elements are built into records by defining functions to process groups of file elements as a unit; records are built into files by defining functions to process groups of records as a unit, and so on, up the hierarchy. Each level supports an important abstraction (see Figure 4-8).

Each access level consists of one or more externally accessible functions (modules) sharing common resources. The connections in control and data among the various access modules induced by the top-down design

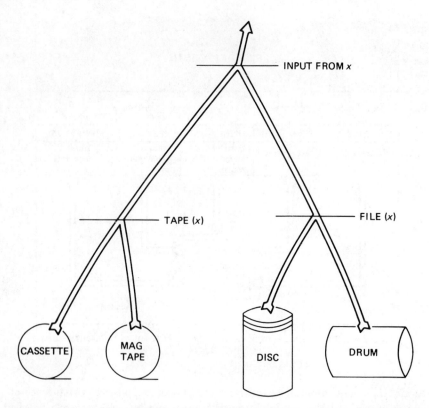

INPUT FROM *x*

TAPE (*x*)

FILE (*x*)

CASSETTE

MAG
TAPE

DISC

DRUM

Figure 4-8. Levels of access for tape and file input are indicated by horizontal lines through information flow lines (note logical cohesion of functions within the accesses; see Section 4.4.2)

hierarchy are limited in a natural way. Every resource used by a program will eventually be represented in a hierarchy whose levels map the needs of the problem into the characteristics of the resource.

The process of hierarchic decomposition of a program into subfunctions (resource access modules) thus generates a hierarchic composition of resource requirements. The SSD (Appendix E) contains provision for Resource Access Requirements Tables to maintain the current state of the access levels in documented, visible form; I give specific rules for the format and content of those table entries in Chapter 12, Program Design Standards.

4.3.3 Data Connection

As I stated in the preceding chapter, an information flow analysis is a natural tool for specifying *what* a program function is in terms of transformations of input data to the output wanted. In design, which specifies *how* the computer is to implement these, it is useful to identify module data interfaces, to identify the precedence of data creation and use among modules, and to promote understanding of the program interactions. For example, if data created in modules A and B are going to be further processed by module C, then execution of A and B must precede C; if A and B do not share data, either may be executed first.

One could conceivably erase all the flow lines from a program flowchart and replace them by lines representing the data structure accesses instead, as a graphic way to identify operations on the data and to display data interconnectivity between executing modules. Such a chart undoubtably would be convincing evidence that analyzing data connectivity can be far more complicated than analyzing program control flow. For this reason, data connectivity design should, from the very first, be made to adhere to a discipline that minimizes module connectivity and organizes it into understandable units. Such a discipline, when coupled with structured control-logic design methods, offers the possibility of maintaining program clarity and correctness in both respects, data flow and control flow.

A *data-connection diagram* is a chart used to depict the same execution submodules (at a given hierarchic design level) of a given module as contained on the flowchart for that module, but with arrows drawn from submodules which create data to those that use the data. The executable modules follow their usual flowchart striping and naming conventions detailed in the next chapter. To distinguish data-connection diagrams from flowcharts, I use the conventions shown in Figure 4-9; data connections are shown as named wide arrows between executable modules, or unnamed wide arrows between a data structure (or enumerated table of such structures) and a module.

Data-connection diagrams, such as Figure 4-10 [26], thus depict the activity of a module as reading the data structures corresponding to incoming arrows, processing, and writing the data corresponding to outgoing arrows. Such diagrams hence display the logical precedence relations with which certain modules must precede others in execution. An analysis technique called *topological sorting* is often useful in revealing an execution sequence for the modules to achieve the intended data precedences.

The topological sorting algorithm is simple [27]:

a. Locate on the data-connection diagram a module such that none of its inputs comes from any module on the diagram.

b. Label this module as first to be executed, and then break (or erase) all of its outgoing data connections.

(a) Simple *data-name* connection

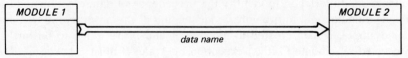

(b) Enumeration of data structures in a connection

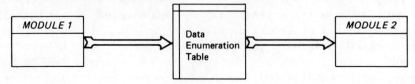

(c) Module external data connection

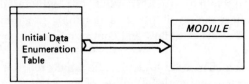

Figure 4-9. Data connection diagram conventions

    c. Repeat this procedure to find each succeeding next-to-be-executed module.

Having such an execution order for modules, a designer may proceed to design control logic to implement module execution in the indicated order.

Topological sorting fails when there are data loops; i.e., modules whose data structures are iterated to reach certain states. In the example shown in Figure 4-11, module A reads data in the Tables T and U to update the contents of U, and module B reads Table U to update Table T. (I shall suppose that T, but not U, was initialized to a known state prior to execution of either A or B.) But what, if any, is the implied execution order of A and B? All that can be said with certainty without further information is that the *first* execution of A must precede the first execution of B.

Topological sorting does, however, identify such loops, as well as the variable nature of the data structures within them. Hence, just as control-flow graphs do not fully describe a program satisfactorily, neither do data-connection graphs. But they can work together as tools for effective design and documentation. Each tends to identify characteristics not visible in the other, thereby not only catching many design errors immediately, but also

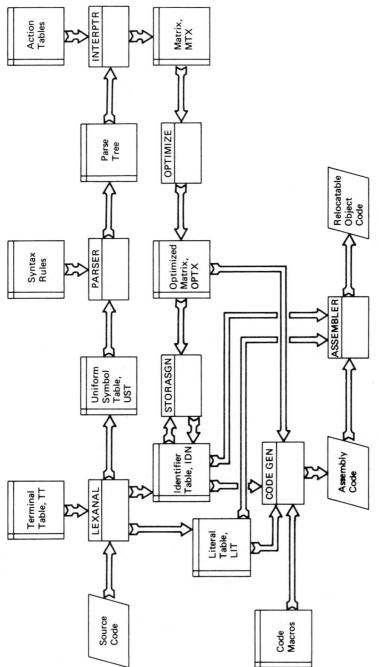

Figure 4-10. A data-flow diagram for a compiler

75

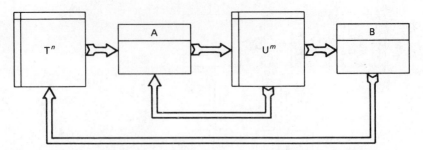

Figure 4-11. Data connection loops (superscripts on the Tables T and U index their contents after the *n*-th and *m*-th executions of B and A, respectively)

minimizing the possibility for side effects when changes are to be made later in the program's evolution.

In summary, data connection diagraming, with accompanying narrative, is another effective tool for the designer's bag. It provides him a means to identify, and then to minimize, data connectivity side-effects among modules. It provides a means of attacking a problem in which questions of control, which often only obscure the solution, are secondary. It fits in with the top-down, hierarchic, modular, structured design discipline. It is a suitable mode of communicating the program organization to project management. It identifies the elements most important to the program mainstream, so that priorities and alternate operational modes can be established.

Probably the most effective use of data-connection analysis will occur at the highest levels of the design. Then, as design progresses, the data interconnectivity becomes more firmly established in the mind of the designer (and reviewer), so graphic aids diminish in value. This is just the opposite from flowcharting, where the control at the top levels tends to be rather non-contributory to understanding, but becomes exceedingly more important at deeper levels.

4.4 MODULARITY IN PROGRAM DESIGN

I have alluded to the need for modularity in program design as a means toward organizing the program into subdivisions (which can be considered separately) to cope with complexity during the development phase, and to cope with side effects when later changes or corrections are made. The first order of business is to be more definite about what *modularity* is and what its characteristics are. In Chapter 2, I defined a "module" as an identifiable subportion of a program that also fits the definition of a "program". Clearly then, each flowchart box and every program statement is a "module" according to this definition.

Certain groupings of such "submodules" then can build other "modules" characterized by [23]:

  a. *Lexical binding.* The submodules appear physically together, as on the same flowchart or on the same code listing page.

  b. *Identifiable proper boundaries.* The collection of submodules has a well-defined, named entry point (at the top) and end boundary (through which it normally exits), and all submodules between these two boundaries belong to that module.

  c. *Named access.* The module can be invoked as submodule of another module by its name.

  d. *Named reference.* The module may invoke other modules as submodules by name.

Such modules I shall distinguish by the term *named modules.* References to such modules on flowcharts are distinguished by the technique of "striping" the flowchart symbol, as shown in Figures 4-9 and 4-10, and for this reason, I shall often refer to named modules as *striped modules.*

Modules are not only characterized by the functions they perform, but also by their connectivity with the rest of the program. Every module possesses what may be termed a "coefficient of modularity", although, at this writing, this measure is rather more intuitive than mathematic.

For the purposes here, such a measure needs to relate modularity to the human capability for understanding a module's function and to the likelihood of side effects caused by later changes in the program. *Side effects* here refer to those changes that have to be made in a program outside a given module as a result of making changes in that module. The two most important measures of modularity by these criteria, according to Constantine [28] and others [23, 29] are *module coupling* and *module strength.* The optimal modular design minimizes relationships between modules (minimal connections) and maximizes relationships among components within each module (maximum strength).

In the remainder of this section, I will present an overview of Constantine's modularity-measure considerations [23, 28, 29].

4.4.1 Module Coupling

Module coupling is a measure of data connectivity between a module and the program in which it is imbedded. Modules may have their own internal (local) data structures, but they must nearly always also access data outside themselves. Such communicated data can either be accessed as arguments or parameters through the calling-sequence interface, or may be passed by direct accesses to global data structures, or else may be referenced to internal data structures of other modules.

Module coupling also measures control connectivity. Modules could conceivably transfer flow of control in awkward ways to internal submodules of other modules; however, this possibility is overtly disallowed by the structured programming discipline to come. But modules may communicate control to other modules in the form of *control data*; i.e., data altering the functional mode of the module.

Modules must at least communicate data or they cannot functionally be a part of a program. Perhaps some modules can get by without any data communication (such as a TOP OF FORM module), but generally, pure data connectivity is a minimum necessary requirement.

Not so the communication of control. Constantine has shown that the explicit passage of control data between modules is theoretically inessential. In a practical sense, however, control data communication is sometimes necessary or desirable.

Coupling measures the independence of modules, one from another; modules that are not coupled are not apt to feel side effects. And obviously, the fewer the *number* of connections a module has, the more that module is apt to be independent of other modules.

Besides the number of connections, the type is important. Meyer's [23] scale of coupling from lowest (best) to highest (worst) is:

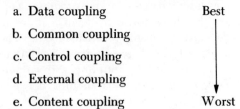

a. Data coupling   Best

b. Common coupling

c. Control coupling

d. External coupling

e. Content coupling   Worst

The scale is not linear, and instances often have to be judged on a case-by-case basis. Figure 4-12 illustrates the 5 types of coupling.

4.4.1.1 Data Coupling

Modules are *data coupled* if one module calls the other, if all input and output communication is in the form of arguments or parameters passed through the call-sequence interface, and if all such parameters are data (not control) elements. Constantine has demonstrated that this form of coupling is sufficient for any program. It, therefore, is the lowest form of coupling.

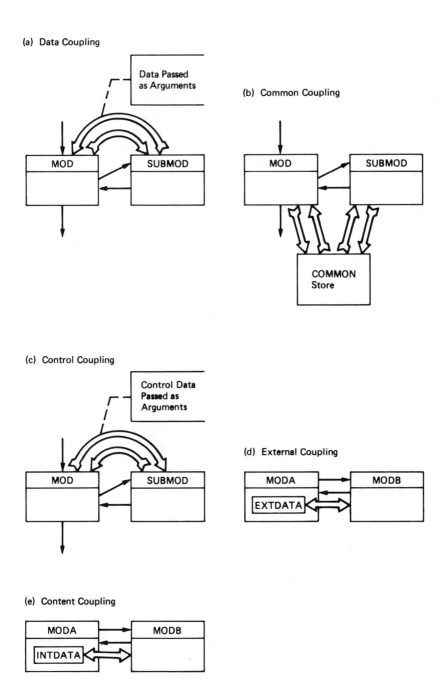

Figure 4-12. Classes of module coupling (solid-line arrows indicate control flow; wide arrows show data coupling)

4.4.1.2 Common Coupling

A set of modules is *common coupled* if they reference data held in a "common pool", or central repository for certain data structures accessible by all the modules. Common coupling creates difficulties because it couples together the entire set of modules using the common pool, without regard to whether the modules have functional relationships or not. For example, if two modules are the only ones to access an array of fixed dimension, say 7, in a common pool, and if it is desired to change that dimension to, say 10, then not only the two modules themselves, but every other module sharing the common pool must usually be recompiled.

Common coupling between unsynchronized real-time programs is especially dangerous because the results of computations very often are unpredictable. Even so, it is generally less caustic than the remaining three forms of coupling.

The disadvantages of common coupling become less severe if common environments can be segmented and localized within minimal subsets of modules that share data structures (e.g., in levels of access). Such measures tend to lower the overall coupling in the program.

4.4.1.3 Control Coupling

Two modules are *control coupled* if one module passes a flag or set of flags (control data) as argument(s) to the other, to directly influence the functioning of the receiving module. Control coupling is not very desirable because the two modules are not very independent; the sending module must usually have some knowledge of the internal processing of the receiving module. That is, a calling module cannot view its submodule completely as a "black box". Such coupling also usually implies low module strength, to be described in Section 4.4.2.

The classification of elements as being either pure data or control data is sometimes a process of judgement. Generally speaking, classification depends on how the *sending* module perceives the data, *regardless* of which module is the calling module.

For example, if module MOD calls module SUBMOD and sends data DAT to it, and if MOD perceives DAT as pure data, then MOD and SUBMOD are data coupled, even if SUBMOD executes differently based on the value of DAT. (This is partly due to the top-down process: MOD places no restriction on *how* SUBMOD performs its function, but merely requires that it process DAT according to the function prescribed.)

In the converse case, if DAT is returned to MOD by SUBMOD , and SUBMOD perceives DAT as data, then the two are again data coupled, even though MOD may execute differently based on the returned value. Here again, the top-down philosophy is at work: MOD has decided how it will function based on DAT, and has required SUBMOD provide it with data to perform that function—SUBMOD is not controlling MOD.

However, if MOD sends a control flag FLG to SUBMOD, and MOD views the value of FLG as a signal for SUBMOD to perform one of its set of functions, then FLG is control data. And conversely, if SUBMOD returns FLG to MOD, and SUBMOD perceives FLG as a request for MOD to perform one of a number of functions, then FLG is again control data.

If control data are communicated via the common store, then the coupling problems are further compounded.

4.4.1.4 External Coupling

Two modules are *externally coupled* if one module refers to elements residing in one module with the elements declared so as to be accessible to other modules. This type of coupling is high because the entire usage or content of a submodule may have to be taken into account to correct an error, or to make a change, or to verify that it does not create side effects.

As an example, suppose module AMOD uses an internal structure DATA, which it declares to be externally accessible. AMOD calls SUBMOD for a service, in which the value of DATA plays a part; upon return, AMOD goes merrily on its way, doing whatever it wishes with DATA. Now suppose that the outside program is to be altered by adding a new module BMOD which in no way

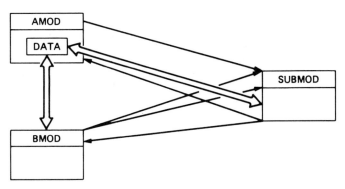

Figure 4-13. Addition of BMOD to AMOD-SUBMOD program, in which BMOD calls SUBMOD and communicates through DATA internal to AMOD

resembles AMOD, except that it could use SUBMOD for the same service it gave AMOD, but based on different DATA to be passed (Figure 4-13).

Suppose BMOD thus sends AMOD a value for DATA and then calls SUBMOD. The next time AMOD executes, it probably crashes because BMOD changed DATA. Recognizing that this would happen, the BMOD programmer could save DATA, set a new value, call SUBMOD, and then, upon return, restore DATA to the saved value. If AMOD and BMOD are capable of concurrent execution, AMOD still crashes.

The point is that BMOD is coupled to AMOD, with which it has no logical connection at all, by external coupling. In addition, all the disadvantages of common coupling are probably present, as well. External coupling thus tends to have an adverse effect on program modification, both in terms of cost and potential bugs, and should be avoided wherever possible.

4.4.1.5 Content Coupling

Two modules are *content coupled* if one module makes a direct reference to the contents of another module, either modifying a statement in the other module, or accessing a set of *internal* data not externally declared.

Another case of content coupling occurs when modules share the same physical code, as may occur when the statements of one module lie physically within another (not as subroutines). It should be obvious that content coupled modules are very dependent upon one another and that a seemingly innocent change in one can easily cause the other to malfunction.

Effective programming does not permit modification of statements or shared code between modules, and therefore does much to minimize content coupling.

4.4.2 Module Strength

The second trait of a good module is its strength, or cohesiveness. The term "binding" is also used in the literature, but I prefer not to use it, as the same term has another meaning to most programmers.

The scale of module strength, or *cohesion*, from highest (best) to lowest (worst) is [23]:

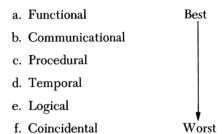

a. Functional   Best

b. Communicational

c. Procedural

d. Temporal

e. Logical

f. Coincidental   Worst

Again, the scale is not linear, and, in fact, items b and c appear differently and perhaps interchanged in two works [23,29]. Functional cohesion is much stronger than all the rest, and the last two are much weaker than all the rest. I will discuss each type and try to show how maximizing cohesion among module components has a positive effect in terms of programming quality.

4.4.2.1 Functional Cohesion

Functional cohesion is at the top of the strength scale. In a functionally cohesive module, all of the components are related directly to the performance of a single function. By a program function, I mean one that performs a prescribed, definable transformation or service. A useful technique for determining whether or not a module is functionally cohesive, is by writing a sentence describing the purpose (function) of the module, and then examining the sentence. If the sentence is a simple declarative sentence in the imperative mood (no commas, and only one verb), if there are no words relating to time or sequence (e.g., "first", "next", "then", "after", "otherwise", "when", "if", "start", etc.), if the predicate contains a single specific object following the verb, and if the verb does not imply a general auxiliary relationship (e.g., "initialize", "clean-up", etc.), then the module is probably functionally bound. I say "probably", because cohesive strength exists in the final code, rather than in the English description.

In practice, however, modules that are judged functionally cohesive by this criterion tend to be characterized by strong relationships among the components within the module: all components tend to be oriented toward a single goal. Such statements as,

```
EDIT SOURCE STATEMENT
MATCH INPUT STRING
PARSE UNIFORM SYMBOLS
OPTIMIZE INTERMEDIATE CODE
```

and so forth, usually describe functionally cohesive modules.

4.4.2.2 Communicational Cohesion

A module with *communicational cohesion* is one in which the components are related through the program procedure (see 4.4.2.3) and additionally, communicate with one another. The submodules either reference the same set of data or pass data only among themselves. Communicational cohesion is higher on the scale than mere procedural cohesion since the module components have the additional bond, that they operate on the same data.

The following statements of module actions are communicationally cohesive:

```
INPUT SOURCE STATEMENT AND ANALYZE LEXICALLY
FIND SIMPLEX SOLUTION AND PRINT ANSWER
FILTER DATA STREAM AND PLOT RESULT
PROCESS TELEMETRY UNTIL LOSS OF QUALITY
IF DATA OK THEN COMPUTE STATISTICS: OTHERWISE
    DIAGNOSE FAILURE AND PRINT MESSAGE
```

The first three of these statements show sequential functions that communicate data between themselves. The fourth is an iterative procedure in which decision and processing components are communicationally related. The last is a conditional procedure in which the condition and each of the two subprocedures share a common data base.

4.4.2.3 Procedural Cohesion

Procedurally cohesive modules are modules whose elements are related in respect to the procedure of the program. Procedural cohesion results, for example, when the problem to be solved is first flowcharted, and then modules are defined to represent two or more blocks on the flowchart. Although this form of cohesion is high on the strength scale because of the close relationship of the components to the problem structure, it nevertheless is not as strong as the two previously discussed types.

The following descriptions of modules are procedurally bound:

```
CLOSE SOURCE FILE, THEN PRINT COST SUMMARY
SWAP IN PARSER WHEN RUNTIME ERROR DETECTED
ACCUMULATE BACKGROUND DATA UNTIL PROCESSOR SEMAPHORE RECEIVED
```

The first is a simple sequence of two functions, the second, a function executed conditionally, and the third, an iterative function. The latter two modules have implied inner functions, CHECK FOR RUNTIME ERROR and

RECEIVE PROCESSOR SEMAPHORE. All three module descriptions exhibit procedural cohesion since the subfunctions of each are related only through the procedure of the program.

4.4.2.4 Temporal Cohesion

A module is *temporally* (or *classically*) *cohesive* if the components of the module form a class of logically related (logically cohesive) functions, all of which are also related in time. Temporally cohesive components are all executed in the same time period; that is, there are no parameters or control data that determine which components are executed and which are not.

The best examples of modules in this class are "initialization", "termination", "housekeeping", and "clean-up". Such modules perform a set of logically related functions (e.g., initialize function f, initialize function g,...) that are all performed together, rather than separately or selectively. Other examples of module descriptions that exhibit temporal cohesion are:

```
SCAN ALL INDICATORS
RESET STACK POINTERS
CLEAR ALL BUFFERS
CHECK STANDARDS AND LIMITS
```

In each case, the functions performed are similar (single verb), but may differ in detail. All functions in each module execute together, rather than selectively.

Temporal cohesion is weaker than procedural cohesion because the relationships between components only exist because of functional and temporal ties; no precedence of operations exists. Such modules, moreover, tend to perform services for other modules (e.g., initialize them) and, therefore, are coupled to each of them.

4.4.2.5 Logical Cohesion

A module is *logically cohesive* if its components perform a class of logically related functions. Logical cohesion is, therefore, much the same as temporal cohesion, except that temporally cohesive module components must additionally all be executed. A logically cohesive module need perform only one or a selected subset of its entire capability of subfunctions when invoked.

Examples of module descriptions exhibiting logical cohesiveness are:

```
INPUT FROM FILE OR TERMINAL
PERFORM ALL I/O
COMPUTE SIMPLEX MAXIMUM OR MINIMUM
```

One clue to judging logical cohesiveness is the following: If the predicate of the module description contains a single verb but does not refer to a single specific object, then the module is probably logically cohesive. If there is indication that the entire set of actions takes place, the module is probably temporally cohesive.

Logical cohesion is clearly weaker than temporal cohesion, because temporally cohesive modules have an additional relationship (that all components are executed together) that binds the components. Since a logically cohesive module must often be passed control arguments, which it must then test to ascertain what action is to take place, and because the similarity of the actions often results in shared code (not subroutines) among the different submodules, such modules reside very low on the strength scale. In short, logically cohesive modules are usually characterized by tricky code that is difficult to modify and by the presence of unnecessary control coupling. Structured programming helps to eliminate the shared code by putting it in separate modules; but such modules are apt to have only coincidental cohesion.

4.4.2.6 Coincidental Coherence

A module displays *coincidental coherence* when there is no meaningful relationship between its components other than, as a coincidence, they lie in the same module and do contribute to the overall program function. Such modules are often created in an attempt to consolidate duplicate coding that may otherwise appear in several modules, or by arbitrary divisions of the program code in an attempt to "modularize". Obviously, since there are no meaningful relationships among elements, module strength is at the lowest scale point.

Understanding of the module purpose is impaired, and one usually shrinks from making any changes whatsoever in such modules for fear that monumental side effects will result. Since such modules have no cohesive purpose, even a minor modification to alter the service requested by one caller can potentially make the module unusable by all other callers. It may even be difficult to identify all of the other callers, especially if these other callers are separately compiled.

4.4.2.7 Composite Strength

Modules may be defined in such a way as to partly or wholly have the characteristics of more than one strength. If a module *completely* exhibits several types of strengths, then it is assigned the *higher* strength. For example, when modules with communicational cohesion also exhibit procedural strength, they are classified by the higher strength, communicational cohesion. Temporally cohesive modules are also logically cohesive, but classified as temporally cohesive.

However, if a module only *partly* exhibits characteristics of several strengths, then it is assigned the *lower* of the strengths. In the following examples, the component and module strengths are as indicated:

```
.INITIALIZE PROGRAM AND THEN GET INPUT LINE
    (temporal)+(procedural)+(functional)=(temporal)

READ ALL SENSORS,CHECK STDS AND LIMITS,AND PRINT REPORTS
    (temporal)    +    (temporal)    +    (logical)    =(logical)
```

In the latter example, there are also the partial attributes of communicational cohesion; sensor data is being checked, the results of which select one of several reports. If the PRINT REPORTS module were to invariably print only one report, then that element is functional, so the module strength moves up to temporal cohesion. If then, in addition, all sensors were read in an identical fashion, and if standards and limits tests are identical except for values in the limits table, then all components probably move up the scale to functional cohesion, and the overall module probably moves up to communicational cohesion.

4.4.3 Guidelines for Modularization

It is only fair to admit that, independent of a module's strength or degree of coupling, there are always instances when any module can be modified in such a way as to make it unusable to all its callers. The scales for strength and coupling are rough indicators of the likelihood that this kind of thing will happen. It is therefore useful to keep these considerations well in mind while the program is being designed. *Design the modules to exhibit high strength and low coupling unless these principles conflict with other design considerations with higher merit.*

The *scope of control* of a module MOD is defined as the set consisting of MOD and all its subordinate submodules. The *scope of effect* of some given decision within a module is defined as the set of all modules whose execution depends on the outcome of that decision.

In the example shown in Figure 4-14, when the decision *d* in module B is true, B invokes D and, in addition, when control is passed back to A, then A invokes C. But when *d* is false, B invokes E, but A does not invoke C. The scope of effect for the decision *d* here is the entire set of modules shown: A, because it calls C conditionally; B, because it executes different calls based on *d*; and, obviously, D and E. In this case, the scope of control of module B does not encompass the scope of effect of the decision *d* within B.

Moreover, B must pass back some information to A, upon which A can then decide whether or not to call C. In some sense then, the test in B duplicates the test in A. At the very least, A and B appear to be control coupled.

This example illustrates that when the scope of control of a module does not encompass the scope of effect of one of its decisions there is higher coupling, some artificial or redundant conditional statements, and probably lower module strength than had this not been the case. One guideline for improving modularity is, therefore, the following: *define program modules in such a way that the scope of control of each module encompasses the scope of effect of every decision within the module.* That is, constrain the effects of all decisions from the top downward through the program structure.

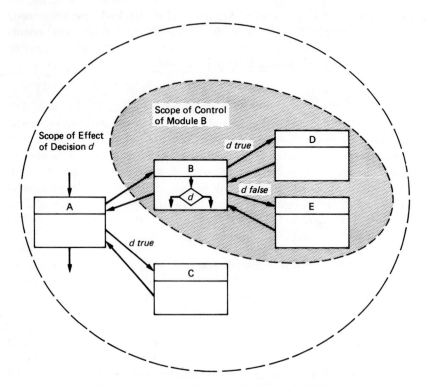

Figure 4-14. A hierarchy of subordinate modules

4.5 ESTABLISHING DESIGN PRIORITIES

Perhaps I have stressed structure and documentation a bit too much in the foregoing sections of this chapter. After all, a design is more than just documentation and structure; it must ultimately produce a program that actually does the intended function. And in most cases, even this is not enough; it must do it *well*.

The quality of a program design can be judged on the basis of how well it minimizes a number of important characteristics that compete for project and machine resources: execution speed, memory used, level of documentation, development cost, development time, cost to execute the program, maintainability of design, etc. If the interrelationships between these characteristics could be known *quantitatively*, as well as the relative merit of each resource, it is conceivable that an optimal program within the constraints could be developed.

However, quantitative measures are seldom (if *ever*) possible, so that optimum programs (in the sense of resource competition) simply do not exist. Design standards, therefore, cannot be expected to produce the best possible programs.

But while competing characteristics may not be *quantifiable*, they usually can be *ordered*, at least subjectively for a given program, in their pairwise relationships with one another, as, for example, "reduced execution time is more important than development cost". Often, it may be necessary to qualify the relationships, as, for example, "reduced execution time is more important than development cost, unless the level of effort required to decrease execution time would result in a contract overrun". Given a set of pairwise relations among competing resources, the designer can then proceed to resolve simple conflicts, which may arise in the design process.

Ranking the competing characteristics by such pairwise dominances can be a very useful tool for addressing and ordering the relative importances of resources from the very beginning of the design activity. Grading the remainder of the design on its merits relative to these characteristics is the province of the project management function, and will be discussed somewhat further in Chapter 10. I also provide sample interactive programs to aid in ranking competing alternatives and grading the design in Appendix L.

4.6 SUMMARY

In this chapter, I have distinguished the design activity as one that generates hierarchic detailings of program specifications into executable units, or modules. The activity has been disciplined to dovetail in with program definition and coding, for the mutual benefit of each.

The program design discipline recommended in these pages starts with the identification of objectives; then an approach is sought to respond to the functional definition in scope, structure, and content. At this point, an embryo program begins to form, first probably as a one-page sketch revealing the upper levels of the program hierarchy into modules and identifying the major flows of data through the program. The designer iterates this sketch until he is satisfied that the configuration meets the program definition, that the modules have as low coupling and as high a cohesion as can reasonably be expected, subject to other competing characteristics.

During this sketching and onward throughout the design, the designer attempts to isolate accesses to resources so as to reduce coupling, through definitions of levels of access.

Hierarchic levels of design tend to postpone design decisions to a level at which considerations are appropriate for those judgements to be made. However, to lower the risk that this may occur inadvertently, I have introduced the concept of a look-ahead design, a sketch of what is coming into the future layers that may impact the current formal level of work.

Once this architectural design is completed to the designer's satisfaction, a formal development of the program procedure begins from the top down using hierarchic layering of subfunction and restricted control flow. When a design portion has been solidified, that design is documented, and then coded and tested within the assumptions valid at that level of the development.

This process continues until the software is complete. Because documentation, coding, and testing are concurrent, major errors have hopefully been averted before the investment in the errored portion has become significant. Errors subsequently detected at a particular design level tend to percolate in side effects downward through the remaining design, hopefully at a lesser cost to correct than had the design not taken place top down.

I have given criteria for design documentation, guidelines for the development of data structures and the allocation of other machine resources, and indices for the qualification of program modularity. Specific design rules based on the concepts of this chapter appear in Chapter 12.

4.6.1 A Design Example: Card Cross-References

Problem: A FORTRAN source program exists on a set of not more than 1000 cards. Write another program for the UNIVAC 1108 to read these cards, extract label and variable names, and then print a sorted list of variables and label names with the card-number cross-references adjacent to each name. The objective for design is rapid execution at a moderate increase in core storage outlay.

Analysis: A 1000-line source program with an average of 8 references per card will have about 8000 card-reference items to be printed. Six-character labels and variable names can be held in one word each of core storage. Hence, if a 10,000 word array were to be reserved for the cross-reference array, then 2048 words could be used for a hash and linkage table (see [30]) to aid in searching for and inserting up to 1023 names, leaving 7952 available to hold card references. Hashing techniques are very efficient as long as the name table occupancy is less than about 80%, or up to about 800 names.

Hashed search and insertion seems attractive, for with 800 names in the table, the average search for a name requires only about [30],

$$\frac{1}{800} \sum_{k=1}^{799} \frac{1025}{1025 - k} = 1.94$$

"probes" per search to find or insert a name. The total number of such events for 800 names plus 7952 card references is thus about 15,500. Afterwards, a quicksort [31] of the name table will require about

$$2(800)\log_2(800) = 15,430$$

comparisons and possible exchanges.

A binary tree search and insertion, on the other hand, if balanced, would take about

$$\frac{1}{800} \sum_{k=1}^{799} \log_2 k = 8.2$$

"probes" per name to find or insert a name. The total number of such events for the 7952 required items is then about 65,200 operations. Sorting the binary tree [32] to insert an item is linearly proportional to 800. The hashing technique is thus clearly the better alternative for this application.

The Program: The reader may note a great similarity between this problem and that given in Section 2.5.2. The problem statement is almost procedural. In it are identified certain implied (functionally cohesive) actions that form the basis for an architectural design: INPUT CARD, EXTRACT NEXT ITEM, SEARCH FOR ITEM, ATTACH CARD NUMBER TO ITEM, SORT ITEMS, SORT CARD REFERENCES, PRINT REPORT. The interface between the first two is the card buffer, and the remaining functions all share the data structure(s) that accumulate the names and card numbers. The first candidate hierarchy diagram for the program architecture is shown in Figure 4-15. The figure also indicates proposed levels of access to the data structures. Some of the other structures needed are not shown, but are known to be present at this point, such as the number of the card just input and the name just extracted.

The next stage of the design details each of the data structures in accordance with the identified functions, which form its level of access. In the INPUT module, the actual input is normally handled via an executive request, READ$, which inserts packed characters into a designated area (another structure inside INPUT). For ease in the scanning needed by EXTRACT, I may specify that INPUT transfer these characters into a 72-word CBUFF, one character per word, right justified.

The design of EXTRACT is by no means trivial—expecially since the source deck is FORTRAN. However, the algorithms for lexical analysis are known [33], so I will not pursue the design of EXTRACT further here.

The functions that repeatedly access the cross-reference array, XREFA, can be accommodated in one pass if XREFA is designed as a linked list, as shown in Figure 4-16. The SORT functions then could have been included into SEARCH and ATTACH by having these latter two modules insert new names and in order into XREFA as they are extracted, card by card, as perhaps in a binary tree. The above analysis shows, however, that it is probably best to sort the name array only once, after all the items have been entered. This not only makes for speed, but also promotes functional cohesion within the modules. However, the sorting of card references can be eliminated by attaching card reference tokens in order, following the "tail" pointer in LINKS (Figure 4-16).

To speed searching and insertion of names, XREFA is shown to consist of a HASH table (see [30]) of names and a LINKS table of linkages to first and last card-reference tokens.

The SORT ITEMS module then sorts both the HASH table and the LINKS array using the name as a key. The SORT CARD NOS module has nothing to do,

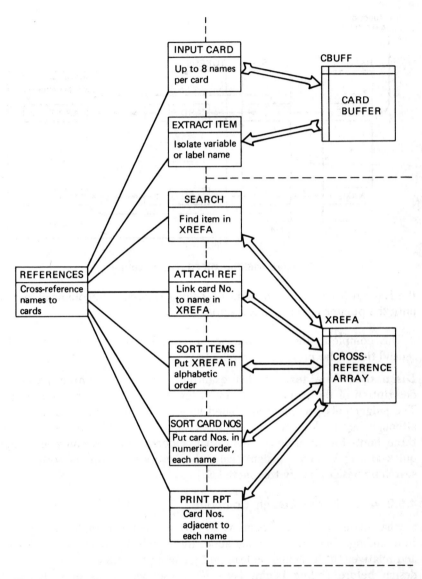

Figure 4-15. The architecture of the card REFERENCES program (dashed lines define levels of access to data structures CBUFF and XREFA)

since all the card-reference tokens are already in sort, and can therefore be eliminated.

The PRINT module now merely scans down the sorted HASH entries in order to find each name. After printing the name, it spaces over and writes

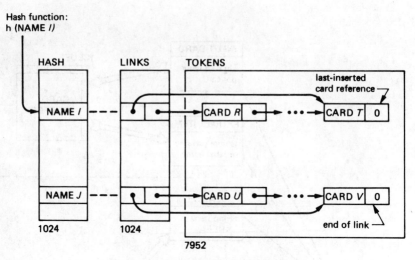

Figure 4-16. The XREFA data structure

the first card reference and each succeeding reference in columnar format until the pointer field contains a zero.

This completes the structural design considerations down through the second tier of the program hierarchy.

Discussion: The text of this example presents a simple narrative description of the major factors and a few tradeoffs in a program design. The judgements presented are based largely on experience and intuition, although more detailed mathematical analyses could have been used throughout—for example, to show that, indeed, hash searching and later quick-sorting is more efficient than other proposed forms of sorting and searching besides binary tree methods.

4.6.2 When is the Design Complete?

I have tried to depict design as an activity that is completely separate from coding. The major learning about the problem is done during design, and relatively little should be learned by coding the design. Changes in the design before coding begins have no consequent costs of coding and debugging. When coding does begin, fewer and less talented people can do the coding; coding is easier to schedule; and coding has become a production job.

A complete design will consist of a specification for coding in which:

- All processing algorithms are specified

- All interfaces, internal and external are defined

- All data structures are defined

- All modules, and procedure of each, are specified

- All error recovery responses are specified

In particular, it should be possible for a person to determine, for any input, the precise path followed in the program from the design, without recourse to the listings.

Coding should begin only after a particular phase of the design has been thrashed through to the point that it is stable. Coding must then be a faithful, direct translation of the design. No short-cuts, no cute code, no coding-level changes to the design—only clear, concise code that is easy to check against the design. The role of checkout is to verify that the design-time assessments of correctness are valid. Errors detected in the design *must* be corrected in the design documentation (SSD).

The Software Specification Document is for people, and people work best in their own language, rather than one created for a computer. Reading the design should not require a translator, nor should it require learning a large data base, nor should it require consulting the listings to find out "the way things really are" in the computer. I will, therefore, attempt in the coming chapters, to provide the means, and continually emphasize the need, for conciseness and clarity in program development.

Problems for Chapter 4

4-1 Design the architecture of a program to simulate a waiting line at an airport ticket counter (see Problem 2-3). Identify levels of access to data structures and present trade-off analyses to justify your choice of manipulations. Retain all look-ahead notes, labeled in order, level, and module.

4-2 Design the architecture of a program to process a stream of telegrams, whereby the number of words in each telegram is counted and telegrams are printed with appropriate spacing on an output medium. Develop the remainder of the problem definition, if needed, as well as the program structure and procedure, in hierarchic levels. Retain all look-ahead notes labeled in order, level, and module.

4-3 Design a data structure and a level of access by which a company skills-inventory (see Example 2.5.2) can be maintained, edited, and queried by employee name or number (for skills) or by skill (for employee names). Refine the data structure and access level to the next hierarchic detailing.

4-4 Give a topological sorting of Figure 4-10. Are there loops? What can be done to remove the loop (if there was one)?

4-5 Analyze a coded program of your choice having 5 to 10 named modules as defined in Section 4.4. Identify the data flow between modules and analyze for coupling type. Evaluate the cohesiveness of the module by giving a short English description, and then try to reconcile that description with the strength of relationships in the code. Identify the scope of control of each module, and the scope of effect of each decision which reaches outside its module.

4-6 Sort the list of subprograms named below into increasing order of module cohesiveness. Name the probable type of module cohesion for each.

a.   INPUT (<*FROM*>*device*, <*INTO*>*buffer*)
b.   ACCUMULATE AND SORT TRANSACTION FILES
c.   SEARCH NAME TABLE.   INSERT NAME IF NOT FOUND
d.   INITIALIZE BUFFER IF READY, CLOSE FILES IF THROUGH,
         AND PROCESS ANY REMAINING DATA
e.   CREATE TABLE OF LITERAL VALUES FOR PROGRAM
f.   READ DATA, DETERMINE ACTION, AND PROCESS ACCORDINGLY
g.   PRINT LINE OF TEXT WITH SPACES INSERTED TO RIGHT JUSTIFY
h.   TRAVERSE A TREE IN POST-ORDER
i.   INVERT MATRIX (A)
j.   MONITOR STATUS OF REAL-TIME PROCESSES

4-7 Sort the module fragments below in decreasing order of coupling, and name the probable type of coupling implied by each (and why, if debatable).

a. INPUT (<*FROM*>*device*, <*INTO*>*buffer*)

b. CALL SUBA (X, Y, Z)

c. DECLARE AND INITIALIZE ALL VARIABLES OF ENTIRE PROGRAM

d. RESET INTERNAL DEVICE CODE AND OUTPUT TO DEVICE

e. SET A TO VALUE IN LOCATION (SUBPROGNAME +358)

f. IF (FLAG>0) THEN JUMP NEXT 68 LINES

g. RING BELL ON TERMINAL (*number*)

h. PARSE INPUT FILE INTO TREE STRUCTURE AND
   DRAW TREE ON PLOTTER

i. DECLARE AAAX EXTERNALLY ACCESSIBLE

j. READ PROGRAM OPTIONS FROM STRUCTURE FILE

V. STRUCTURED NON-REAL-TIME PROGRAMS

In 1968 and 1969, Edsger Dijkstra [6,34,35] produced a set of ideas and examples for clear thinking and construction of programs to begin what is now referred to as *Structured Programming*. He set forth a methodology that formed a powerful tool in mentally connecting the static text of a program and the dynamic process it invokes in execution.

Böhm and Jacopini [36] had, in 1966, indicated that it is possible to write programs using only the control logic structures consisting of sequence, two-outcome decisions, and restricted looping. Mills [12], early in 1972, set the mathematical foundations for structured programming, binding the ideas of Dijkstra, Böhm, and Jacopini together in a way which initiated the transformation of programming methodology from a private craft to an engineering practice.

5.1 STRUCTURED PROPER PROGRAMS

Mills defines a *proper program* as one which can be flowcharted and has only one entry point and one exit point, every point reachable from the entry point. His structured programming theory encompasses only such proper programs.

In this and the next chapter, I extend the concept of structured programs to include certain types of non-proper programs. Such non-proper programs are often times unavoidable in programming, such as when traps or interrupts are involved. They are, at other times, very desirable and useful constructs (when program failure has been detected, for instance).

5.1.1 Basic Theorems

There are four basic mathematical results (Böhm and Jacopini [36] and Mills [12]), which are central*:

1. <u>*Top-Down Corollary*</u>: *Every proper program logic can be represented by one of the three structures:*

(a) *DO f THEN g*

(b) *IF c THEN f ELSE g*

(c) *WHILE c DO f*

where f and g are proper programs each with one entry and one exit, c is a determinable condition (i.e., a test) and IF, THEN, ELSE, WHILE, and DO are logical connectives.

2. <u>*Structure Theorem*</u>: *Every proper program logic is equivalent to a program obtained by iterating and nesting the structures (a), (b), and (c) above.*

3. <u>*Correctness Theorem*</u>: *If a program is structured as in (2) above, and if the domain of the data-space on which f operates in (c) is not redefined dynamically† in the looping process, then the correctness of the entire program can be proved by successively proving that the data spaces for each structure at each level of iteration, or nesting, are transformed in the specified way.*

4. <u>*Expansion Theorem*</u>: *The freedom by which a proper-program logic f may be refined into one of the forms (a), (b), or (c) above is limited as follows:*

(a) *DO g THEN h can replace f whenever there exists a functional decomposition of f into g and h in which f = h(g); i.e., f is the result of the program logic h operating on the computer state at the completion of g.*

---

* These are not listed in their order of mathematical proof given in [12], but in their order of logical precedence.

† Refer to Section 9.1 for a somewhat relaxed generalization of the looping qualifications.

(b) *IF c THEN g ELSE h can replace f whenever a logic condition c can be found whose domain is the same as that of f. Then g and f are fully determined.*

(c) *WHILE c DO g can replace f whenever a function g can be chosen which, when iterated, ultimately reaches f. The condition c is determined as that condition which recognizes that g has reached f.*

Flowcharts for the canonic constructions (a), (b), and (c) are shown in Figure 5-1. The interesting fact concerning these flowcharted structures is

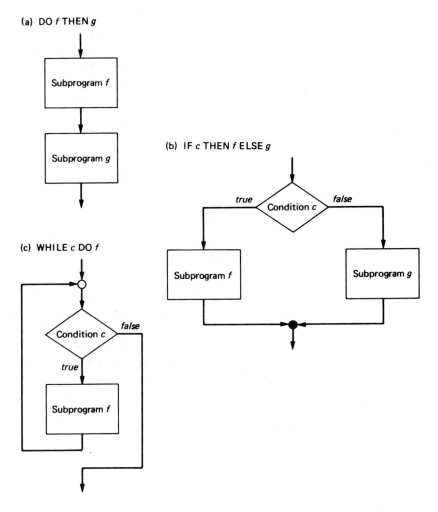

Figure 5-1. Canonic program structures (*true* is always drawn as the leftmost branch of a decision)

that each has only one entry (at the top) and one exit (at the bottom). Furthermore, each of the subprograms inside the structures are entered at the top and exit from the bottom. Thus, it can be seen that program flowcharts formed by inserting any one of the three structures as a subprogram of any of the three (i.e., by iterating and nesting these three structures) can literally be read from top to bottom. Programs formed of such iterations and nestings are examples of *canonic structured programs*.

5.1.2 Other Structures

Needless to say, there is no particular merit to limiting program structures to the minimum three* necessary to represent all proper programs. After all, the theorem merely states that programs *can* be so represented; it doesn't say they are efficient. In fact, two other structures, shown in Figures 5-2 and 5-3, are generally accepted as valid program structures, along with those in Figure 5-1. I additionally use the structure in Figure 5-4 as a simplified convention. The multiple-decision structure is certainly derivable from the binary decision structure by mere concatenation, and the reader may convince himself that the DO f WHILE c structure is representable as the structure shown in Figure 5-3(b).

The reason for including such structures in the permitted canonic set of programming constructions is obvious: they are simply related to the minimum set and they tend to yield programs that are more understandable and efficient than the minimum set.

Each of the structures, as previously indicated, has *one* entry point and *one* exit point. The iteration of any of these in any way results in a structure again having only one entry point and one exit point. Furthermore, programs made by iterating and nesting the allowed structures are *planar*; that is, they can be flowcharted on one page (if large enough) without any intersecting program flow lines.

5.1.3 Structure Notations

Before proceeding, it is convenient to introduce some terminology regarding flowchart structures.

---

*The minimum is actually only two, as IFTHENELSE is not theoretically needed, but can be replaced by the use of two WHILEDOs and a structure flag (see problem 5-10).

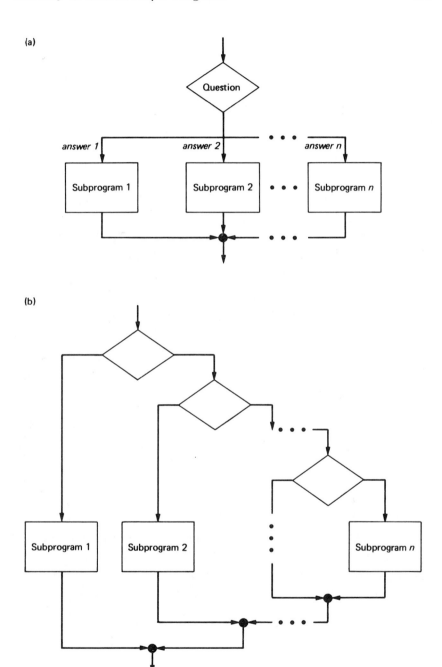

Figure 5-2. Multiple-branch decision structure and its equivalent binary-decision structured program (outcomes of all decisions are always drawn in case order from the left)

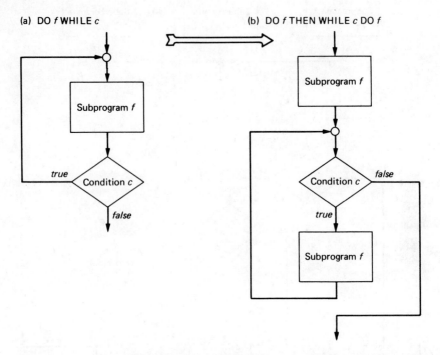

Figure 5-3. The DO *f* **WHILE** *c* **structure and its equivalent form using subprogram duplication and a WHILE** *c* **DO** *f* **structure**

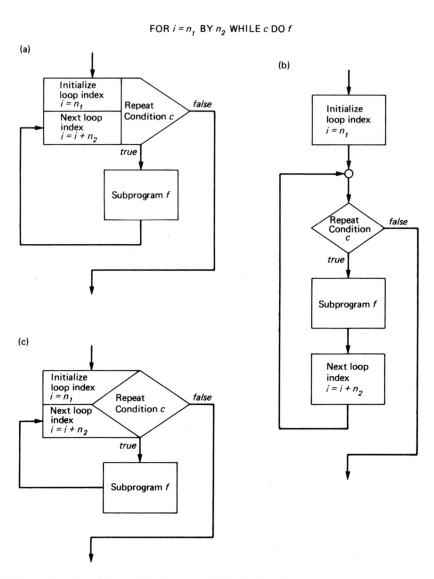

Figure 5-4. Special notational symbol for indexed loops: the flowchart (a) represents the structure (b), and (c) is an alternate form of the convention in (a)

5.1.3.1 Designating Flowchart Elements

Abstractly, a flowchart is composed of flow lines and nodes. The nodes can be grouped into four categories (see Figure 5-5): *process nodes (or p-nodes), decision-nodes (or d-nodes), loop-collecting nodes (or lc-nodes),* and *decision-collecting-nodes (or dc-nodes).* These categories are indicated on flowcharts by flowchart symbols having distinctive shapes. *P*-nodes are given a variety of shapes to indicate the procedure involved [8] and *d*-nodes are diamond-shaped. Collecting nodes of both types are commonly annotated only by the meeting of flow lines; however, for the treatment in this monograph, they will always be denoted by circles, open for *lc*-nodes, and filled for *dc*-nodes.

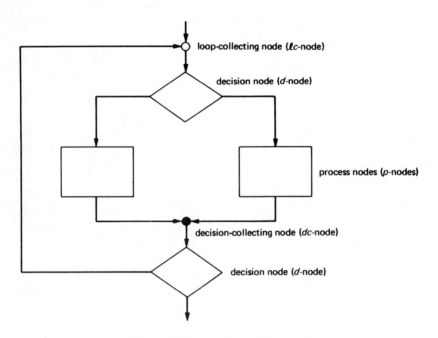

Figure 5-5. Elements of a flowchart

Flowcharts are always to be drawn such that binary decision nodes always have *true* to the left. Multiple-decision nodes are always drawn with outcomes in logical case order from the left.

5.1.3.2 Dewey-Decimal Numbering Scheme

The ANSI technique used for denoting hierarchic flowchart expansion is *striping* the box to be expanded, as shown in Figure 5-6. The striped module is given a procedural name, *NAME*, a cross-reference identifier, *x*,

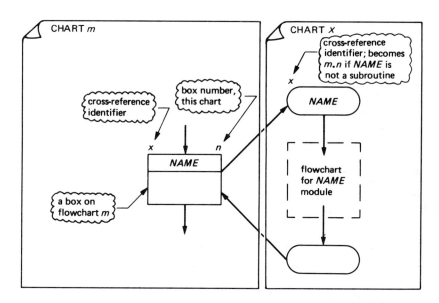

Figure 5-6. Hierarchic expansion of striped flowchart symbol

and a number, *n*, on its current flowchart. I shall augment that method as follows. If the current flowchart identifier is *m*, then the box can be uniquely identified as the Dewey-decimal number *m.n*, and this number can be used for cross-referencing as long as no ambiguity arises. In such a case *x* need not appear at the point of striping.

Striped symbols can refer to hierarchic expansion in one of three ways: (a) *subprograms*, which can either be segments of in-line code or procedures that, on normal termination, continue execution always at the same point in the program; (b) *internal subroutines*, which are segments of code invoked at several places in the 'program, which always return, upon completion, to the point of call, and which are part of the body of the program; and (c) *external subroutines*, which are subroutines (returning to the point of call) whose designs are external to the program (e.g., library subroutines) and not described in this set of documentation. I have previously referred to such program segments as *striped* or *named modules*. Notations for these three cases are illustrated in Figure 5-7.

The hierarchic place that a module occupies in a design is denoted by its Dewey-decimal cross-reference. For example, suppose that on a flowchart numbered *m*, a box numbered *n* refers to a procedure (not subroutine) to be expanded later in the design process. Then the flowchart for that later expansion is made Chart No. *m.n*. One reading the flowchart wishing to trace out *how* the function in box *n* of flowchart *m* is achieved, merely has to locate Chart No. *m.n* to proceed.

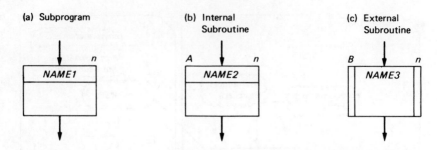

Figure 5-7. Striped symbols: *n* **is the module number on this chart;** *A* **is a numeric or alphanumeric chart number where the hierarchic expansion of that subroutine begins; and** *B* **is a designation that indicates where interface information can be found**

More specifically, suppose a striped module appears on Chart 1.2.6, and has the number 5. Then one can state that box number 2 on Chart 1 was expanded as Chart 1.2; on that chart, box 6 was expanded as Chart 1.2.6; and module number 5 may appear expanded later as Chart 1.2.6.5.

The reference to a flowchart, however, cannot always be cross-referenced this way because subroutines, which can be called from many places, would not then possess a unique chart number. Therefore, each subroutine is assigned its own unique level-one chart number. One convenient way of distinguishing procedures from subroutines is by assigning an alphanumeric chart number for subroutines; for example, S6 refers to Subroutine 6, T4 to Trap routine 4, etc. The choice of an alphanumeric designator can be used to group subroutines with common properties together in documentation. Expansions within subroutine flowcharts follow the normal numbering: for example, S6.4.2 refers to the box numbered 2 on Chart S6.4.

5.1.3.3 Numbering Flowchart Nodes

One natural way of numbering graph nodes is the so-called *pre-order traverse* method. A pre-order traverse of the chart enumerates the boxes on the flowchart as follows (see Figure 5-8).

Starting at the top of a structured flowchart, number boxes and loop-collecting nodes sequentially down the chart until a branching node is sensed. Number this node. The general rule to be followed upon reaching a branching node is to take the leftmost branch for the numbering sequence. When a decision-collecting node is encountered, return to its corresponding decision node, and if it has a yet-unnumbered branch (or branches),

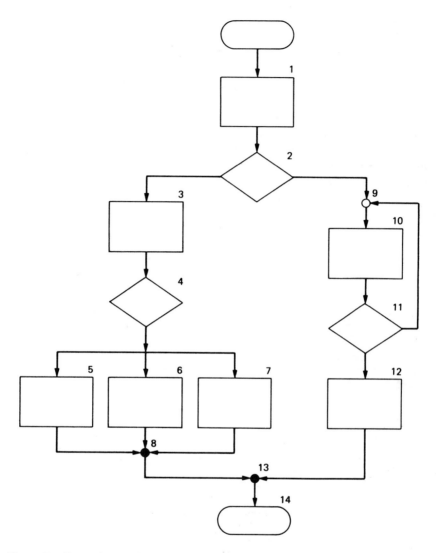

Figure 5-8. Pre-order traverse of structured flowchart nodes; decision-collecting nodes and loop-collecting nodes for WHILEDO structures are often left unnumbered, depending on intended coding language (see Section 7.3.1)

then proceed to number the leftmost of these branches; if all of its decisions have all branches numbered, then continue on.

5.1.4 Structure Graphs, Program Trees, and the Tier Chart

The *structure graph* of a program is a representation showing the control connections between striped modules. The graph has a root node (which represents the main program) at the "top" of the graph. A set of lines are drawn from this root node to each of the nodes representing striped modules that appear on the "flowchart" of the main program. For each such new node added to the structure chart, a set of lines is drawn to each of its striped modules, as depicted in Figure 5-9, until the entire set of striped modules is represented on the graph, properly connected. For example, if a subroutine is called several times in various program modules, corresponding connections appear on the structure graph; if a module is recursive, the graph contains loops. Because modules can be recursive or may invoke subroutines, the structure graph is likely to be non-planar (crossing connection lines).

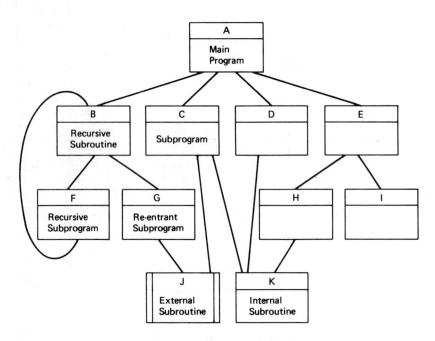

Figure 5-9. The structure graph of a program (note the loop around recursive modules, and multiple ancestors (calls) of subroutines)

The *program tree* is a somewhat simpler version of the structure graph containing no recursive modules. Rather than drawing the several (possibly crossing) lines to a common node for each subroutine of the structure graph, the program tree treats each subroutine call as a separate node, which then begins its own (identical) subtree, as shown in Figure 5-10. Such a graph is again planar, but each subroutine appears as a subtree as many times as there are calls to that subroutine.

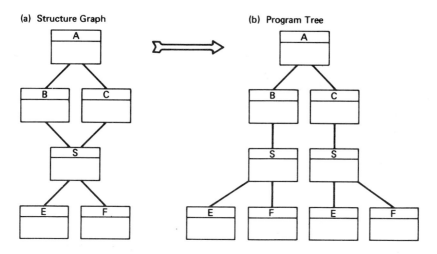

Figure 5-10. Conversion of a non-recursive structure chart to a program tree

Mills' proof of the correctness theorem is based on the representation of programs as trees. The tree diagram is also useful in identifying the separate roles that a subroutine plays in a program when changes need to be made. From it can be assessed the effect of these changes on the remainder of the program. But, as a general tool, the program tree probably loses its effectiveness because of its tendency to become quite large.

The *tier chart* of a program resembles the program tree and is, in fact, derived from it. The tier chart is merely a listing of the program tree node names in order of hierarchic degree, as shown in Figure 5-11. Each *tier* of the chart consists of all modules possessing the same degree of hierarchic nesting from the main program (root). Subroutines may appear more than once in the program tree; however, only one instance of the subroutine subtree is kept on the tier chart, that having the least nesting degree. If a subroutine appears twice at the same (least) degree, only the first, in order of module numbering, is kept on the tier chart.

As previously explained (Section 5.1.3.2), the main program, each subroutine, and perhaps some major subprograms, all begin at Dewey-decimal-level 1. Each of these then has its unique level-1 flowchart number; subprograms of these modules build onto the Dewey-decimal notation in a prescribed way.

By this convention, a subroutine that first appears at tier 4 in the top-down development process then begins its own hierarchic expansion again

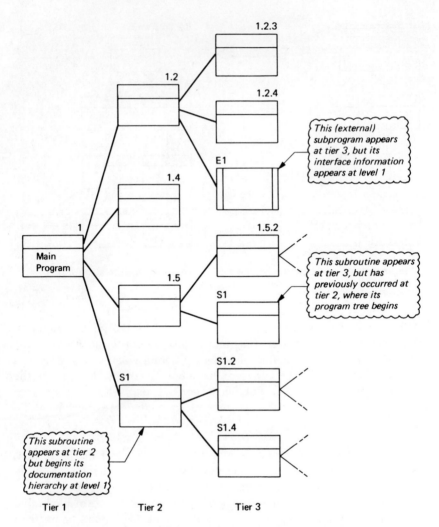

Figure 5-11. Organization of program into hierarchic design tiers

at documentation-reference-level 1, such as S1. To avoid confusion, I thus refer to the depth that a module appears in the program tree as its *tier number,* and its documentation reference depth as its *level number.* (Note that in a program without subroutines or separate level-1 major subprograms, the tier numbers and level numbers coincide.)

The main use of the tier chart is as a tool for keeping track of which modules are currently being worked on, which have been completed, and which are yet to come at the next immediate phases of effort. More discussion on the use of the tier chart appears in Chapter 10.

5.2 HIERARCHIC EXPANSION OF PROGRAM DETAIL

Structured programs can be organized into the hierarchic program segments (discussed in the previous chapter) such that each segment is at most some prescribed size, say one page, with entry only at the top and exit only at the bottom of each segment. Segments can refer to other segments at the next level, each by a single name, to represent a generalized data-processing operation at that point. This property of readability is a major advantage in testing, maintaining, or otherwise referencing program segments at later times.

Figure 5-12 illustrates a structured program created by nesting and iterating the structures given in Figure 5-1. The main program structure is of the WHILE c DO f type, where f is a sequence structure. The sequence structure f is of the DO g THEN h type, in which g is a function-box and h is an IF d THEN i ELSE j structure, and so on.

In this simple illustration, all the detailed program subfunctions are shown explicitly, all on the same flowchart, all on the same page. In more complex programs, however, all the detail cannot be hoped to fit all on the same page. How can such programs be represented for human comprehensibility, when many pages of flowcharts comprise a program?

Decomposing a given program function into one of the three basic forms necessitates the invention of: (a) two proper program subfunctions, f and g, for DO f THEN g; or (b) two subfunctions, f and g, and a condition c for IF c THEN f ELSE g; or (c) one subfunction, f, and a condition c for WHILE c DO f.

Each of the subfunctions, being proper, can likewise be partitioned into subfunctions, and so on, until the functional detail of each sub...subfunction is simplified to any required degree.

This process makes it possible to limit the size of a program unit to that most convenient for understanding, say, a one-page flowchart, or one page of program-code. Each of the subfunctions, by the definitions in Section 4.4, can be called a module. Each module which requires further detailing, or *expansion*, can be relegated to its separate page as a procedure— subprogram or subroutine—for a later level of design.

The expansion theorem defines the freedom available in expanding any functional specification into a structure at the next level. To expand a given program function f into the form "DO g THEN h" merely requires choosing any two pairs g and h whose successive application leads to f. The invention of an "IF c THEN g ELSE h" program to replace f is equivalent

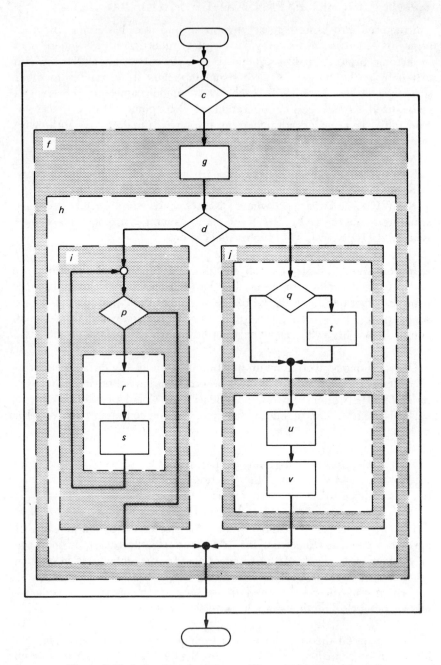

Figure 5-12. A structured program with nested substructures

to partitioning f into non-intersecting subfunctions g and h, and the invention of a "WHILE c DO g" program to replace f is equivalent to the determination of a suitable g which, when iterated, ultimately reaches f.

The only freedom in an "IF c THEN g ELSE h" construct is the choice of the condition c, which then splits f into determinable functions g and h. The only freedom in a "WHILE c DO g" construct is the iteration process g, for c is then fully specified as that condition under which the iteration of g has produced f. Any other supposed freedom is illusory.

Mills' structure theorem and top-down corollary state that any proper *program logic* can always be *represented* by one of three primitive structures, or by iterations and nestings of the three. This doesn't mean that such a program can always be *written*. For one thing, there may not be enough storage to accommodate the entire program. However, insofar as the abstraction of the program matches reality (see Section 2.5) Mills' theorems apply.

By way of illustration, Figure 5-13 shows that any of the three basic structures can be used to create a program "FILL A" to insert up to 100 numbers into array A. The function to be accomplished in each box is clear and each version of the program can be *proved* to perform the required function. However, if the *algorithm* by which each subfunction is to be realized is also to be detailed, it can be expanded at the next hierarchic level, as illustrated in Figure 5-14, which expands the function appearing in Figure 5-13(a).

Note the use of the name "LOOP" appearing in the striped box of Figure 5-14(a) and in the entry symbol of Figure 5-14(b). This is the ANSI standard [8] notation for hierarchic expansion of flowchart functions. Notice also that the correctness of each hierarchic segment of a program depends only on the segments already written or read, and on the functional specifications of any additional segments referred to by name.

The correctness theorem assures that a program, proved correct based on the functional specification of its modules, does not have to be *re-proved* after each of its modules has been designed in later levels of the hierarchy to satisfy its specified requirement. Because of the simplicity of control structures and hierarchical nesting of functions, the control complexity of a structured program is approximately linearly proportional to the program length; that is, the program control logic can be understood by an argument related linearly to the length of the program (see Chapter 9).

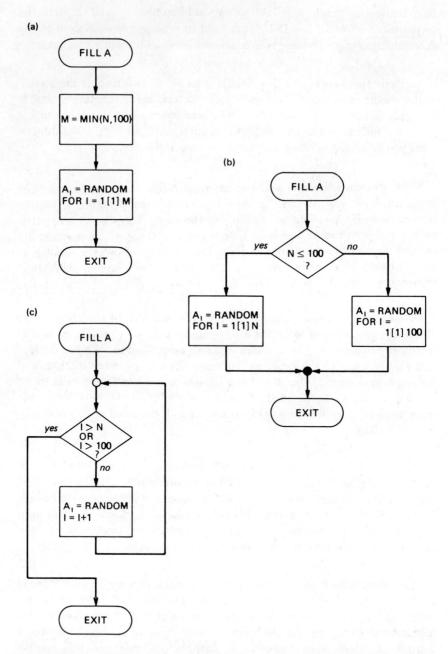

Figure 5-13. Three realizations of the program, "Fill the first N elements of array A with random numbers, available through the function RANDOM; the maximum dimension of A is 100, and the variable I is available as an index, initialized to 1"

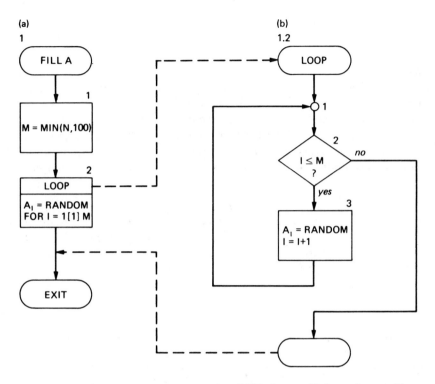

Figure 5-14. Hierarchical expansion of "LOOP" box, which performs "A_I = RANDOM for I = 1 [1] M" in Figure 5-13(a)

5.3 PROGRAM CORRECTNESS

A computing process can be viewed as a succession of machine states dictated by the input data. Generally, the number of possible input sequences, and hence the number of possible states, is so great that it would take an impossibly long time to demonstrate them all on a computer of practical speed. While it is possible to test the logic flow of a program in finite time, demonstrating the correspondence of the actual output to that required under given input is what takes so long.

How else can we assess a program to be totally correct? Program correctness is a question of predictability. Given a function f, however specified, and a program F, then F can be verified to perform the function f only by comparing of the input and output data sets of F against the transformations specified by f. If not by enumeration, then perhaps by formal mathematical means.

Hoare [37] has argued that formal proofs are possible in concept, and Mills [12] has shown that, if such be the case, then these proofs can be applied to structured programs in a simplified way. In particular, for structured programs, proof of correctness turns into a series of nested problems, each of which is one of three simple types, which can be prescribed in advance. It must be remembered, however, that a formal proof is merely another formal statement of about the same size as the program it refers to, and, without any automatic aid, is also subject to just as many human errors. Moreover, rigorous, formal proofs by humans are generally prohibitive in the amount of work required for a program of any size.

It has also been argued that there is no such thing as an absolute proof of logical correctness; there are only degrees of rigor, as "technical English", "mathematical journal proof", "formal logic", etc., each of which is an informal description of mechanisms for creating agreement and belief in a process of reasoning.

Automatic program provers have not been forthcoming either, although some progress has been reported [38,39,40] and it has furthermore been hinted by Elspas, *et al.*, [38] that the generalized prover might be equivalent to just enumerating all the cases in the first place.

5.3.1 Assessment of Correctness

Programs must be correct, or at least they must operate in a way that *appears* to be correct, to be useful. The degree to which the program appears correct can be termed its *index of reliability*, or its *confidence level*.

Currently, human intelligence is the only general means available to check program reliability. Therefore, another reason for the concise expression of programs is to remain within the limits of human understanding. Computers are often used to test the response of the program to certain "typical" input data sets, but it is up to the human to design the tests (sometimes with computer aid) to assure that the program operates within a qualifiable level of confidence.

Nevertheless, test hypotheses can be formulated on a systematic basis, and technical judgements can then be applied to determine the level of validation that is feasible and desirable for a given program. *The correctness problem comes down to the demonstration of agreement between a functional description and a program behavior.*

But formal proofs are infeasible and fallible, and complete testing is impossible in all practicality. We must be content with not being able to demonstrate program correctness on a rigorous scale, and settle for an *informal assessment* of the program functioning.

What information must accompany a program to permit an assessment of correctness on any reasonable scale? The first requisite, of course, is that the program *functional behavior* be known. It is an *absolute necessity* that the response of a program to every input stimulus be checkable. If what a program is supposed to do, given a certain input, has not been defined at all, then the resulting output cannot really be said to be incorrect, regardless of *what* it is.

One typical, though sometimes subjective, method for program behavioral specification is the "principle of least astonishment" default. According to this principle, one expects rational operation of the program in its more pathological moments in keeping with similar situations that were envisioned and specified.

The second requisite is that the program must be readable (documented) enough to permit a feasible proof. For structured programs, only that level of detail sufficient to assess correctness on an individual module basis is needed. Documentation certainly should not be *overdone*. But, neither should it be *underdone*.

I shall defer further discussions of criteria and procedures for increasing probable correctness and program validation to later chapters of this monograph, so as to include considerations necessitated by real-time programming, as well as other constraints.

5.3.2 Recursive Subroutine Correctness

Program segments that may call each other as subroutines are termed *recursive*. Certain subroutines can be recursive with themselves; these are said to be *self-recursive* subroutines.

Mills' proof of the correctness theorem assumes that each striped module can be replaced directly by the program it represents at each level of the hierarchy, and assumes that this process ultimately terminates. He then uses finite induction to demonstrate that correctness of a program is provable. However, coroutines and recursive subroutines do not satisfy this hypothesis, because the substitution of coding or a flowchart for the subroutine call never ceases. Does the correctness theorem then apply to such routines?

The answer is *yes*, at least for recursive subroutines, a direct consequence of the top-down hierarchy and the functional correctness of segments at every preceding level in the hierarchy. If a program is designed top-down and proved correct at each level prior to going on to the next level, then each subfunction in the algorithm at the correct level is *defined* and *independent* of the algorithm used at later levels to realize it. It does not matter if the subfunction definition is the same as that of the function itself. It is the job of the correctness proof at that level to show that the algorithm given, having one of its subfunctions the same as the function, actually terminates and produces the specified result.

5.4 STRUCTURING UNSTRUCTURED PROPER PROGRAMS

Mills' proof [12] of the structure theorem provides a constructive method to convert any proper program (i.e., one entry, one exit) into a structured program using only the basic canonic forms given in Figure 5-1. The method does not produce particularly efficient structured programs, but they are, nevertheless, structured. While I do not necessarily advocate turning already operating programs into structured programs just for the sake of having structured programs, the procedure by which programs can be structured is an instructive one.

Once the reader sees how any proper program *can* be structured, he will know better how to devise structured programs from the beginning for his own designs. He can always resort to the Mills algorithm to structure his own program, or perhaps to other methods such as that of Ashcroft and Manna [41], but, more likely he will develop a natural ability to create structured designs on his own.

I have introduced structured programming as a discipline and methodology to aid in human comprehension and orderly program development, but that does not mean that the code resident and operating in the computer itself necessarily has to be structured. Just as for any programming language, compilers can be made to optimize the object code to be executed. A compiler for a structured programming language may well optimize using *proven* algorithms to unstructure the object code in specified ways. In that case, even though structured programs may *appear* in their source form to be less machine-efficient than unstructured programs, this need not necessarily be the *actual* case.

While the structured programs that result from applying Mills' method to existing programs are perhaps less efficient than the existing programs, there is no indication that entire programs designed in a structured way from the very first are any less efficient than an unstructured design written to do the same job. The reason for this is that a structured design facilitates thinking, so that a better product naturally emerges.

5.4.1 Mills' Method

I shall describe Mills' method itself as if it were a structured computer program. The algorithm I give does not appear in this exact form in Mills' paper, but is, in essence, the same. It does not, for instance, include some rather obvious refinements for producing more compact flowcharts.

The algorithm stated below makes use of a "flowchart stack", a structure for storing and retrieving as-yet-unstructured flowcharts on a last-in, first-out (LIFO) basis. The procedure furthermore yields structured programs with DO...WHILE loops, rather than WHILE...DO loops.

MILLS ALGORITHM:

.1 CONVERT all multiple-branch nodes into their binary-branch equivalents. Create specific binary lc and dc nodes where flowlines meet.

.2 INITIALIZE the flowchart stack to contain only one flowchart, namely, the entire program. Initialize the Master flowchart as a blank page with an entry flowline at the top.

.3 WHILE the stack is not empty, perform the following procedure:

.4   REMOVE the last-entered flowchart for current consideration.

.5   SCAN down from the top of the retrieved flowchart, drawing all flowlines and p-nodes (these are already structured) on the Master flowchart, until a d- or lc-node is reached.

.6   IF a d-node was reached in the scan

.7   THEN DRAW the d-node on the Master chart and partition the remainder of the flowchart being scanned into flowcharts fc_1, fc_2, and fc_3, as defined by Figure 5-15.

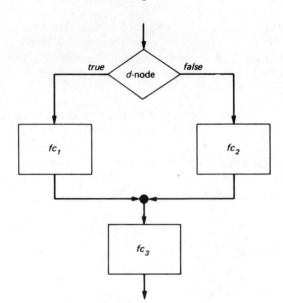

**Figure 5-15. Partition of a flowchart after a *d*-node
is reached in Mills' algorithm**

Any of the fc_i may be trivial (only a flow line). fc_1 and fc_3 together comprise the entire set of flowchart nodes reachable from the "true" output of the node. Similarly, fc_2 and fc_3 together comprise the entire set of nodes reachable from "false"; fc_3 is comprised of that set of nodes common (and separable) to the two paths.

.8   PLACE the non-trivial, non-structured flowcharts among fc_1, fc_2, and fc_3 on the stack, the largest (most nodes) first. (Placing the largest on the stack first minimizes maximum stack depth.) Draw trivial or structured flowcharts on the Master flowchart, and leave space on the Master for the charts put on the stack.

.9   OTHERWISE the node reached is an *lc*-node. Hence,

.9.1   CONSIDER the next mode.

.9.2   WHILE this node is not a *d*-node,   perform steps .9.2–.9.7 below.

.9.3   IF this node is an *lc*-node,

.9.4   THEN CHANGE the *lc*-node to a *dc*-node, and move it into the returning flowline, as shown in Figure 5-16. Continue at .9.6 below.

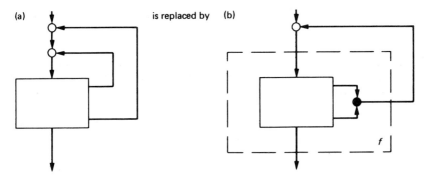

Figure 5-16. Combination of *lc*-nodes in Mills' algorithm

.9.5   OTHERWISE, it is a *p*-node. Hence,

JUMP* the *lc*-node below the *p*-node, draw the *p*-node on the Master chart, put the *p*-node in the returning flowline, and redefine the remaining flowchart as *fc'* (Figure 5-17):

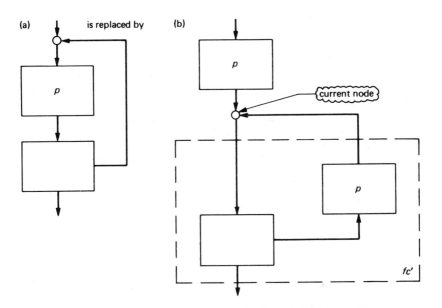

Figure 5-17. Duplication of *p*-node inside loop in Mills' algorithm

.9.6   CONSIDER the next node, then

.9.7   REPEAT from step .9.2 above until a *d*-node is reached, at which time continue on.

---

* This step can be refined so that a duplication of *p* may not be necessary.

.9.8–.9.10 SPLIT fc' into fc'_1 and fc'_2, and insert flag* *set* and *test* nodes as shown in Figure 5-18 to form flowcharts fc_1 and fc_2.

---

* A new flag must be used for every nesting of a loop within another loop. Mills uses the convenience of a flag stack for this purpose; upon entry to the loop (the *lc*-node), the stack is "pushed" down to access an unused flag, and upon exit (after the final flag test) the stack is "popped" up to release the flag for later use.

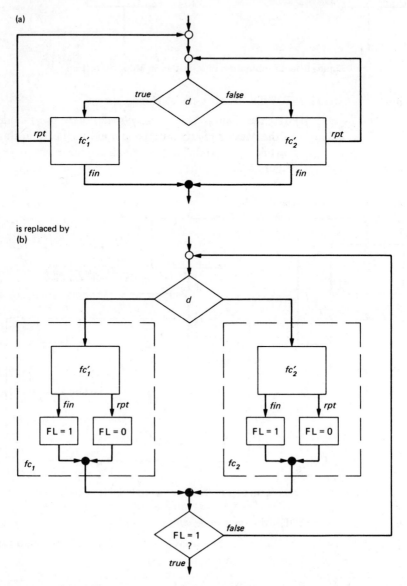

Figure 5-18. Splitting the flowchart inside a loop after a *d*-node by Mills' algorithm

.10   PLACE the non-trivial, non-structured flowcharts among fc_1 and fc_2 on the stack, the largest (most nodes) first. Draw the d-node and the flag-test node on the Master chart, as well as any trivial or structured fc_1 or fc_2 not stacked. Leave space on the Master for stacked charts.

.11   REPEAT by going back to step .3 for another chart until the stack is exhausted, at which time

.12 STOP. The Master flowchart is now structured.

Notice, in the statement of the algorithm above, that certain key words are capitalized and that parts of the narrative are indented and blocked in a way which modularizes the algorithmic steps and reveals the flowchart nesting levels. The algorithm as it stands *is* a structured program; it's just written in English rather than some definite (and non-ambiguous) programming language. The indenting convention can be used as an alternate to flowchart production of programs. More detailed information concerning indenting and structured-program languages appears in later parts of this monograph. A flowchart of the algorithm appears in Figures 5-19 and 5-20.

As seen in the algorithm above, it may be necessary in the course of a structured design to introduce flags and tests for flags solely for the purpose of achieving the topology indicated by the Structure Theorem. However, an examination of the procedure shows that such *flags are only strictly necessary in loops* that require more than one test of the loop-termination condition within the loop, and in which the processing of data subsequent to one end-test invalidates the results of any later retest needed. The flag in such cases is introduced to record the outcome of the first end-test. Introducing such auxiliary flags may be desirable, even when not required, as for example, when a condition is to be tested several times in a program, and a flag test is faster and simpler to code than the corresponding condition test.

Auxiliary flags set to indicate the outcome of a test condition for later use in order to achieve a certain structured design, whether required or desired, are referred to hereafter as *structure flags*.

5.4.2 Examples Using Mills' Procedure

To give a little familiarity with structured programs and methods for turning unstructured designs into structured ones, I will work out a few simple examples. From these examples, the reader will hopefully be able to see many shortcuts and reductions that can be made in the Mills' procedure. The first two examples are simple enough that the separate steps of the structuring procedure are not shown, only the resulting structured program.

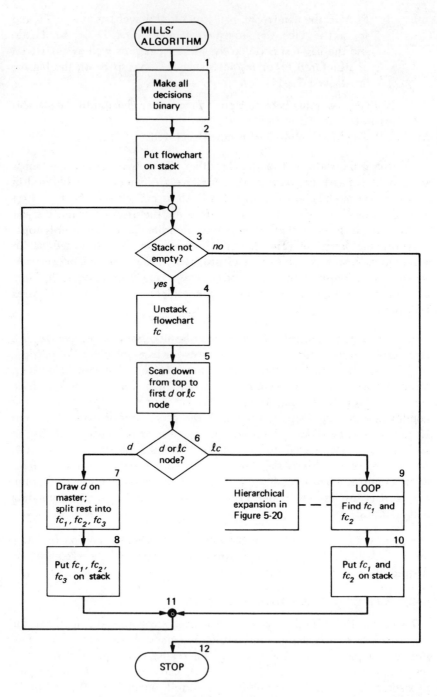

Figure 5-19. A flowchart for Mills' algorithm (flowchart numbers correspond to steps given in the text)

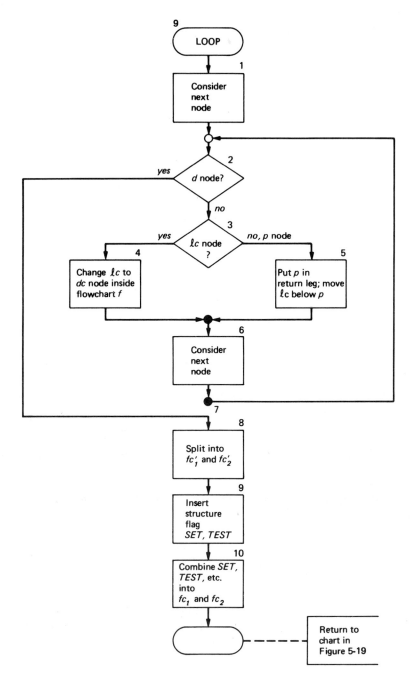

Figure 5-20. Hierarchical expansion of the LOOP subprogram appearing in Mills' algorithm (Figure 5-19)

Example 1. In the following example (Figure 5-21), note that the function D must be duplicated to achieve the structure requirement.

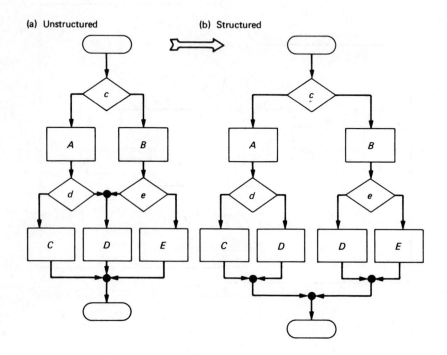

Figure 5-21. Example 1 using Mills' algorithm (no structure flag required)

Example 2. The following construct (Figure 5-22) is widely used; some advocate its inclusion as a valid structured program for the form **DO** *A* **LEAVE IF** *c* **ELSE** *B* **AND REPEAT.**

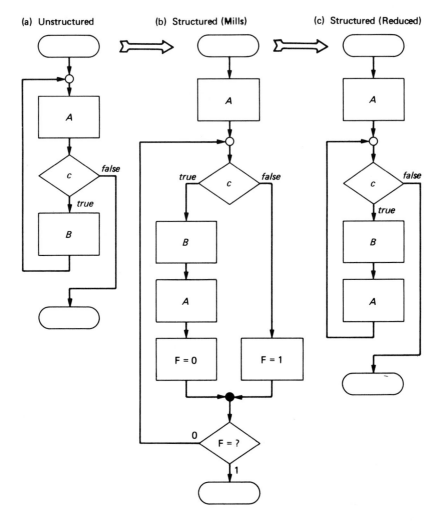

Figure 5-22. Example 2 using Mills' algorithm and reduction to get rid of an unneeded structure flag

In this example, Mills' procedure duplicates the function A and introduces a structure flag F to achieve a structured flowchart. In this case, however, the flag is not needed, as shown in the rightmost flowchart, part (c) of Figure 5-22. An alternate structuring procedure, in which the duplication of A is unnecessary, is shown in Figure 5-23.

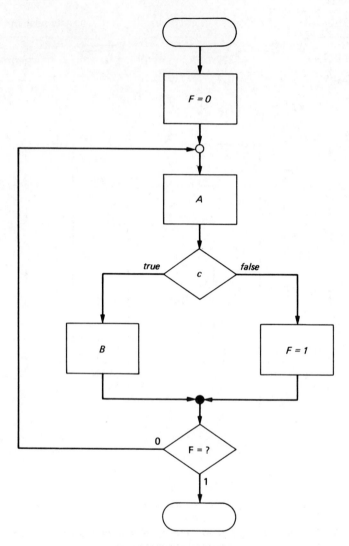

Figure 5-23. Alternate structured solution to Example 2 using a structure flag to avoid duplication of A

Note, in this last construction (Figure 5-23), that the structure flag F is initialized to zero at the beginning, and not changed to unity until the looping is complete. In this case, the only program overhead required to structure the given flowchart is a flag cell, initializing it at the beginning, checking it during looping, and setting it (and a final check) at the end. When A and B are rather large or time-consuming program segments, the overhead is negligible.

Example 3. The last example of this section is from John Flynn of the Jet
Propulsion Laboratory; it is quite a bit more complex than the previous
two we have seen. For this reason, the following structuring steps are more
detailed. The given chart is that shown in Figure 5-24.

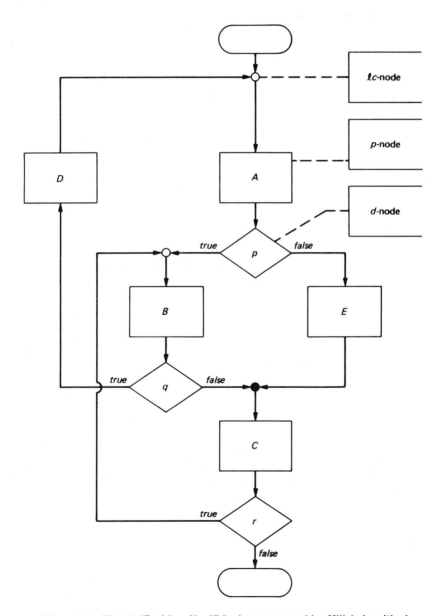

Figure 5-24. Flynn's "Problem No. 5" (to be structured by Mills' algorithm)

The first steps are the placement and retrieval of this chart from the chart stack, and the initialization of the Master chart to the entry flowline. Scanning for a *d*- or *lc*-node stops at the first node, an *lc*-node. The next node is the *p*-node, *A*, which is put on the Master chart and duplicated into the returning flow line; the collecting node is then moved below *A*. The flowchart between this point and the end is labeled fc_1. The progress at the end of the first steps is shown in Figure 5-25.

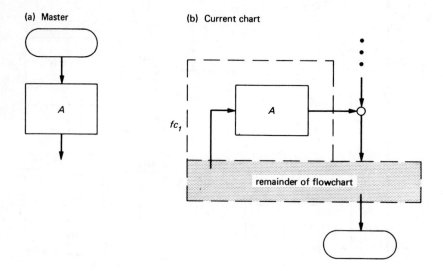

Figure 5-25. First steps to structure Example 3

The *d*-node with the condition *p* is detected next, whereupon fc_1 above is split into fc_2 and fc_3 (see Figure 5-26(b) and (c) below). The *lc*- and *d*-node labeled *p*, together with a *d*-node labeled "F1 = ?" and the returning flowline are put on the Master chart as shown in Figure 5-26(a). Flowchart fc_3, having the most nodes, is stacked; then fc_2, on the flowchart stack. (Note the reversal of the *true* and *false* legs of fc_3 at this stage for readability.)

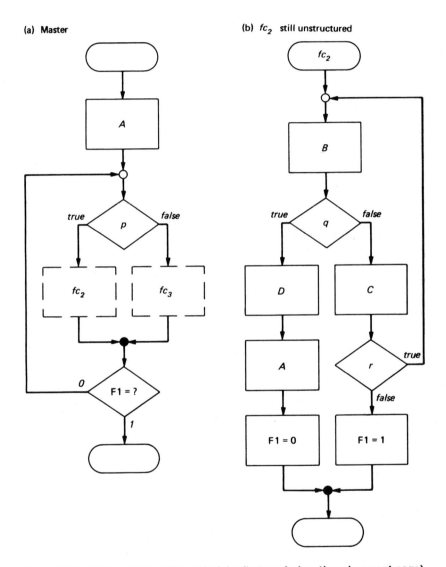

(a) Master

(b) fc_2 still unstructured

Figure 5-26. Configuration at the end of the first cycle (continued on next page)

(c) fc_3 still unstructured

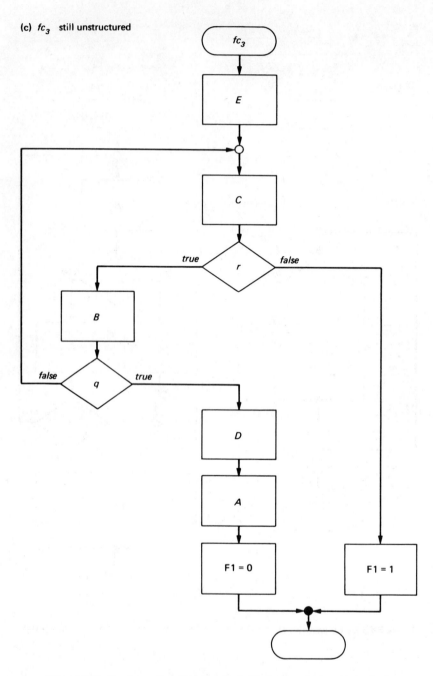

Figure 5-26. Configuration at the end of the first cycle (continuation)

The process then iterates: fc_2 is fetched from the stack and processed. At the end of this cycle, fc_2 is structured, and appears as Figure 5-27, which is then drawn onto the Master chart.

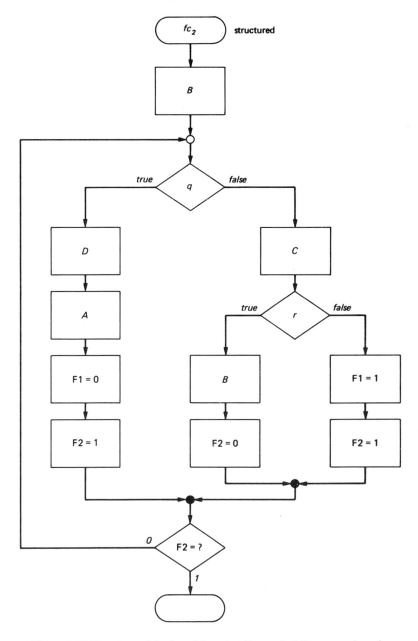

Figure 5-27. Structure of fc_2 is achieved at the end of the second cycle

On the next iteration, fc_3 is retrieved, and E and C moved to the Master chart. The remainder after applying Step .9.6, resulting in fc_4 in Figure 5-28, is stacked for the next iteration.

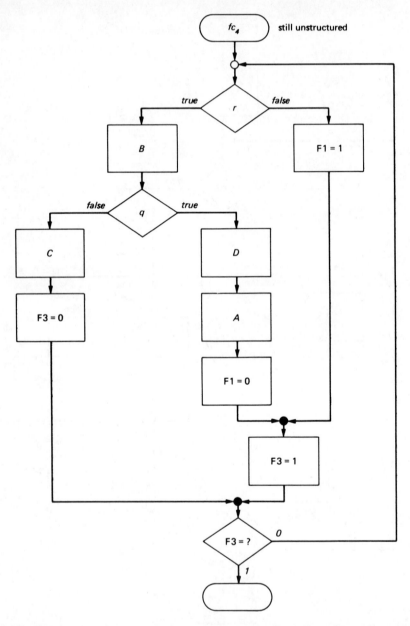

Figure 5-28. Flowchart stack at the end of the third cycle (remainder of fc_3 after application of Steps .5 and .9.6)

Finally, the next iteration structures fc_4 and places it on the Master flowchart, which is now complete, and structured as shown in Figure 5-29. (Note that the previously reversed *true* and *false* legs have been restored to their initial order.)

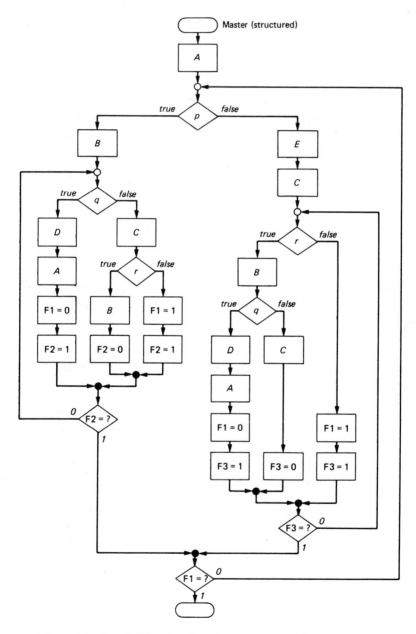

Figure 5-29. Flynn's "Problem No. 5" structured by Mills' algorithm

5.4.3 Efficiency of Structuring Programs

The expansion of a simple 8-box flowchart by Mills' algorithm into a 30-box chart is hardly what one would call "efficient" in either memory utilization, speed, or perhaps even understandability. But then, much of the duplication in memory can be avoided by making A, B, C, and D subroutines, and the flag-sets and tests do not introduce a large speed overhead either if A, B, C, and D are long-duration processes in comparison.

As for understandability, one at first has a natural tendency to believe that the original is more readable than the final structured result. But the original is deceivingly complicated: the various looping paths intermingle to the extent that one cannot really tell (until after much study) just what the state upon entry to any box is, or when (and under what circumstances) the program terminates, or then what the results will be. The structured version avoids this difficulty to a great extent by its top-down development and controlled looping. It identifies separate distinctive actions as separate program modules, even though they were the same originally. Thus a looser coupling probably occurs between modules in the structured version, because each replication of a function is not playing its total role played in the unstructured program.

If the designer had decided to program Flynn's example in a structured way from the first, he could have been more efficient. As shown in Figure 5-30, the duplication or subroutining of A, B, C, and D is not really necessary at all, and the structured design only has 14 boxes. The design uses one structure flag and combines the tests p and r with structure-flag tests. Because no boxes are repeated, there is probably tighter coupling among modules.

But *is* the program depicted in Figure 5-30 a *better* program than that shown in Figure 5-29, and is either better than the one in Flynn's original problem? The answer is *no*—they are equivalent functionally. The structured forms even take slightly more memory and execution time. But several other questions are equally relevant: How long would it have taken a designer, starting with a functional requirement, to come up with and establish the correctness of each of the three? Which is most readible and understandable? Which most naturally fits a top-down logical development, problem to solution? What length of time would be needed to debug logical errors in each? With what degree of ease and with what side effects can alterations be accommodated in each version of the program and its documentation?

More and more programmers are discovering that the answers to these latter questions tend to favor the structured, top-down approach. In

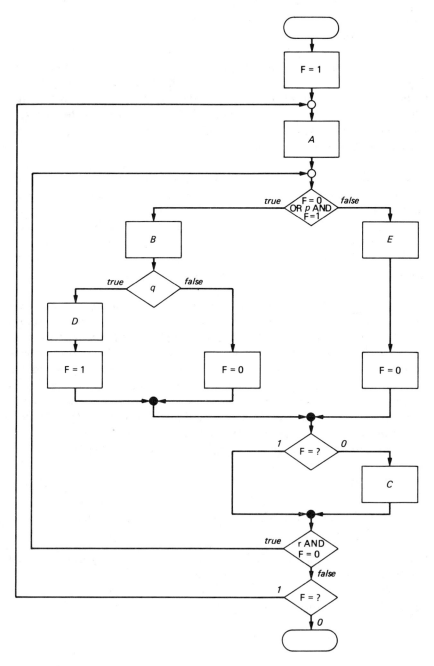

Figure 5-30. Another solution to Example 3, in which no function boxes are duplicated

response to the side effects question, for example, suppose that there is an error or a change to be made in Flynn's program, and suppose that it has been determined that module C of the original problem is at issue. Any proposed alteration of C must be checked to verify whether it will work or not under all conditions of execution. But the conditions under which C is invoked are masked by the convoluted connectivity of the original problem to the extent that the effects of a proposed change are apt to be very difficult to assess. The version in Figure 5-30 is quite a bit better because the connectivity is structured; but still, the single occurrence of C has placed a burden on the evaluation of side effects.

On the other hand, the 30-box version has 3 copies of C on the chart, each executed under different conditions. Hence, one can probably identify more easily whether or not a change proposed for one of the C modules also works for the others. If it does, then the change can be made. If not, then separate C modules are needed. If C were programmed as a subroutine, the change would then have to be executed conditionally, according to the conditions in effect when C was called.

Another general method for structuring an arbitrary unstructured program was devised by Ashcroft and Manna [41]. Their method employs iteration with an index variable and a multiple-branch decision logic to route program control to the proper next function. Each series of actions on the original flowchart is assigned a value of the index variable; in the structured version, then, the outcome of each decision sets the index to its proper next action value, whereupon the program repeats at the multiple branch. The solution to Flynn's "Problem No. 5" using this method appears in Figure 5-31. In this figure, none of the original functions or decisions have been repeated, but eight settings of the index variable and two flag tests have been necessitated.

5.5 PROGRAM STRUCTURES FOR NON-PROPER PROGRAMS

Structured programming, as I have presented it so far, forms the basis of an attractive software design and production methodology applicable to *proper* programs—those that have only one entry and one exit. I have argued that such programs developed using top-down, modular, hierarchic, structured programming techniques tend to be easier to organize, understand, modify, and manage, especially when the structure-set includes other simple extensions of the minimal three, as shown in Figure 5-32. However, there are typical cases where the strict adherence to the "one-entry one-exit" rule for a program or program module is a *hindrance*, rather than a *help*, to effective software development.

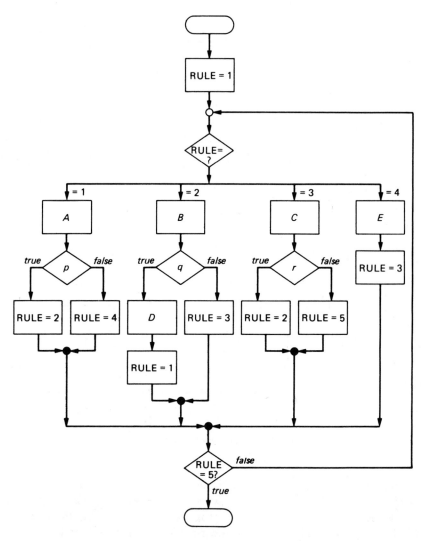

Figure 5-31. Another structured solution to Example 3 in which no functions are duplicated (note the use of multi-valued flag and decision structure)

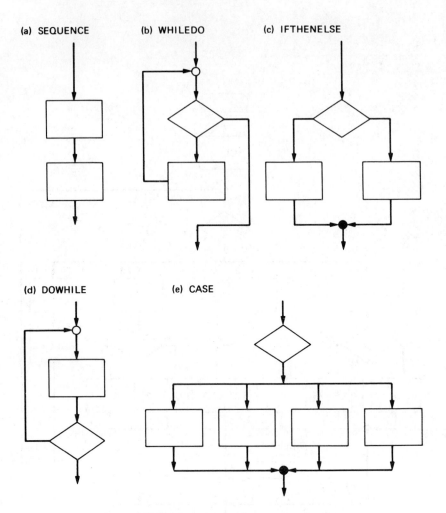

(a) SEQUENCE   (b) WHILEDO   (c) IFTHENELSE

(d) DOWHILE   (e) CASE

Figure 5-32. Extended canonic program structures

Structure for the sake of structure should not overrule structure for the sake of clarity. One notable example of such counter-productivity occurs when one is designing a program that is capable of detecting the existence of situations for which further processing in the current mode is either useless or unnecessary. Often, in such cases, the most desired, most logical, and most clearly understood course is to divert program control to a recovery mode or back to the user/operator for subsequent decision making and manual operations (Figure 5-33).

The alternative to programming abnormal exits of a module is to introduce structure flags as necessary to force these exits to the normal exit

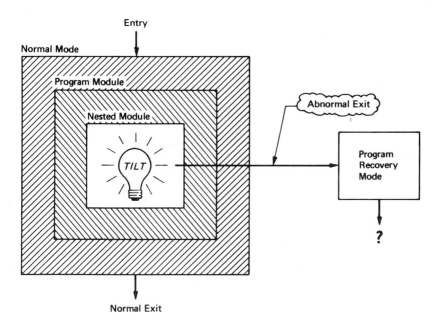

Figure 5-33. Abnormal exit from a nested structured program

point. However, this flag then has to be tested each time a "normal" action in the program comes up for execution. If an abnormal condition has occurred, the normal action must be bypassed (see Figure 5-34). Bypassing is necessary until an appropriate nesting level is reached so that the appropriate recovery procedure can be invoked in a properly structured way. This not only introduces a clutter of excessive, distracting detail to slow down the programmer, but it also creates a somewhat larger, slower program. Hence, besides interfering with programmer effectiveness, strict adherence to canonic proper-program structures causes the program itself to suffer.

It may also be the case, in many of the higher level languages, that some statements can cause unavoidable, automatic branching to prespecified or default program locations when certain conditions occur. For example, in FORTRAN, executing the file-input statement can result in normal input (the program continues at the next statement), an end-of-file condition (the program branches to a prespecified statement), or a file-error condition (the program branches to a separately specified statement). "Structured programming" (using canonic structures) is thus not possible whenever such statements appear.

(a) Unstructured   (b) Structured form of (a)

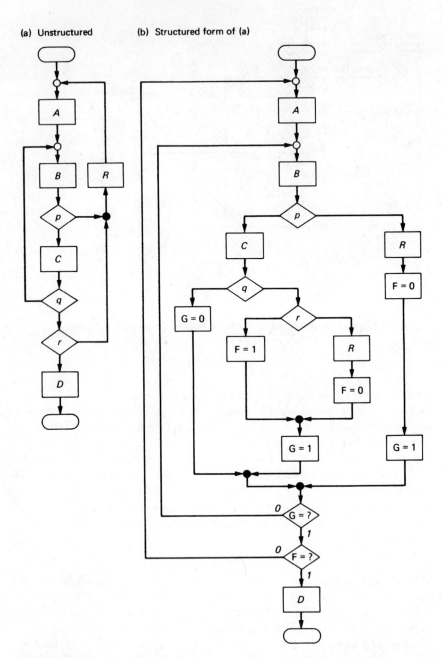

Figure 5-34. Bypass program in which *p* and *r* are tests that indicate further execution is useless; *R* is recovery module, which then initiates program restart

5.5.1 Criteria for Structuring Multi-Exit Modules

The context of structured programming obviously needs to be extended, in such cases, to include constructs that fit the language and that will tend to increase design productivity and program efficiency. But great care must be taken in extending the basic set of structures so as not to undo (or potentially undo) the progress that canonic structures have contributed to software development. Mills' proof of the correctness theorem depends on the "one-entry one-exit" character of programs. Permitting modules to have multiple exits (or entries) can, therefore, be a very dangerous policy unless that policy is limited to justifiable situations where correctness is not impaired. Candidate structures to augment the canonic set should satisfy at least the following criteria:

a. The top-down development and readability of the program design must not be impaired by the extended structures.

b. The hierarchic, modular form of the program must be maintained using the extended structures.

c. Program clarity and assessment of correctness on an individual module basis must not be jeopardized.

d. The situations under which an alternate exit of a module is permissible must be limited to special situations where the need is clear and desirable, or where it is unavoidable.

e. The new structures must conform to the same codability conventions used for the canonic set, such as modular indentation of lines of code, easily identifiable entry and exit points, and clear connectivity of program modules.

5.5.2 Structures for Multi-Exit Modules

Iterations and nestings of canonically structured proper program modules always result in proper programs. Whenever a branching (one entry, multiple exit) node appears in a structure, there also appears a collecting node and one or more process nodes within the structure arranged so that the global view again has only one entry and one exit.

The extension of this philosophy to modules having multiple exits suggests the following simple extension to structured programs (Figure 5-35).

The entire structure is a proper module, although module A obviously is not. However, if the function A has been stated explicitly enough that the two exit conditions are determinable, based on entry conditions to A, then proof of correctness is conceptually the same as for an IFTHENELSE

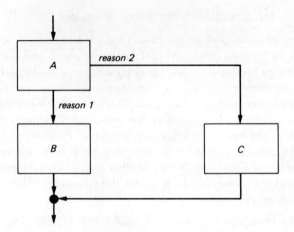

Figure 5-35. Multiple exits configured into an IFTHENELSE-like structure

structure. I shall use the following convention (Figure 5-36) to denote and emphasize the condition for that other exit.

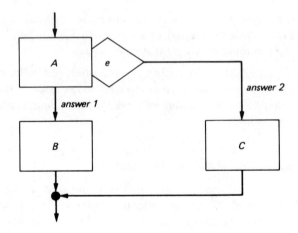

Figure 5-36. Multi-exit program configuration with exit condition explicitly annotated

The condition or event *e* under which the exit occurs is directly displayed for more clarity and better understanding.

When there are more than two exits, these can be accommodated by another configuration (Figure 5-37), analogous to the CASE structure.

Box *A* in Figure 5-37 represents, for example, the way end-of-file and file-error conditions are actually treated in programming languages such as

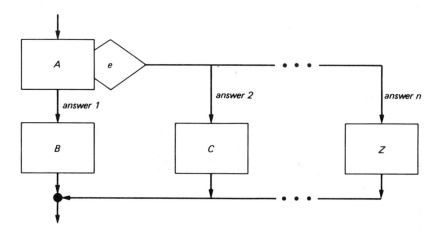

Figure 5-37. Multi-exit CASE-like configuration with exit condition explicitly annotated

FORTRAN. Using the configuration shown permits file input modules in such languages to take a structured appearance not otherwise achievable.

Normally, I draw the collecting node of CASE and IFTHENELSE constructs directly under the bottom vertex of the decision symbol. However, the exits in Figures 5-36 and 5-37 are unusual exits from a module, so I do not. Normal flow is straight down.

Looping structures could similarly be extended by this technique to yield the four configurations of Figure 5-38. However, the case for permitting such structures is a weak one, because the configurations in Figures 5-36 and 5-37 serve to bring the design back into a structured form. Such structures do not satisfy the criterion "the need is clear and desirable, or unavoidable". I shall not include them, therefore, in the set of permissible program structures.

Structures (a) and (d) of Figure 5-38 represent program examples that endlessly process streams of input data until the data quality falls below a specified event *e*, at which time some alternate procedure is invoked.

Structure (b) represents a program *A* in which *e* senses an abnormal condition: *B* is a recovery module that initializes *A* for another try.

Structure (c) could find application, for example, when information is being inserted at a terminal by *A* for processing by *B*. If *e* detects an error, the program returns to *A* for correct input; otherwise, it continues.

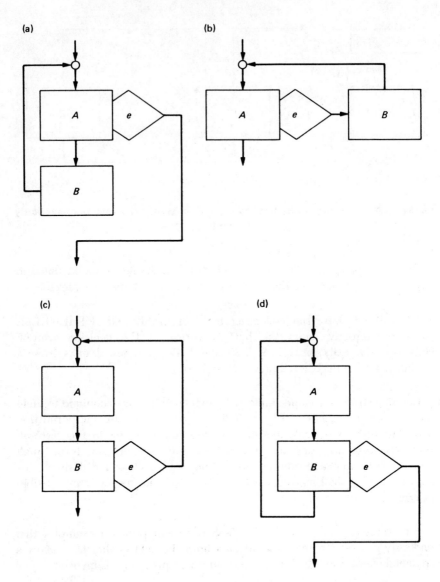

Figure 5-38. Conceptual looping configurations for multi-exit structures

5.5.3 Hierarchic Expansion of Multi-Exit Modules

The configurations in Figures 5-36 and 5-37 certainly satisfy the first four criteria for extensions to the basic proper structures, at least when viewed macroscopically. But what happens when a multi-exit function (box) at one level expands (to a flowchart) at the next hierarchic design level?

Using top-down hierarchic-expansion methodology, one starts the design of the module at the next level with a functional description of the module and the conditions under which the several exits occur. He then proceeds to design an algorithm to perform the intended action using the usual canonic structures. In addition, he perhaps finds occasion to use one of the extended configurations. At some point then, he breaks away from proper program constructs to divert the flow of control to the alternate module exit(s). He does this by replacing a box normally appearing in a structure by an exit symbol, as shown in Figure 5-39.

The resulting flowchart has one *normal* (structured) exit point, and one or more *extra-normal* (unstructured) exits. It is worthwhile pointing out again that the extra exits may derive from perfectly normal, non-pathological events. For example, when reading data from a file, it is a very common practice to read until an end-of-file indication occurs. Hence, the alternate exit from a box labeled "input from file" taken when the end-of-file occurs cannot be said to be an "abnormal" event. I shall refer to it rather as a *paranormal* exit (*para* from Greek meaning "beside"), to differentiate it from the (normal) exit taken after the more usual, stated

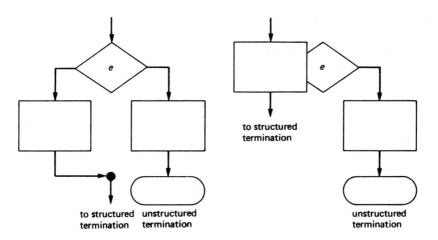

Figure 5-39. Modes of generating multiple exits in otherwise structured programs

function (reading elements from the file) has taken place, and from a truly *abnormal* exit (one in response to an abortive event).

Paranormal events thus lie between the normal and abnormal; they are the simple "alternate exits" that should be allowed in the software designer's bag. They will permit him, among other things, to create modules which can recover efficiently from minor failures in the program or from erroneous input data.

On the flowchart of a multi-exit module, several occurrences of each paranormal exit might appear, as depicted in Figure 5-40. How does such a flowchart stand in relation to the criteria I gave earlier? The flow through the chart does not appear disorganized, nor do any of the first four criteria seem violated; some branches just terminate early, back to an activity defined and assessed to be correct at a previous hierarchic level. The expansion of a multi-exit symbol as a separate flowchart thus does not seem objectionable according to the given criteria, at least whenever the invoking events are unavoidable or when an early exit is clearly desirable.

However, if a multi-exit chart such as that in Figure 5-40 were to replace its flowchart symbol at the previous level in the hierarchy, the new expanded chart would have crossing flowlines. A simplified case of this is illustrated in Figure 5-41.

Non-planar flowcharts are particularly annoying to anyone trying to understand a program, because crossing flowlines detract from readability, reduce clarity and understanding, impair assessment of correctness, and attack the program organization generally. Flowcharts with on-page connectors to avoid the crossings are no better. Programming conventions that can lead to such difficulties are of questionable utility and are clearly a violation of the criteria I stated earlier.

The violation comes as the result of substituting the flowchart with paranormal exits back in place of the simple box at the earlier level. Neither of the flowcharts—that with the multi-exit box, nor its expansion at the next design level—is objectionable on a separate module basis. For example, there is no objection to having Figure 5-41 be the next-level embodiment of box *A* in Figure 5-37. But there is objection to substituting Figure 5-41 for box *A* in Figure 5-37 because then the flowlines become jumbled. In Chapter 7, I shall reconsider this issue in the code for such modules, since flowlines in the code tend to be less visible than they are on flowcharts.

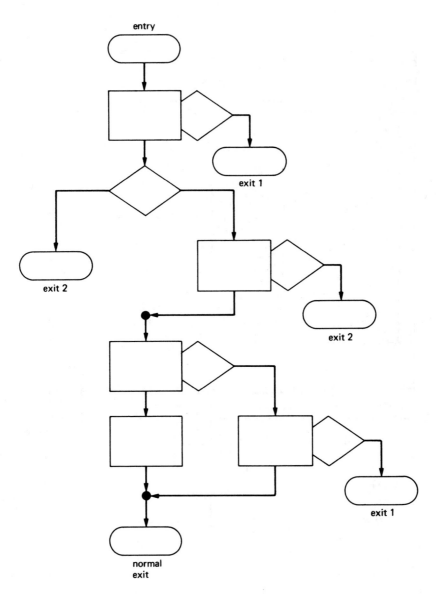

Figure 5-40. Possible expansion of a module with two extra-normal exits

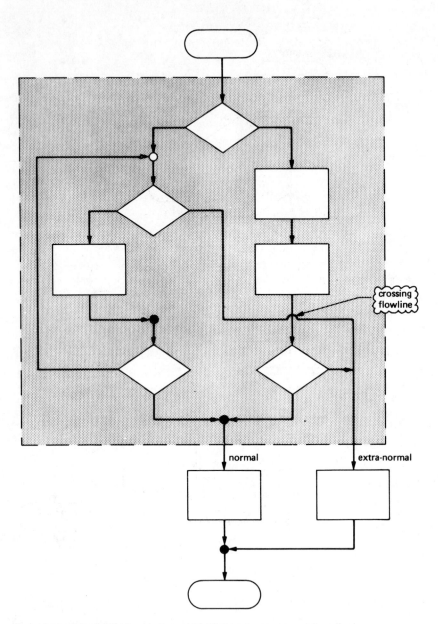

Figure 5-41. Crossing flowlines can appear when the flowchart of a multi-exit box replaces the box

The exit points of canonic structures, coded or flowcharted, are readily located, because they invariably either appear at the bottom or result as the immediate consequence of the loop test at the top. Logical flow in nested structures having exits somewhere in the middle is naturally going to be harder to read and follow, even if the flowchart remains planar. Hence, even if flowlines don't become jumbled as one flowchart replaces its box at the preceding level, the resulting chart is very apt to be less readable, because of the lack of uniformity in substructure exit conventions. The lesson here is that *paranormal exits from canonic structures should be used sparingly.*

Canonically structured flowcharts at one hierarchic level can replace a striped symbol at the preceding level without violating any of the criteria given earlier. But in order to avert such difficulty with the extended structures, one must accept the following guideline: *Do not redraw flowcharts at one level, substituting flowcharts from the next level for multi-exit striped modules.* Fortunately, this restriction is superficial in a top-down *design*, because flowcharts are developed *from* striped symbols, rather than vice-versa. I discuss the implications of this philosophy upon coding modules with multiple exits in Section 7.1.2.

5.6 ABNORMAL TERMINATIONS OF STRUCTURED PROGRAMS

The programming structures discussed so far extend structured-programming techniques to cases where programming normal events using canonic structures could prove counter-productive. However, there may be *abnormal* contingencies encountered during a top-down design that may not have been fully identified at earlier levels. In order for the program to perform correctly, these abnormal situations must be dealt with, and hopefully *not* by redesigning the previous levels.

For example, it may be known intuitively ahead of time that some arithmetic operations can result in overflow-errors under certain (perhaps unknown) input conditions. But it may not be known, until an actual algorithm is designed, just where the overflows will occur, or what the input conditions that cause them will be.

In other cases, there may be knowable, specifiable contingencies that represent abnormal departures from the program's normal functionings, which the program must respond to (or recover from). A decision table (see Chapter 8) drawn up for this program would likely classify such abnormal conditions into the "ELSE-rule" category—all cases not specifically defined by the program's intended behavior under normal, error-free input.

In some cases, recovery procedures can be instituted by the program itself; in others, operator intervention may be required. Different types of abnormalities will conceptually require entirely separate recovery procedures. For example, a program which generates a report from several files may conceivably be asked to complete the report because some identifiable parts of the report may yet be useful, even though one of the files continues to be read occasionally in error. However, in the same program, execution may be halted and control returned to the operator if one of the files cannot be found.

Abnormal exits from many unstriped modules are often overlooked because the abnormal exit is implied in the code for that module. A flowchart box labeled "A=B+C" would, for example, be coded in FORTRAN as "A=B+C"; but if A and B are large enough, an overflow trap automatically kicks the control to some error-handling procedure. Yet these connections are seldom put on the flowchart. Indeed, if such implicit actions were required to be drawn onto flowcharts, as in Figure 5-42, few "structured programs" would exist. And imagine all the confusion trying to follow the jumbled mess of lines!

A similar statement holds concerning abnormal terminations of striped modules. In order for us to be able to design and program using what *appears* to be structured programming techniques, it is usually necessary for us to suppress the flowchart connections for abnormal situations, at least down to that design level where an abnormal event is sensed explicitly and an explicit branch to the recovery procedure appears. But if program modules (unstriped, as well as striped) may have abnormal contingencies whose connections may not appear in an explicit form at a given design level, then program response can only be fully and readily assessed if the conventions for suppressing the connections are easily remembered, fully understood, and rigorously adhered to.

Of course, it may be entirely possible that a program can invoke a recovery procedure and return to normal processing in a purely structured way. Such cases, even though induced by abnormal events, nevertheless can be handled by the normal- and paranormal-exit structures already discussed. It is the others that must be covered by the convention.

The following rule for displaying abnormal terminations seems, to me, to be most in keeping with the first four criteria given earlier: *Flowchart lines showing abnormal terminations exiting from modules may be omitted at all hierarchic levels beyond that at which the recovery module first appears on a structured flowchart; this higher-level flowchart will also show the abnormal-exit flowlines from the modules (within which unstructured exits occur) to the appropriate recovery modules.* Such omissions at later levels are permissible, provided the rule for such exits is clear, easily remembered, and rigorously adhered to.

Figure 5-43 depicts a chart at which a particular abnormal termination first appears. The recovery procedure appears as a module (here named RECOVERY) executed whenever the abnormal error event occurs in later levels. The exploded views of striped submodules of *B* being aborted do not show either the *error* condition or the module termination symbol labeled "RECOVERY" unless there is an explicit need to do so (e.g., when *error* is actually tested as an unstriped module), or unless showing them contributes to readability, understandability, assessment of correctness, etc. As the latter of these represents an optional case, the abnormal exit can appear merely as a comment, as shown in Figure 5-44.

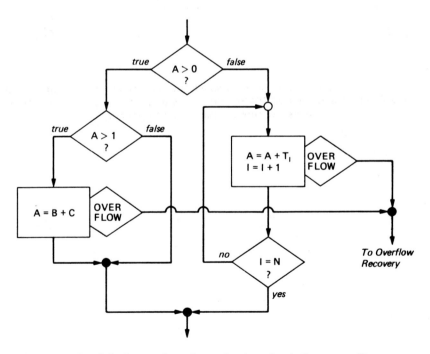

Figure 5-42. Implicit abnormal contingencies in a simple "structured" program

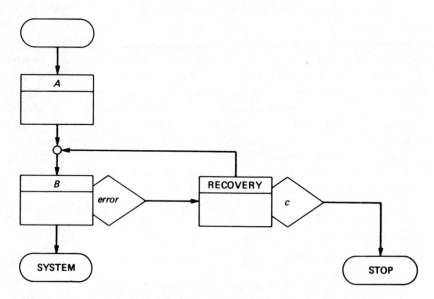

Figure 5-43. A program A **THEN** B, in which an occurrence of *error* during the execution of B initiates the **RECOVERY** procedure (if no recovery under criterion c is possible, control returns to the operator)

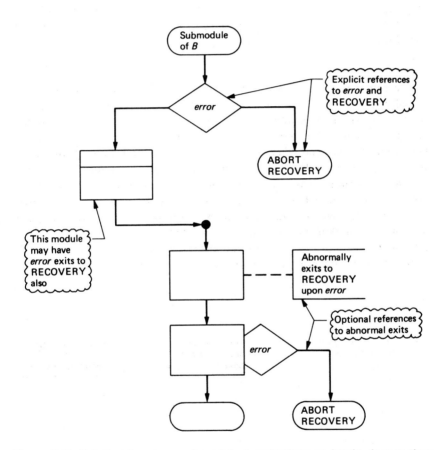

Figure 5-44. Notation for abnormal module terminations at levels deeper than
RECOVERY

5.7 LABELING FLOWCHART EXITS

There is obviously a need for correct and consistent labeling of the exit terminals of a module flowchart, so that the reader can tell immediately and with certainty whether it is a normal, paranormal, or abnormal subprogram exit, or a subroutine return. Further, he must be able to locate the procedure next to be executed, following the exit easily and unambiguously.

The conventions summarized in Figure 5-45 (of which only a subset may actually be operable within a given system) contain a type designator within the terminal symbol, and in some cases, an additional number designator that labels the outcome. This number, denoted by n in the figure, can be optional whenever all outcomes are indistinguishable to the preceding flowchart level. The number becomes mandatory if outcomes are distinguishable. The normal exit of a flowchart need not be given an outcome number, but is always assumed to be labeled "0". The CRISP (Control-Restrictive Instructions for Structured Programming) language (Chapter 7) implements such paranormal EXIT and RETURN by setting an OUTCOME flag to n prior to resumption at the previous level. This flag can be tested to determine appropriate action, as in Figure 5-46.

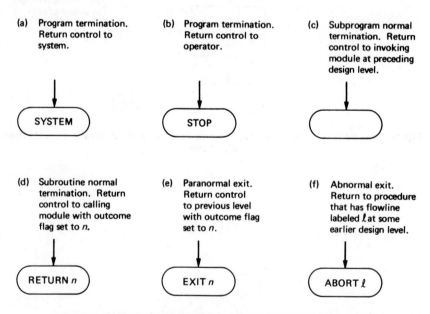

(a) Program termination. Return control to system.

(b) Program termination. Return control to operator.

(c) Subprogram normal termination. Return control to invoking module at preceding design level.

SYSTEM   STOP

(d) Subroutine normal termination. Return control to calling module with outcome flag set to n.

(e) Paranormal exit. Return control to previous level with outcome flag set to n.

(f) Abnormal exit. Return to procedure that has flowline labeled l at some earlier design level.

RETURN n EXIT n ABORT l

Figure 5-45. Module termination symbol annotation conventions

(a) MODULE with paranormal EXITs

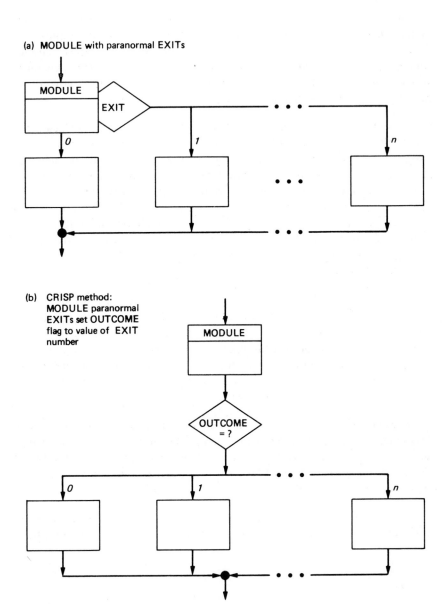

(b) CRISP method:
     MODULE paranormal
     EXITs set OUTCOME
     flag to value of EXIT
     number

Figure 5-46. Paranormal EXITs and RETURNs

5.8 SUMMARY

I have approached "structured programming" not as a coding methodology in this chapter, but rather as a flowchart design discipline. By doing so, I have not had to consider how the flowchart topologies translate into any particular programming language. Ultimately, of course, codability of the flowcharts has to be addressed, and I do so in Chapter 7, showing, by the way, that coding can also take a highly structured form.

I do not wish to have the reader believe that I necessarily advocate the use of flowcharts as the primary expression of the procedural design of a program. Whether this should be the case or not depends on whether flowcharts are economically supportable by the programming system. However, they do form excellent tutorial aids for my present purposes, and that is the principal reason I have used them thus far. In Chapter 7, I will show a mathematical equivalence between flowcharts and CRISP code structures, and thus in Chapter 17, I am able to discuss the components of a programming support system that makes the design documentation take the most useful, desired form.

Upon inspecting a variety of programs, one is very apt to see many programs that look like "structured programs" because they religiously adhere to the canonic restricted-control structure, but which, on closer inspection, are quite unreadable and contain bugs. One is also apt to find programs that look "unstructured", but which are quite understandable and entirely correct. *The final measures of quality and readability of a design are still inherently dependent on human ingenuity.*

To accommodate some of the inherent difficulties associated with "canonic" structured programming, I have introduced additional structures to increase programming productivity. These structures permit efficient designs of programs that must terminate their normal activity to initiate an other-than-normal activity.

The next chapter carries structuring one step further, into the realm of programs that may contain interruptible or concurrently executing parts.

Problems for Chapter 5

5-1 Structure the flowchart below using only the extended canonic structures shown in Figure 5-32: (a) by Mills' algorithm, and (b) by another method of your invention.

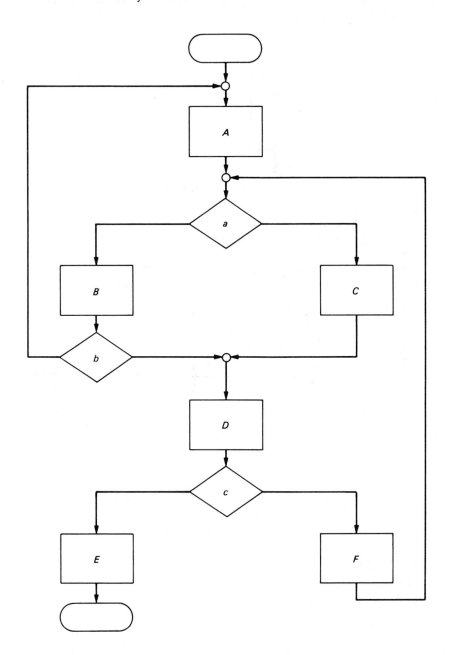

5-2 Prove that the structured flowchart generated by Problem 5-1(b) has the same function as the given flowchart. Make as rigorous a proof as you can.

5-3 Structure the flowchart below using only the extended canonic structures of Figure 5-32: (a) By Mills' algorithm, and (b) by another method of your own invention.

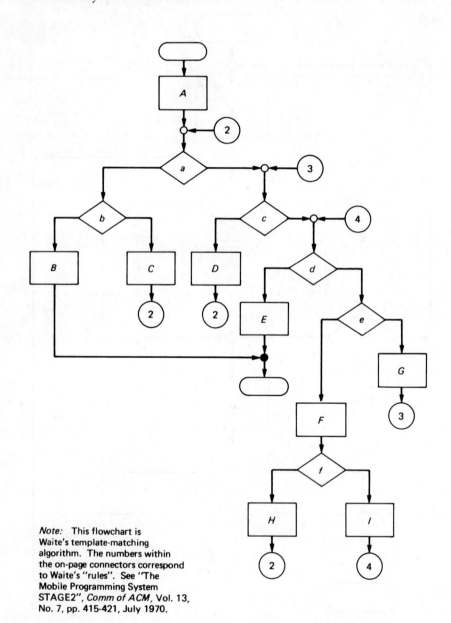

Note: This flowchart is Waite's template-matching algorithm. The numbers within the on-page connectors correspond to Waite's "rules". See "The Mobile Programming System STAGE2", *Comm of ACM,* Vol. 13, No. 7, pp. 415-421, July 1970.

5-4 Prove that the flowchart of Problem 5-3(b) has the same function as the given flowchart.

5-5 Draw a structured flowchart for a subroutine that uses recursion to compute n!. Prove that the program function is actually n! for all n≥0. What does the program do if n<0?

5-6 Flowchart the skills inventory program of Problem 4-3 as a structured program using hierarchic levels of flowcharts, such that each flowchart fits on one 8-1/2 × 11-in. page and with no more than 10 boxes per page. Number flowcharts as discussed in Section 5.1.3.2.

5-7 Prove in Step .10 of Mills' algorithm that the stack depth is minimized by placing the largest flowchart on the stack first.

5-8 Prove that structure flags are necessary only in loops that require more than one test of the exit condition within the loop and in which the processing of data subsequent to one end test invalidates the results of a later retest.

5-9 Flowchart the first level of a program that inputs data from a sequential data file. The format of the data on the file and the structure to hold the data in memory are to be defined at later levels of the design. Account at this level, however, for the error and end-of-file traps that occur when a read is attempted.

5-10 Show that IFTHENELSE can be made using two DOWHILE structures, one following the other, by the introduction of a flag variable to terminate the loop selected after one iteration.

VI. REAL-TIME AND MULTIPROGRAMMED STRUCTURED PROGRAMS

The program structures in the previous chapter provide a natural means for writing non-real-time programs in a top-down way. But real-time, interrupt-actuated programs and multiprograms often have many (perhaps implicit) entry points, many exit points, perhaps simultaneous computations, etc., and so these are inherently much harder to understand than non-real-time programs (which are usually hard enough, even when aided by the structure requirements imposed in the last chapter). There obviously needs to be an extension of the top-down structured design and production techniques to such programs. This chapter addresses that need.

The physical constraints of the computing system and the complexity of the programming process might at first seem to be of secondary importance to the computational problems to be solved. Yet, programming efforts typically are dominated by the human incapability to comprehend the total picture of what is really going on in the computer on an instant-by-instant basis.

A single computer with but one central processing unit can only process instructions sequentially, whether on an interrupt-priority, queued-priority, or background basis. We normally think of a computation as a set of operations applied to data to solve a given problem, and we know that these operations must be carried out in a certain order to ensure that the results are correct. We realize that many computational requirements do not imply a strict operational sequence; some of the operations, to be sure, must be carried out before others, but others may be carried out in arbitrary order, or in parallel, if there are other processors available for concurrent computation.

Sequential processes thus closely reflect how we think. But a computer must often be called on, for efficiency, to process certain operations out of their normal sequential order. For example, suppose two independent user programs, time-sharing a computer, are regularly interrupted by the system executive, to deactivate the one currently active and to pass control to the inactive one. In this example, the computer sequences back and forth between the two processes (which could be operated concurrently), and, in fact, the two programs appear to each user as if they are being simultaneously processed (except for the speed factor). Whether concurrent processes are multiplexed or multiprocessed, many of the attendant programming problems are much the same.

This chapter also addresses some of the inherent differences between programming real-time and non-real-time processes.

6.1 ATTRIBUTES OF MULTIPROGRAMS

In the remainder of this chapter, I shall refer to operations, processes, and computations. By way of review (Chapter 2), an *operation* refers to a finite-time execution performing a time-independent function based on its input. In this sense, each instruction, and indeed each of the non-real-time programs of the previous chapter, may be viewed as operations. A *process*, on the other hand, refers to a sequence of such operations performed one at a time. Two or more processes that have overlapping or interleaved operations are *concurrent* processes.

6.1.1 Program Interrupts

According to ANSI vocabulary standard definitions [7], an *interrupt* is the stopping of a process in such a way that it can be resumed. A particular type of interrupt is a *trap* (Figure 6-1), which is an unprogrammed conditional jump to a known program location, automatically activated by hardware with the location from which the jump occurred recorded. By this definition, a process that has placed a processor in a stopped state awaiting input data before continuing has been interrupted, but not trapped.

Trap interruptions to normal program sequence can be classified into three categories: (a) interrupts caused or actuated by specific internal operations in the program, such as overflow, underflow, input error, etc.; (b) interrupts resulting from external contingencies in response to internal program operations, such as disk or magnetic tape endfile, input buffer full, etc.; and (c) interrupts resulting from external events not prompted by internal program operations, but to which the program must respond, such as a real-time clock, emergency stop (BREAK), etc. Although a program responding to such contingencies is not a proper program, top-down procedures can still be developed and applied to aid in understanding and to provide discipline to the design process.

The program structures introduced in Section 5.5 of the previous chapter are useful in the handling of *dedicated* or *predictable* interruptions in the normal sequence of operations. Such events, you may recall, are indicated graphically by merging the function with the event actuating the interrupt, as exampled in Figure 6-2. The resulting control logic is then similar to the IFTHENELSE structure.

Particularly useful examples of this structuring convention are the handling of disk and magnetic tape end-of-file indicators, as shown in Figure 6-3.

The use of such program structures promotes top-down readability and simulates the form of a proper program in the design. Either subprogram 1 or subprogram 2 is executed, but not both; either may result in other-than-normal termination procedures discussed in the previous chapter. As will

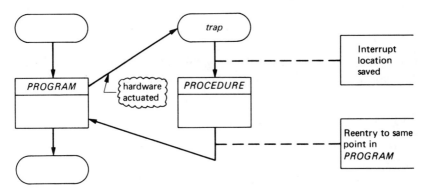

Figure 6-1. Hardware *trap* event causes *PROGRAM* interruption to service *PROCEDURE*

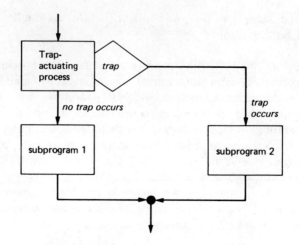

Figure 6-2. Dedicated-trap program structure

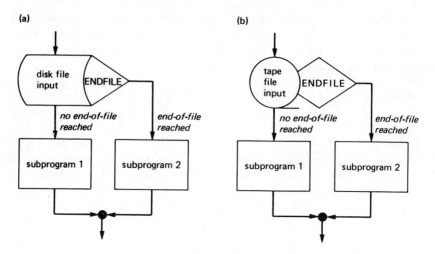

Figure 6-3. End-of-file trap program structures

be shown in the next chapter, the program code for these constructions can also appear to be structured in a highly organized way.

6.1.2 Multiprogram Interrupts

Interrupts that cannot be made to fit the structure illustrated in Figure 6-2 (or similar extensions of those given in Section 5.5) yield truly improper programs. It is specifically this type of interrupt that causes problems in understanding real-time programs. Obviously, a subprogram actuated by a real-time trap is manipulating the computer state in some way which can affect operations in the interrupted program. Programs having this type of interrupt I shall refer to as *multiprograms.*

Multiprogramming can easily be an order of magnitude more difficult to understand than mere sequential programming because of the interruptable aspects of process execution and because of the possibility that, once a program has been interrupted, its pertinent data state can be changed in a damaging way before the eventual resumption of its previous activity. Clearly, such a difficulty must be averted at all costs.

A typical multiprogram interrupt is illustrated by the structure in Figure 6-4. Once the interrupt occurs, a subprogram executes, and control returns to the point in the program where the interrupt occurred. If there is a functional invariance between the interrupted segment and the interrupt program, then the two segments could well have been executed independently by a parallel processor, if one were available and if the difference in execution speed were immaterial. Therefore, multiprogramming is, in many ways, a more general concept than concurrent programming (multiprocessing) because the program segment and the interrupt subprogram can be viewed as potentially concurrent. Certainly, the inherent problems of *concurrent programming* must be averted as a subset of the problems attendant on multiprogramming.

The structure to be imposed on real-time concurrent processes is modular partition into sequential activities which can be programmed separately and then combined for execution in a way that allows for

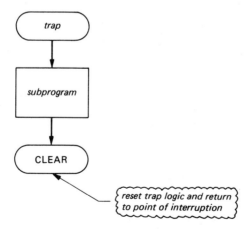

Figure 6-4. Multiprogram interrupt (returns after execution of *subprogram* to point where interruption occurred)

precise assertions concerning the data space before and after each activity [42].

In order for real-time sequential programs to simulate true concurrent or parallel structures, any process interrupted by a multiprogram trap must be permitted, at a later time, to continue on to its normal termination. Subprograms actuated by such traps must thus eventually return control after execution to the point where the interrupt occurred (or else pass directly to an abnormal termination point). Three permissible forms are depicted in Figure 6-5.

Interrupt structures that exit to other points in the program violate the top-down aim of structured design. They, therefore, must be forbidden.

The only conceptual differences between structured real-time multiprograms and programs with structured concurrent segments are imposed by time-response constraints and interrupt priorities. In a hard-real-time situation, interrupts may be triggered by external events which require response within a very short time, before a certain condition evaporates. Parallel programs may not need to react in the same hard-real-time-constrained way. Furthermore, the priority of a trap subroutine ascribes a level of CPU privilege to that routine; the multiprograms may thus communicate or share resources in a slightly different way than parallel programs do.

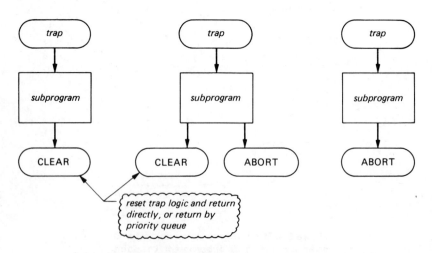

Figure 6-5. Multiprogram-interrupt structures

6.1.3 Resource Sharing

Certain resources, by their very nature or by the nature of the operation with which they are accessed, must be dedicated exclusively to only one operation at any given time; these I will call *devoted resources*. Other resources, which I call *mutual resources*, can be engaged in simultaneous operations when certain stated limitations are met.

Memory cells form one example of devoted resources. The reader can well appreciate that it is impossible to make meaningful statements about the net effect of parallel computations which are able to change the contents of a shared cell location simultaneously (or change and read it simultaneously). Rather, when one process is storing, other processes must be excluded from accessing that location in any way, storing or reading.

A physical resource that interconnects producing and consuming processes is a *buffer*. If it possesses the capability of holding simultaneously many products to be consumed, the buffer can be viewed as a mutual resource of the processes involved. The resources being buffered are said to be *temporary resources*.

If one process stores data into, and another process retrieves data out of, a first-in first-out buffer (queue), then simultaneous use of the buffer by the two processes is permissible except when the buffer is empty (and possibly when it is full). Hence, the buffer is a mutual resource of the two processes under the stated limitations, and, in this case, the mutual resource is composed of devoted resources (memory cells) as subunits.

A mutual resource need not necessarily be made up of devoted subunits. For example, a read-only memory may service any number of parallel processes without any doubt of the theoretical (as opposed to implementable) outcome of accesses. However, *any mutual resource whose state is capable of being changed must contain devoted subunits to comprise that part of the resource whose state is alterable.*

6.1.4 Concurrent Program Structure

Two or more processes are concurrent when their operations overlap (or interleave) in time. Processes result in computations, which are applied to resources (CPUs, memory, files, magnetic tapes, printers, etc.).

On a flowchart, concurrent processes are indicated as illustrated in Figure 6-6. The parallel lines at the top and bottom of the figure represent the *limits of concurrency*. Entering the top of the figure, execution is sequential; then $P_1, \ldots, P_n$ are executed concurrently (or interleaved); and after all the concurrent processes are *complete*, the overall process continues sequentially again at the bottom. The upper line is sometimes called *fork*, and the lower, *join* [25]. Others have called these *cobegin* and *coend* [43]. I shall use the former.

Each of the processes P_i depicted in Figure 6-6 may itself contain forks and joins, and so on, iterated to any desired level, as illustrated in Figure 6-7.

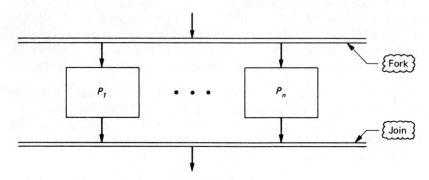

Figure 6-6. ANSI-standard flowchart [8] representation of concurrent-mode processes $P_1, \ldots, P_n$

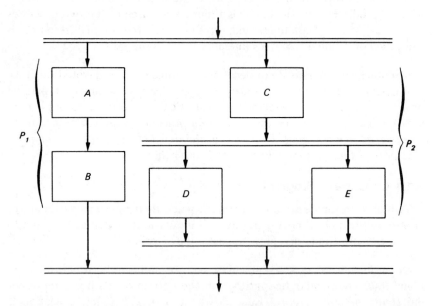

Figure 6-7. Nested concurrent processes (processes *A* and *B* are functions executed in sequential order to form process P_1; the function *C* is executed prior to the initiation of the parallel processes *D* and *E*; together these form process P_2; and P_1 and P_2 are executed in parallel)

Parallel processes generally progress at independent rates, although operations in one branch of a fork may be synchronized to mutually exclude or precede operations in another. Inasmuch as parallel processes represent simultaneous operations, and a join returns computations to a sequential state, it is clearly impossible to recontinue the sequential mode simultaneously at two different points. Furthermore, parallel processes cannot join and proceed with the sequential mode until all the branches of the fork terminate, either normally or abnormally.

In keeping with the philosophy given in previous parts of this work, it is reasonable, as a structure requirement for parallel processes, to forbid one process from disrupting the action in a parallel branch of the fork except when that disruption is an abnormal termination of the entire parallel structure. Each process, therefore, eventually reaches its join by normal termination, and a set of parallel processes terminates normally only when *all* of its component processes have normally terminated. Processes reaching the join earlier than others must wait until all the others have reached the join.

For concurrent programs, there are certainly other control-structure topologies that can be dreamed up and that some might even find useful. However, none appear in this work. If there was an advantage in the use of structured control flow in sequential programming, this advantage becomes almost a necessity in concurrent programs, insofar as program reliability is concerned. The doubting reader is referred to the work of Brinch Hansen [42].

6.1.5 Consistent Concurrent Processes

Concurrent processes that operate on non-overlapping sets of variables or physical resources are said to be *disjoint*. A simple example of a disjoint process is illustrated in Figure 6-8. Ten records to be input from a card reader are to be output on a line printer. Input and output resources are separate, and hence may be used simultaneously. However, in order to keep the records themselves from being a shared resource, two separate record buffers, RCDIN and RCDOUT, are used; RCDIN is copied into RCDOUT during a time when the card reader and line printer are not in parallel.

Disjoint processes are an example of a somewhat wider class of consistent processes called *non-interacting* processes. A set of concurrent processes is said to be non-interacting when resources can be used by each concurrent process without synchronization.

For example, non-interacting processes P_1 and P_2 may both read a variable v so long as neither changes its value; but if P_1 changes v, then P_2 may neither read nor change it with consistency (unless synchronized). In

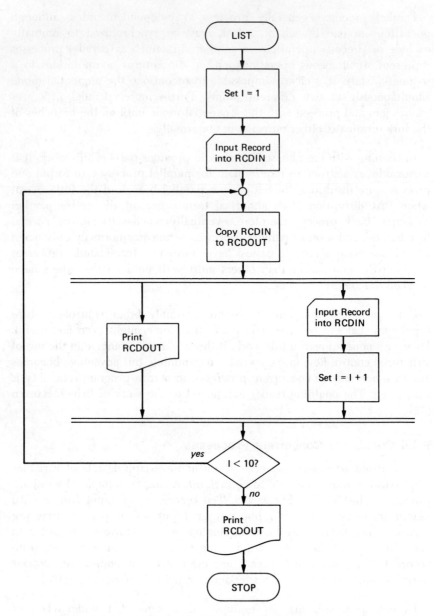

Figure 6-8. Card-listing program with concurrent input and output

the former case, P_1 and P_2 are non-interacting, although not disjoint; in the latter, P_1 and P_2 are interacting. These situations are shown in Figure 6-9.

Other processes, which can access and change the state of common variables or other shared physical resources, are said to be *interacting*.

(a) Disjoint

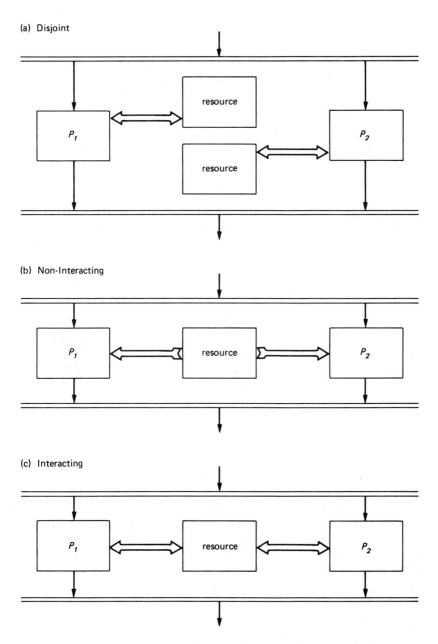

(b) Non-Interacting

(c) Interacting

Figure 6-9. Concurrent process (wide arrows indicate data connectivity between process and resource)

Interacting processes must make some provisions for excluding certain operations on shared resources from simultaneous occurrence. This principle is called *mutual exclusion.*

When the resource to be accessed on a mutually exclusive basis is a data structure (e.g., variable, array, queue, record, stack, etc.), then the process using the structure is said to be in a *critical region* with respect to that structure.

The work of Dijkstra [43] indicates that mutually exclusive use of a shared resource among concurrent processes of equal priority must be arbitrated by a program or device external to the processes involved and having higher priority. Such a program or device (or combination of the two) is called an *arbiter.* Arbitration of a shared resource between one process and an interrupt process with higher priority, however, may not need higher authority to guarantee mutual exclusion (see Section 6.4.3 later in this chapter), but can be handled within the higher priority process at a loss of program structure.

It is the job of the arbiter to assure that resources which *should* be devoted to their operations *are actually* devoted. That is, it must be able to enable certain operations involving shared resources and to exclude others in time. The scheme by which the arbiter constrains the ordering of operations in time is known as *synchronization.* Interacting processes must be synchronized if they are to be consistent. By making arbitration a service of the operating system, program structure of the type previously described is possible.

6.1.6 Program States

Before addressing what is needed to make concurrent programs synchronizable, let me mention that a process may be in any one of a number of *states.* A typical process state diagram appears illustrated in Figure 6-10. The UNINITIATED state is, of course, that state before the process has begun; upon initiation, the process enters the RUNNING state, during which time it performs its programmed computations. At various times, it may enter a WAITING state until certain events can take place in other processes; then it continues running. Finally, it exits to the TERMINATED state. During the time it is running or waiting, however, it may happen that other processes may require, and thus be permitted, to preempt some or all of the resources allocated to the current process. In such cases, the process may be said to enter a DORMANT state until such time as its needed resources can be returned.

During the WAITING state, CPU time is not required; hence, preempting the CPU resource and giving it to another process during this

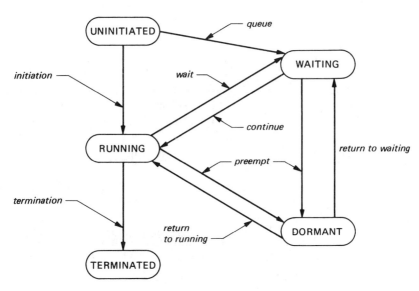

Figure 6-10. A process state diagram showing five states and actions that cause the changes in state

time does not really preempt a needed commodity, so the process need not enter what I have called the DORMANT state. However, if some of the other resources need to be reassigned during WAITING and are actually preempted, then the processor does enter the DORMANT state.

The scheduling of resources on a preemptive basis and control of the DORMANT state is generally the province of a higher-level privileged process (an *executive*), beyond the scope of the present discussion. I shall only address the fundamental needs attendant to synchronization and arbitration (see Section 6.4).

6.2 MULTIPROGRAM DESIGN REQUIREMENTS

In real-time program development, the designer sets the interrupt policy and subprogram queueing strategy, determines the individual subprogram durations, and verifies that the operating program can meet its real-time-event deadlines. The analysis of event timings often influences what computations need to be made, as well as the way they need to be programmed, and, of course, the reverse is also true. However, the structured methodology simplifies the design job by separating proofs of computational correctness from proofs of timing correctness.

6.2.1 Consistent Program Constraints

If there are errors in a program, there must be some facility for diagnosing what they are and where they occur. Error detection at run time is practically impossible unless programs have a functional behavior to permit errors to be reproduced under controlled circumstances. In addition, no system can be said to be operating correctly when its processes are "deadlocked" in attempting to perform their intended functions.

Program design methods should therefore be constrained so as to encourage these two qualities in programs, as a first step toward achieving correctness. I will refer to programs that satisfy the following two constraints as *consistent programs*:

a. *Repeatability*: The results of all computations must be reproducible in a practical sense in spite of logical errors, which may be present.

b. *Deadlock-Free*: It must not be possible for the program to reach a state in which two or more concurrent processes are waiting indefinitely for conditions that will never occur.

As a direct consequence of the repeatability requirement, Hoare [44] has shown that two more provisions are necessary for consistent concurrent programs:

c. *Speed-Independence*: The results of computations in one process must not be dependent on the rate at which computations are made in a concurrent process.

d. *Resource Protection*: Data and physical resources of each process must be guarded against inadvertent or malicious interference by other processes.

The latter of these seems rather obvious, but it is by no means a trivial commodity to achieve. Many present-day computers have lock-out features that can separate instruction and data sets of processes from each other and from other processes. Other computers do not. In either case, there must be great care in overseeing the allocation of common resources. I shall address some aspects of process protection in a later section.

The necessity of the speed-independence provision may appear surprising at first; we normally *envision* real-time concurrent processes as communicating data back and forth and using resources in a very time-*dependent* way. However, it is extremely difficult for us to *comprehend* the combined effects of a large number of intricate, interacting activities that evolve nearly simultaneously at independent rates. On the other hand, our understanding of *what* a single sequential process *does*, will not generally depend on its actual execution speed. All our understanding requires is the knowledge that operations are performed one at a time, and that certain assertions concerning the data space can be made before and after each operation.

Because the dynamic behavior of external events is possibly very unpredictable, and because of the lack of influence that an operation can exert on its own execution rate (which itself may be dynamic, if processes are interleaved in time), and because of the general inability of humans to understand concurrent processes in terms of their absolute speeds, the necessity of speed-independence is unmistakable. Besides, speed-independence does not prevent time-dependent *interaction* among concurrent processes; it just makes it possible to program assuming that the responses to given inputs will be the same, regardless of how slowly or quickly the computations are carried out.

Obviously, when incoming events occur too rapidly for the program to respond, the program output is again likely to contain unreproducible errors. We may, therefore, add another necessary condition for consistent programs:

   e. *Deadline Integrity*: Processes must meet appointed timing deadlines.

Programmers who knowingly violate consistency requirements, do so with great risk. They must do so knowing, that while they may well reduce a program's overhead once it is correct and working, it may not be possible to reproduce errors, and hence, some errors are going to be difficult, if not impossible, to fix.

Some may argue that all errors can be perfectly reproducible in any program if only the program could be subjected to the identical input sequence, timing, and process interaction in effect when the error was detected. But here the human aspects again become a factor; it is too big a chore for human intelligence to keep track of all the simultaneous goings on in a large real-time system, much less design a program that can react differently to each of the slightly different situations which can occur. Therefore, to the extent that errors can be identified on a *practical basis*, those events causing time-dependent errors must be classified as non-reproducible.

I thus limit my concern in the remainder of this monograph toward generation of programs in which computations can be verified independently of other concurrent operations.

6.2.2 Resource Arbitration Requirements

Where multiprocessors are concerned, there *must* be a *hardware arbiter* to provide the mutually exclusive accesses to each unit of devoted resources (resources shared among processors and accessed one at a time). In simple computers with concurrent CPU and I/O processors, the arbiter is usually a simple device that "steals" infrequent memory cycles from the CPU during I/O operations, thus interleaving CPU and I/O operations in time.

Inasmuch as arbitration is a process capable of changing the state of a shared devoted resource (namely, by reassigning it from one process to another), it follows that it must act on a privileged basis, taking priority over any other processes desiring use of that resource. Each process using a devoted resource must go through a procedure (see Figure 6-11) by which it: (a) invokes the arbiter to request the resource and waits until the resource is granted, then (b) uses the resource, and, finally, (c) invokes the arbiter to release the resource.

The hardware arbiter for parallel processors is more complicated than that needed to multiplex a single processor's resources among multipro-

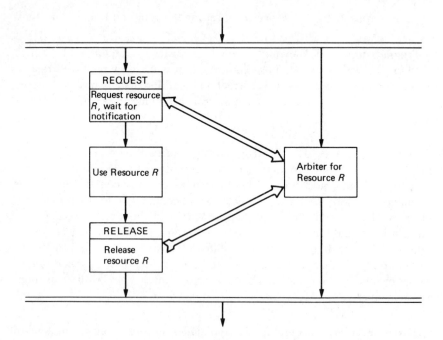

Figure 6-11. Structured interaction of a process and arbiter (wide arrows show data connections between the requesting process and the arbiter)

grams. For a true multiprocessor, the hardware arbiter must have properties equivalent to the following [42]:

a. The arbiter may be invoked by either of two commands, which I will call REQUEST and RELEASE.

b. If the arbiter is invoked while it is BUSY, the process identifier(s) and command type(s) are entered in a hardware queue.

c. If the arbiter is invoked simultaneously by two or more processes when the arbiter is NOT BUSY, and the queue is empty, the arbiter is granted to one of them immediately, and the identifier and command type of the other(s) are entered in the hardware queue.

d. When the arbiter is granted, a function corresponding to the invoking command (REQUEST or RELEASE) is performed, and the arbiter is marked BUSY until the function execution is complete.

e. If the arbiter is NOT BUSY and the hardware queue is NOT EMPTY, then the next action in the queue is granted.

f. The process invoking the arbiter is placed in a waiting state until the arbiter is granted to that process and its command-function has completed its execution.

6.2.3 Resource Protection Requirements

The simultaneous presence of data and programs belonging to co-existing processes requires that something must be done to protect processes from each other. In larger multiprogrammed installations, some measure of protection comes from services provided by an existing, privileged operating system. In smaller applications or applications where an entire computer is dedicated to a fixed set of related, hard-real-time tasks, and where the operating system is less elaborate, the user may have to achieve protection by some other means.

Guarding against inadvertent (or malicious) destruction of data or misuse of any other resource is not easy, and a satisfactory general solution is not yet known, to my knowledge. One can, however, identify some of the characteristics of the solution.

Brinch Hansen [42] classifies protection according to two aspects: operations and security. Resources are characterized not only by the functions and meaning attached to their use, but also by the operations by which they are accessed and by the authority to make such accesses.

For example, suppose that a numerical array with known dimensions can be operated upon in several well-defined ways, such as termwise addition with an equally-dimensional numeric array. There are unpermissible operations, such as addition with an array having different dimensions. But even the permissible addition must, at times, be temporarily banned, as is the case when another process is engaged in a permissible operation changing some of the array elements. There may also be permanent bans needed to guard against malicious processes accessing the array at all.

Hence, three attendant problems are associated with protecting a resource:

a. Authority recognition.

b. Identification of resources and permissible operations.

c. Checking that operations on a resource stay within its limits of integrity.

Programmers must identify to what extent these three are needed by their programs, and to what extent the operating system fulfills these needs. Any shortcomings must be taken care of by implementing such accommodations into the operating system or by inventing accommodations for each potentially interfering program segment. Those accommodations falling outside the operating system domain must become programming standards and should be documented as a necessary part of the inter-process interfacing requirements.

At least one language, Concurrent Pascal, combines the concepts of levels of access (Section 4.3.2), resource protection, and synchronization into a single concept, called a *monitor* [45]. A monitor is a level of access to a shared resource and provides both arbitration among users at run time and check of access rights at compile time. A monitored resource can only be accessed via interface functions that hide the resource from the outside users; synchronization is implemented within the monitor; and parts of a program attempting to directly access any resource within a monitor definition are caught by the compiler.

6.2.4 Synchronization Requirements

Mutual exclusion of shared devoted resources alone is not sufficient to satisfy the concurrency requirements. Other known criteria for proper process synchronization include the following [44]:

a. When a devoted resource has been requested by one or more processes, it must be granted by the arbiter to one of them within a finite time.

b. When a process has acquired a devoted resource, it must eventually release it again.

c. When a process has requested, used, and released a devoted resource, its request for use must not remain in the request queue.

d. While a process is using a devoted resource, it must make no assumption concerning the state of any other process with which it shares that resource. No assumption concerning the relative speeds of the various processes must be made. Processes may even be in the DORMANT state when not using a shared resource (as long as no real-time deadlines are missed).

Other additional features are sometimes useful, or contribute to more efficient synchronization, but are not required by consistency, such as:

e. The waiting state should not waste CPU time endlessly. (Wasting CPU time during a waiting process is sometimes called the *busy form of waiting.*)

f. The arbiter should be "fair" in its policy by which resources are granted to requestors.

The subject of "fairness" in arbitration is entirely application-dependent, and will consequently be left open; the discussion in Brinch Hansen [42], however, is very informative and recommended reading.

6.2.5 Requirements for Deadlock Prevention

A *deadlock* results when a parallel process lies in a waiting state for conditions that will never hold. Deadlocks are also called *stalemates* or *deadly embraces.* A process in the waiting state cannot transit out of the waiting state until another process releases it. Hence, deadlocks occur when each of the deadlocked processes is waiting for one of the other to act, and all are unable to do so. Deadlocks can involve *permanent resources* (those that can be used repeatedly by many processes, such as line printers, card readers, etc.) and *temporary resources* (ones that are produced by one process and consumed by another, such as signals, messages, etc.).

For a deadlock to occur involving permanent resources, it is known [46] that four conditions must simultaneously hold:

a. Sets of permanent resources have been acquired by two or more processes for their mutually exclusive use.

b. The deadlocked processes are in the waiting state, awaiting their needed, but unacquired, resources.

c. Certain subsets of these resources, which, if reassigned to other processes, could break the deadlock, either cannot be released or cannot be preempted to the proper process.

    d. Two or more of the deadlocked processes are capable of acquiring their needed resources in partial allocations, and the resources lacked by each deadlocked process have been acquired by others.

The obvious solution sufficient to prevent such deadlocks is to choose design rules by which all of the four conditions will not simultaneously be true. Negation of (a), of course, cannot be allowed, as it would permit simultaneous access to devoted resources (forbidden by the consistency requirement). Furthermore, it is natural for processes to wait for a resource being used elsewhere, so negation of (b) does not seem feasible, although it can be combined with the negation of (c) to form what is called *preemptive reallocation.*

Preemptive reallocation forces some processes to release resources temporarily in favor of others, on a priority basis. Such scheduling is sometimes impractical on many resources (such as magnetic tapes, etc.) and inefficient on many others. It sometimes may be required, however.

The most generally suitable possibility for preventing deadlocks comes in the area of proper resource allocation to user processes. The simplest technique for allocation that prevents deadlocks is the allocation of *all* resources needed by a process at one time (*complete allocation*). In such a case, joint processes must operate on disjoint sets of resources; if that is feasible, it presents a simple solution. However, computational efficiency can usually be enhanced by resource sharing, and when that is the case, the decreased efficiency engendered by complete allocation is often too dear a price to pay for deadlock protection.

Allocation algorithms exist [42] by which a master arbiter can make very flexible use of the system resources. The idea behind such algorithms is the allocation of resources in nondeadlocking sets.

As an example of such an algorithm, suppose P_1, P_2, and P_3 are three concurrent processes that require resources A, B, C, and D. As illustrated in Figure 6-12, P_1 requires A, B, and C, while P_2 requires B, C, and D, and P_3 uses only A. If the arbiter has granted B to P_1, it will not then grant C to P_2, as C will be required to complete P_1; but it can grant D to P_2. Similarly, it can grant A to either P_1 or P_3 because, if given first to P_3, then A will only be used for a finite time, after which it can be reassigned to P_1.

The arrangement of resources into acceptable non-deadlocking sets and the algorithms associated with arbitrating the allocation (both in the *sequence* that resources may be granted to each user as well as *which*

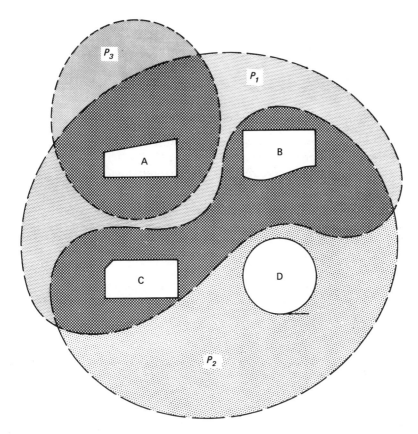

Figure 6-12. Resources *A*, *B*, *C*, *D*, and processes *P₁*, *P₂*, and *P₃* using them

resources may be granted to him) is a topic beyond the scope of this work. I recommend the interested reader to the book by Brinch Hansen [42] for further discussions of deadlock prevention by resource allocation.

Deadlocks may also occur in the use of temporary resources. However, in order that a deadlock involve temporary resources, such as messages, it is necessary that either a buffer is full and a PUT is being executed, or a buffer is empty and a GET is being executed, or both.

Deadlocks involving temporary resources can be averted if one programs according to the following rule [42]: *a temporary resource must never be produced unless it will eventually be consumed, and a temporary resource must never be expected unless one will eventually be produced.*

The following design rules are sufficient to ensure that this stipulation holds:

a. Provide a consistent interface between the producer and consumer processes with regard to where the next temporary resource will be available.

b. Design so that, within each process, all operations that produce or consume temporary resources eventually terminate.

c. Provide processes producing temporary resources and requiring the return of like or other resources with an empty (buffer) element into which the returned resources can be delivered immediately.

d. Make all communications complete in the sense that, when one process has consumed a resource produced by another, the consuming process requires no further resource from that producer for the current transaction.

These four rules are not the only sufficient conditions for temporary resource deadlock prevention; other sets of sufficient rules can also be formulated. It is important that any set of rules proposed for use be known to be sufficient, however.

6.3 SYNCHRONIZATION METHODS

Synchronization, or the scheme by which the arbiter constrains the ordering of operations in time, can be designed, to a great extent, to fit the needs of the problem and the limitations of the resources involved. In this section, I shall discuss three typical methods: buffering, semaphores, and conditional critical regions.

6.3.1 Synchronization by Message Buffering

As I indicated earlier, not all shared resources need to be devoted, but can be mutual resources between two processes. In the case of cooperating processes, where resources are apt to be temporary (i.e., produced by one process and consumed by another), there still has to be some *physical* resource (i.e., buffer) capable of holding the product of the producer (e.g., a message) until it can be used by the consumer, and the use of this physical resource must be arbitrated.

The producing process may use the buffer in the cycle

REQUEST (*buffer*) ⎫   or merely
PLACE (*message,buffer*) ⎬   PUT (*message,buffer*)
RELEASE (*buffer*) ⎭

which will copy the data structure *message* into the designated *buffer*. The consuming process may similarly use the buffer in the cycle

REQUEST (*buffer*) ⎫ or merely
TAKE (*message,buffer*) ⎬ GET (*message,buffer*)
RELEASE (*buffer*) ⎭

which removes information from the designated *buffer* and places it in the *message* structure.

As I have shown the arbiter calls above, PUT and GET operate the buffer on a mutually exclusive basis, whereas they only *need* to be mutually exclusive when the buffer is empty (and sometimes, when full). The arbiter can accommodate such cases by using a second argument of the REQUEST call above, as

REQUEST (*buffer,top*)

or

REQUEST (*buffer,bottom*)

where *top* and *bottom* are pointers within *buffer*. A request for access to *buffer,top* is a request for access to a different data location than to *buffer,bottom*, except when the buffer is empty (or full, if circular). Hence, the arbiter can exercise mutual exclusion on these different locations accordingly.

6.3.2 Synchronization by Semaphores

The simplest mode of synchronization is the communication from one process to another that a particular event has occurred. The shared resource in this case can be a timing signal from one processor to another, a program-actuated trap, or a flag to be set by one process and tested by another.

In any case, the temporary resource can be regarded as a simple message, and all operations which access or activate that message must exclude each other in time in a consistent (error-reproducible) way. The only difference between these messages and the ones considered earlier are that the messages considered here take a much more primitive form—mere occurrences.

If the communicated event in question can happen more than once during the life of a given process, the recipient may need (in order to prevent deadlocks) a way of knowing whether the message he is now examining is the same as an earlier notification, or is, in fact, a new message, informing him that the same event has reoccurred. He has one of two alternatives: he can mark the current message himself for later identification, or he can establish an agreement with the sender to distinguish the messages.

But if he marks messages himself, he runs the risk of missing one or more messages that arrived during a time he was otherwise occupied. If that risk is untenable, he must require that distinguishable messages be sent.

Dijkstra [43] introduced the *semaphore* as a simple device for handling such communications. In its simplest form, a semaphore S is a data structure composed of a variable s whose value is

s = (number of messages sent) − (number of messages received)

and a queue q, which contains a list (if not empty) of processes currently waiting for the signal. In this form, each "receiving" process "consumes" one of the transmitted messages.

Both the send and receive operations yielding synchronization via semaphores access the count variable, and must therefore be mutually exclusive in time. The subprograms invoked by the semaphore arbiter in response to SEND(S) and RECEIVE(S) requests are similar to those found in the generalized resource arbiter (see Section 6.4.2). But, because of the simplified nature of semaphores, they can be implemented somewhat differently, as shown in Figure 6-13.

Synchronization via a semaphore takes place as follows. Somewhere in the program before forking, s is set to zero and the queue emptied. A positive value of s thereafter will be equal to the number of sent, as-yet-unreceived signals; a RECEIVE(S) request thus causes no waiting but reduces the value of s. If $s = 0$, more RECEIVE requests have been encountered than SENDs; hence, the processes issuing RECEIVEs are inserted into the queue q and put into the WAITING state until more SENDs occur. When a SEND occurs with a non-empty q, a process identifier is immediately removed from the queue and the corresponding process removed from the waiting state; otherwise, when the queue is empty and a SEND occurs, s is augmented.

The SEND and RECEIVE operations for a semaphore are similar to PUT and GET for a message buffer, except that the buffer for a semaphore is realized as the count variable.

6.3.3 Conditional Critical Regions

It is sometimes the case that a process, say P_1, inside a critical region (i.e., it owns data on a mutually exclusive basis) must wait for a condition c to come true, but the condition c is based on critical-region data to be supplied by another process, say P_2, temporarily locked out. So P_1 must release its resources in favor of P_2 to avoid a deadlock, but immediately request those resources again so that it may continue after P_2 has completed its critical region and enabled condition c. The situation appears

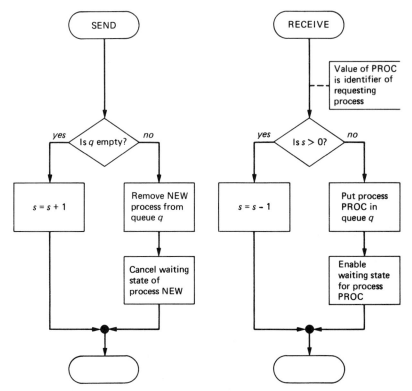

Figure 6-13. Mutually exclusive SEND and RECEIVE operations on a semaphore
$$S = s:q$$

flowcharted in Figure 6-14; part (a) shows the temporary release and re-request of the critical resource, and part (b) introduces an equivalent AWAIT function. (Brinch Hansen's *await* function [42] is similar to this, but more sophisticated in queueing the resource rerequests so as to avoid "busy waiting" for c to come true.)

6.4 CONCURRENT PROGRAM DESIGN METHODS

So far, I have been addressing the requirements for programming a design and the tools for assuring that the programs are consistent, deadlock free, and meet deadlines. Such tools do much to relieve the designer's mind of details inherently structural in nature, but control-logic-flow structures and resource protection do not address other problems, such as timing conflicts or constraints, data connectivity, resource assignment, memory management, etc. The techniques given in this chapter have addressed the characteristics of good real-time programs, rather than the creation of the algorithms and data structures that form these real-time programs.

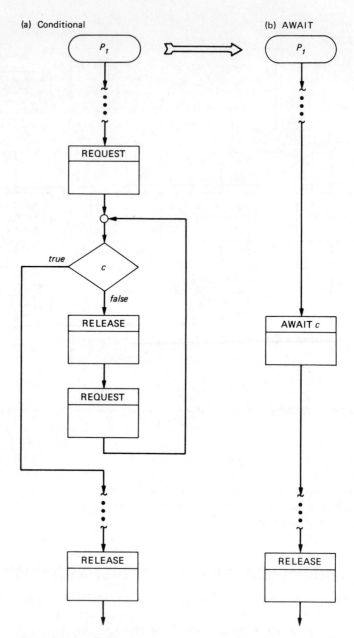

Figure 6-14. Conditional critical region and the AWAIT function

The design ease for a given application is greatly influenced by the aptness of a language for describing that problem and for arriving at a solution. The suitability of a candidate language can be gauged by how well it permits the user to abstract the (large) problem into smaller abstractions, each with only relevant details appearing at that level, to focus his attention appropriately on these details, and to manipulate and evaluate design decisions and parameters.

It would be nice if the problem-solving and analysis language could be the same as the implementation language, for then there would not need to be an extra translation of that design description into implemented procedures, data structures, etc. Thus, the power of a language with respect to a particular problem may be measured by the number of statements required within that language to implement the solution to that problem. Higher-level languages intrinsically hide a great quantity of implementation detail from the problem solver. Therein lies their power, but only in special circumstances does any one programming language seem to conceal the proper level of detail so as to be appropriate for describing the system design also, especially for real-time systems.

For this reason, graphical and symbolic representations are rife in software designs. Besides flowcharts and data-flow diagrams, one finds finite-state-machine graphs, timing-interaction plots, state-transition networks, data-structure diagrams, etc., used throughout the design process. Each describes an aspect of the design in a different set of abstractions; the particular description/analysis tool used in a particular instance depends on how concisely it portrays the relevant issues and conceals the irrelevant ones.

Whatever methods used for describing a non-real-time program design must be augmented (and perhaps, replaced, at certain levels) in real-time designs by descriptions of the time-critical interactions among the various processes involved. The program code cannot stand alone to document the design rationale or analysis.

6.4.1 Real-Time Program Structures

I have shown two forms of interrupt-handling structures in previous sections of this chapter. The first is the IFTHENELSE-like dedicated trap structure shown in Figure 6-2, in which one of two subprograms, but not both, executes in response to a process that can potentially cause the trap to actuate. The second is the fork/join concurrent structure shown in Figure 6-6; each of the processes in the structure executes exactly once (barring abnormal terminations) leaving the "fork" before entering the "join".

Real-time process-control applications, however, are typified by *repeated* executions of trap routines in response to *recurrent* external events. Once a trap has been enabled and armed (external signals enter a priority hardware or software queue and are eligible to cause activation of the trap routine), the trap routine executes each time the computer detects that the external event has occurred. Background and interrupt processes are concurrent processes—their operations overlap and interleave in time. But the iterative nature of the trap executions is not correctly represented by fork-join flowcharts (Figure 6-6), and the true form (Figure 6-1) lacks the aesthetic benefit of a structured appearance.

For this reason, I use the convention shown in Figure 6-15. It merges the ANSI-standard symbols for parallel processes with the interrupt/terminal symbol. The fork symbolizes that point in the background program at which the trap first becomes eligible to interrupt (probably the enable/arm instruction), and the join is that point beyond which the interrupt is no longer eligible (probably the disable/disarm instruction). The priority p (if pertinent) is shown by annotation.

This structure may be iterated within each of the processes shown. For top-down development integrity and consistency, it is necessary to make certain restrictions. In Figure 6-16, it is fairly evident that the priority of T_3 must exceed that of T_1, otherwise T_3 would never activate F. The structure convention I have presented means that T_2 may interrupt C, T_3 may interrupt E, and, certainly, T_1 may interrupt A and C. The question is, should T_2 be allowed to interrupt T_1 or T_3?

The answer is that design and analysis considerations should probably set interrupt priorities to assure that process deadlines are not missed, rather than have them assigned as a consequence of top-down hierarchic development. And since process durations cannot be rigorously prespecified by a top-down design, the hope of a top-down proof of timing correctness is fiction anyway. As a result, deadline errors are apt to

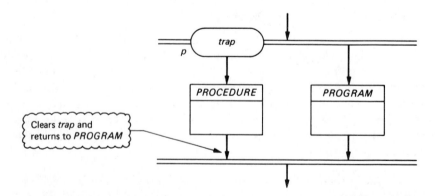

Figure 6-15. Concurrent background and real-time trap-actuated processes

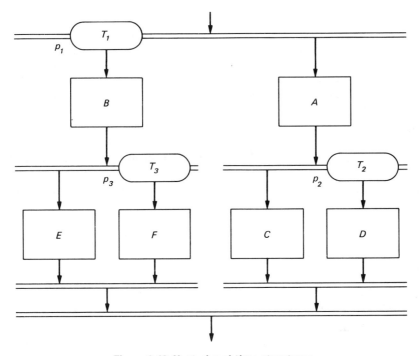

Figure 6-16. Nested real-time structures

manifest themselves late in the development and be difficult to correct without massive redesign.

For this reason, many will prefer to design trap routines and their background interfaces from the bottom up, at least on a preliminary basis. I do not consider this a violation of the top-down design principle, but rather, another instance of the engineering "look-ahead" technique described in Chapter 4. Inasmuch as trap routines tend to be very short anyway, the departure from true "top-down" practice is vestigial.

Synchronization of a real-time multiprogram in a single-processor system is then only slightly different than it is for the concurrent programs previously discussed in this chapter. The same statements concerning consistency apply to real-time programs equally as well as they do to concurrent programs. However, arbitration may be implemented differently.

6.4.2 Resource Arbitration Methods

A simple attempt at sharing a single resource R among N concurrent processes $P_1,\ldots,P_N$ of equal priority, using only a hardware simultaneous-memory-access arbiter, is shown in Figure 6-17. Each of the processes has a need to perform a subprocess involving the resource over and over. The program segment shown uses a flag to arbitrate which process shall gain possession of the resource. Initially, FLAG is set to 1.

When the program reaches the fork, only the process P_1 can activate and use R. Not until "FLAG=2" is encountered can another process—this time P_2—acquire R and use it. When P_2 sets FLAG=3, then next uses R, and so on. The processes thus arrange for mutually exclusive use of R by alternating cyclically, $P_1...P_nP_1...P_N...$, etc. However, the program is *not consistent*, for, say P_1 terminates; then after P_N has released R and has set FLAG=1, none of the other process can begin. The program deadlocks because P_1 is scheduled next to use the resource, but P_1 has terminated, and lies dormant, waiting at the join until the rest have also terminated.

The reason why the scheme above fails to be consistent is not just because it was a bad design to begin with; indeed, any such attempt would have failed! A hardware arbiter on single load and store operations is just not enough to provide arbitration of resources on a larger scale. Something else is needed.

Since it is fundamental to real-time multiprograms and multiprocessing, arbitration is usually handled by executive requests to the *operating system*. However, in some minicomputers or dedicated process-control applications, arbitration may be handled differently. In the next few pages, I shall discuss the inner-workings of arbitration so that the reader can realize what provisions must be made to make programming of consistent, equi-priority, concurrent processes possible. I will address non-equal-priority real-time resource arbitration later (Section 6.4.3).

The functional integrity of a devoted resource must be maintained from first use to as long as required by a process. For example, if a shared variable is given a value in one process and that value is used later in the same process, another concurrent process may not change that variable (unless it can assuredly return the variable to its former value by the time it is needed).

Before reserving a resource, a process may sometimes be able to *test* the availability of that resource, and if not available, to go on to something else in the meantime. When a process *requests* a resource, however, it must be prepared to wait until the resource has been freed and assigned to that process.

A shared resource may take many forms: a single variable, a whole complex data structure, a line printer, etc. Regardless of the units of access, program consistency requires that each devoted unit of a shared resource must have associated with it: (a) a facility by which a process may REQUEST

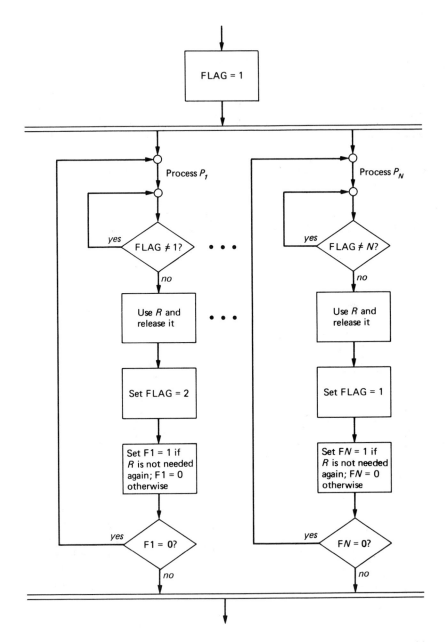

Figure 6-17. Simple synchronization of a resource among several processes (the program, however, is not consistent)

the resource, (b) a facility which causes a process to wait until the resource has been acquired, and (c) a facility by which a process can RELEASE the resource to other processes.

These functions of an arbiter are illustrated in Figure 6-18. Since RELEASE and REQUEST access and change shared commodities, and since many processes may call them concurrently, they must be mutually exclusive operations; hence, even the arbiter calls require an arbiter at a higher authority. At the highest level, arbitration requires a hardware device to permit only one process at a time to perform either REQUEST or RELEASE operations. Not only are REQUEST operations mutually exclusive with respect to other REQUEST operations, but with respect to RELEASE operations as well, and vice versa.

With a simple hardware device to make REQUEST/RELEASE subroutines mutually exclusive operations, other arbiters can be programmed. It is not necessary to have one hardware arbiter for each resource, one will do for

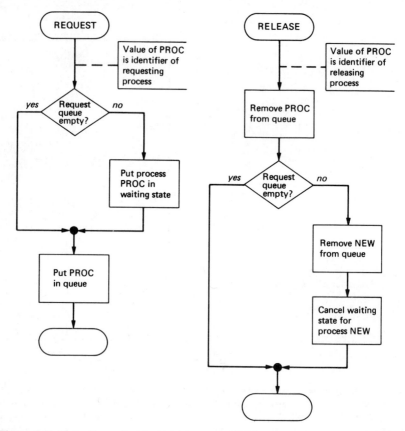

Figure 6-18. Mutually exclusive REQUEST and RELEASE functions of an arbiter

all when properly programmed. It may often be advantageous, in the interests of execution speed, however, to have more than one.

The hardware arbiter for a multiprogrammed single CPU computer can be realized by triggering the two highest-priority traps via program instructions to call REQUEST and RELEASE subprograms. Since individual instructions in a single CPU are time-exclusive operations, since neither REQUEST nor RELEASE subprograms call each other, and since the multiprograms are initiated by traps having lower priority than those assigned to the arbiter, mutual exclusion of the two arbiter functions is assured. Further, no hardware queue is required; however, the arbiter must be able to ascertain which of the multiprograms has invoked the arbiter. (See Section 6.4.3 concerning relaxation of arbitration between a higher-order interrupt program and the program it interrupts.) This is usually no great difficulty, as the identifier of the current process can be maintained in a program register.

Again, only one hardware arbiter is required (the two program-actuated traps), but more may be used to increase operating efficiency. Whenever an arbiter controls more than one resource, it is necessary to call the arbiter using a resource identifier as an argument. A separate request-queue for each resource is then maintained by the REQUEST and RELEASE subprograms shown in Figure 6-18.

6.4.3 Arbitration Among Real-Time Processes

Real-time multiprograms sharing a single CPU are actuated in response to external events assigned to priority interrupts. When a higher-priority process interrupts one of lower priority, it (usually) executes to its termination before allowing the other to recontinue. The higher-priority process is not, therefore, in jeopardy of having the states of any of its resources altered by the lower-priority process while it is executing. If no yet-higher-priority processes access these resources, then that process has gained mutually exclusive use of them for the process duration. It need not appeal to a higher authority for arbitration. If a lower-priority process was not accessing those resources when the interrupt occurred, the trap process may go ahead and use them.

If the overall program is to be consistent, however, the lower-priority program(s) must thus have some way of either preventing the higher-priority interruption from occurring, or communicating to the higher-priority process that a shared devoted resource is busy. In the latter case, the higher-priority task must have some way of transferring CPU control back to the low-order process, just long enough to permit it to complete its use of the resource. Then the higher-order task resumes.

A simple example of this type of control interconnectivity and loss of program structure is illustrated in Figure 6-19. Arbitration takes place within the trap process T: Before the background process B—or trap process with priority less than T—uses the resource, it sets BTURN true, as a signal to T not to preempt the resource. When T activates, if BTURN is false, T may be certain that B is not using the resource, and so may use it, reset the priority-trap logic and return to the point of interruption. However, if BTURN is true, T registers its intention to use the resource by setting TTURN to true, and returns CPU control to the point of interruption *at the same level of priority* (the trap-priority logic has not been reset). If T had interrupted a task T_1 with lower priority, the CPU would complete the lower-priority task at the higher priority, and so on, until control eventually passes back to B. Then B would finish using the resource and resume T as shown. I have labeled the two unstructured control connections between B and T as $1 and $2.

Aside from there being a lack of structure here, arbitration in this case is also somewhat unfortunate, because it has inverted the order of priority between processes T and T_1, which do not share resources at all! To repair this misfortune, when BTURN is true it is necessary for T to locate and use the return address (and the saved state) of the lowest-priority suspended trap process T_1 (that's the one that interrupted B) to return directly back to B. The repair is shown in Figure 6-20. Upon resumption of T (control passes through $1), the "state-save" area of the lowest-priority active trap will have to be replaced with appropriate data to assure proper resumption at $2 after T is complete. (This implies a common save-mode for all trap routines). When T completes, it reassumes the saved state (that of B if T is the only active interrupt), clears the trap logic, and returns (to $2 if T was the only trap active). How intricate the control has become!

The configuration shown thus requires some increased overhead to avoid a higher-authority arbiter. The situation, however, becomes much more complicated if more than two processes share a devoted resource, and it is probably wiser to use the higher-authority arbiter to queue all requests for a resource until it has been released. Upon release, control passes to the highest-priority waiting task.

The *ad hoc* configuration in Figure 6-20 not only does not extend to arbitration among more than two user processes, but, moreover, its non-structured control interconnectivity detracts from readability. Even if multi-exit modules RELEASE and REQUEST are used, as shown in Figure 6-21, the cross-connectivity is still distressing. However, this sort of interconnectivity and overhead is inherent when real-time priority-driven processes are synchronized without having arbitration administered by the operating system.

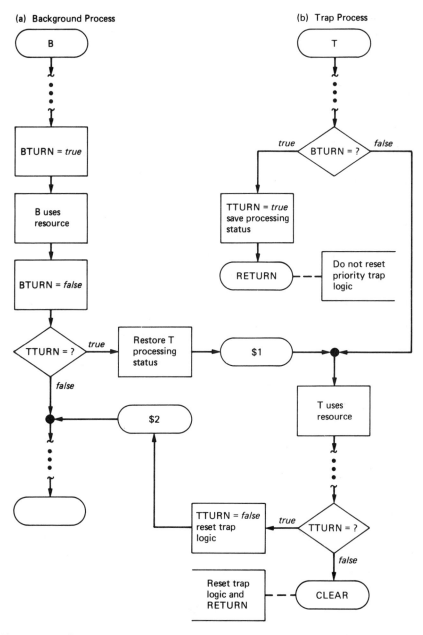

Figure 6-19. Unstructured arbitration of a devoted resource between a background process B and a trap process T (no other process shares the resource)

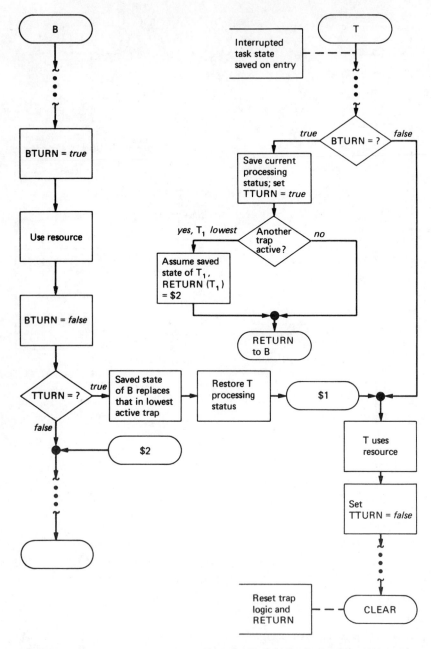

Figure 6-20. Unstructured arbitration of a resource between background process B and trap process T in which trap priorities are preserved

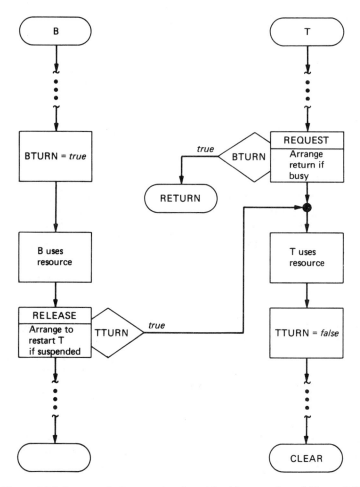

Figure 6-21. A somewhat more structured-looking version of Figure 6-20

6.4.3.1 Arbitration by Priority Reassignment

Some computer systems (or operating systems) permit processes to declare priorities of their subtasks. Others permit the traps to be disarmed (prevented from entering the trap routine) without being disabled (prevented from entering the hardware queue). In either case, it is sometimes possible to cut down on the arbitration overhead. If priorities are reassignable, the REQUEST merely becomes a reallocation among the priorities using the resource to favor the current process. RELEASE then restores the original priorities. Alternatively, if interrupts can be disarmed without disabling, then the REQUEST function can disarm any higher-priority traps that may access the resource.

In either case, however, it is not merely the resource *use* that is prevented, but the *entire trap process* in which that use occurs. Such drastic means should thus only be allowed into a design when there is demonstrable assurance that the program integrity is not violated. For example, if the time required by a lower-priority task to use a resource is small, or can be made small (perhaps by segmenting the resource into mutual subunits), and if no real-time deadlines are critical within this time, then lock-outs of higher priority tasks are generally permissible.

6.4.3.2 Relaxation of Consistency

There are also instances where global program consistency is achievable, even though some program segments may be inconsistently programmed. For example, if a background process B reads a structure written by T, then T can write into that structure and set a flag to communicate to B that he has done so. Then B resets the flag, reads the resource, and checks the flag again; if still reset, the reading was okay. If the flag had been set, however, B would have to reread the structure, presuming that, in doing so, no deadlines are missed. (See Figure 6-22.)

There are also situations in which inconsistency can be identified to cause no problem. For example, suppose a consistent program continuously monitors and controls a hardware device, such as a receiver or command modulation assembly in a deep-space tracking station. Its operation mode has been selected and set by a control-data structure initially stored, but can be altered while the program is running by piecemeal, low-priority entry of new control data via an operator keyboard terminal. During this entry, the program is adapting in a piecemeal fashion to its new control data, and if an error occurs, its repeatability is questionable. However, once the program is reconfigured, it runs consistently again.

In each case, the designer must analyze the effect of not arbitrating and prove that momentary inconsistency does not violate the program specification.

6.4.3.3 Higher-Priority Arbitration

When all the special techniques one can think of (and prove to work) to gain mutual exclusive use of a resource fail to apply in a case at hand, there is always higher-level arbitration to fall back on. The real-time arbiter I shall describe here makes use of four program-instruction-actuated traps, the highest priority traps available. I spoke of such REQUEST and RELEASE traps earlier in Section 6.4.2. The other two I shall call ENTRY and RESUME; every other trap routine save these four has ENTRY as its first module and RESUME as its last, beyond which it resets the interrupt logic and returns to a process at lower priority. (See Figure 6-23.)

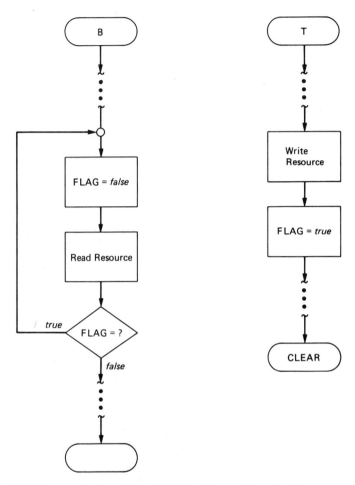

Figure 6-22. Communication of a data structure written by trap process T to background process B without arbitration

Processes accessing a shared devoted resource do so by actuating the REQUEST and RELEASE traps, possibly passing a resource-busy-queue name, if more than one resource are to be arbitrated. Figure 6-24 shows flowcharts for the four trap routines. Four are needed because mutually exclusive use of the priority P index is required.

The ENTRY module saves the entry state (registers and address for resumption of the suspended process) on a stack indexed by P, the current priority. RESUME unstacks the saved state, resets the trap logic, and resumes execution at the saved resumption location. REQUEST sets the resource queue TURN entry at the current priority level *true* to indicate its intention

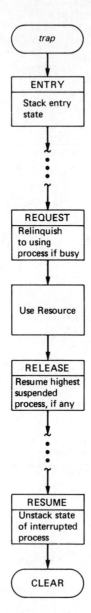

Figure 6-23. Structured configuration of trap processes (all have ENTRY and RESUME; those using a shared devoted resource also have REQUEST and RELEASE)

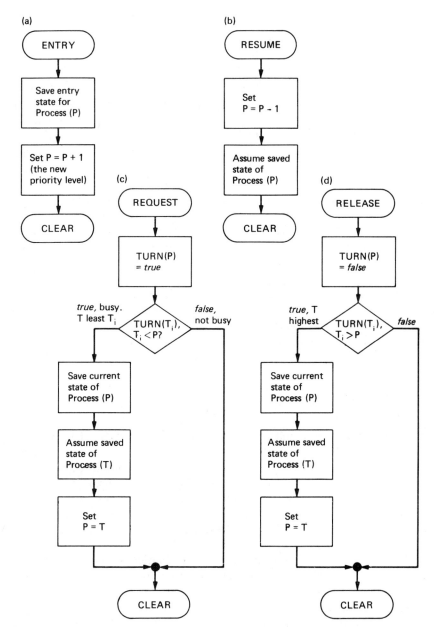

Figure 6-24. Program actuated trap routines for real-time, single CPU, priority arbitration

to use the resource; but if some other process T is using it, then T is the least index having a true TURN entry. In such a case, REQUEST saves the current state (registers and resumption location), retrieves the saved state of the interrupted process currently owning the resource, and resumes that process at the priority level of the latest REQUEST.

When a process RELEASES a resource, it removes its *true* flag from the TURN queue; if any higher-priority tasks have registered intentions to use the resource, the greatest TURN index T with a true value will correspond to that highest priority waiting task. The same sequence of state transformations used in REQUEST follows, to resume execution of the higher-priority task, now free to use the resource.

The uniformity of all usages of shared devoted resources permits the suppression of the control flow connections between REQUEST/RELEASE modules in processes; such connections are understood as a standard operating mode. Whenever a trap process requests a resource, it may expect that that resource will be granted within the maximum time needed by any trap of lower priority (including REQUEST/RELEASE overhead). The real-time program designer may thus build modules using entirely the same structured programming techniques as does the concurrent process designer, except that he must additionally analyze and keep track of timing schedules, planning so that no deadlines will be violated.

6.5 CONCURRENT STRUCTURE DESIGN

In Chapter 5, I presented an architecture by which sequential programs may accommodate a certain set of situations wherein the normal canonic structures prove awkward, but where multiple (paranormal) exits from a module seem both desirable and effective. I also gave rationale and criteria for the use of such structures, and I produced a flowchart notation that represents the use of these constructs in much the same way as other program constructs use branches in the canonic set.

The same types of arguments as appear in Chapter 5 to substantiate the use of paranormal exits, when applied to real-time programming structures, reveal that the spawning of concurrent processes (the establishing of concurrent processes, cognate to branching in a sequential program) may, at times, also not conveniently fit into the strict fork-join form, which I have been discussing so far. Rather, one can readily identify situations in multiprogramming where the strict adherence to fork-join structures is either impossible (a fault of the operating system), or else, extremely awkward (usually in lower level langauges).

6.5.1 Paranormal Entries into Concurrency

There is advantage in extending the permissible set of multiprogram control-logic structures to permit the unconditional spawning of concurrent processes from within a striped module, as is illustrated in Figure 6-25. The striped module shown is much the same as the multiple-exit striped modules of Chapter 5, except that the processes *A* and *B* shown are not selectively processed, but are both executed concurrently.

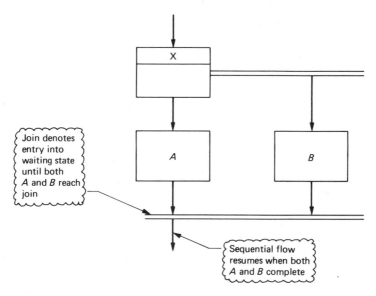

Figure 6-25. Convention for denoting the entry into concurrent mode nested within module X (process *B* is concurrent with *A*, as well as some portions of process *X*)

Selective spawning of a concurrent processes is also desirable at times, and a convention for structuring these situations is shown in Figure 6-26; the event or condition that causes the "striped fork" to activate can be attached to the module symbol as shown as an aid in the top-down correctness assessment of the program. When both conditional and unconditional entries into the concurrent mode appear within a striped module, the two conventions can be merged, as shown in Figure 6-27. If many such processes are spawned, the convention in Figure 6-28 can be applied.

On flowcharts that expand a given striped module into its algorithm of component submodules, entry into the concurrent mode can then be denoted as shown in Figure 6-29, which represents the next level expansion of the striped module in Figure 6-27. Concurrency is signalled by the occurrence of parallel lines across a flowline, and module departures are

represented by regular ANSI-standard terminal symbols. Unstructured
(paranormal) departures of flow from the flowchart connect to corresponding concurrent processes designated at the earlier flowchart level. When
more than one concurrent paranormal exit appears, it is necessary to label
these by number or process name. Both labeling techniques are illustrated
in Figure 6-29.

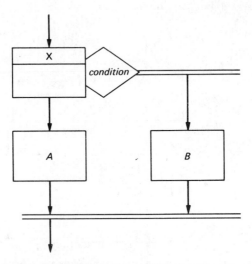

**Figure 6-26. Convention for denoting the conditional entry into a concurrent mode
nested within module X (process *B* is conditionally concurrent with process *A*, as
well as some parts of process X)**

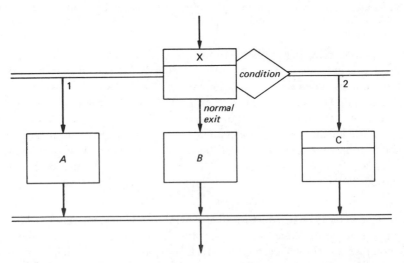

**Figure 6-27. Paranormal concurrent structure showing both unconditional entry
into concurrent mode on the left, and conditional entry, on the right**

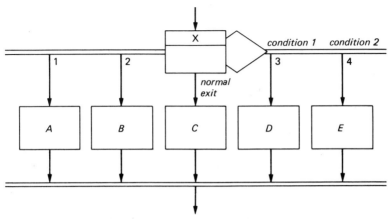

Figure 6-28. Generalized paranormal concurrent structures; the module X has both unconditional (on the left) and conditional (on the right) concurrent departures

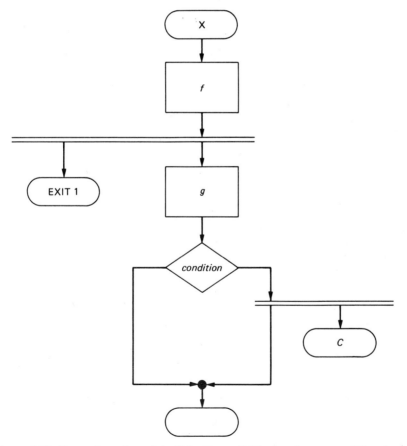

Figure 6-29. Expansion of module X in Figure 6-27, showing unconditional and conditional structured paranormal departures into concurrent mode

6.5.2 Event-Actuated Concurrent Structures

Another structure often needed for designing programs with concurrent processes is one that permits the activation of a concurrent process repeatedly for the performance of a task, invoked during the execution of another on-going process. The convention for declaring such tasks is shown in Figure 6-30; it merges the ANSI-standard symbols for concurrent processes (the parallel lines) with the interrupt/terminal symbol. The fork symbolizes that point in the invoking program at which the concurrent task is declared (to the operating system usually) available for invocation when *event* occurs, and the join is that point beyond which the event no longer may invoke the task.

The event that invokes the process, shown as A in Figure 6-30, can be an external interrupt, a call for an executive service from the operating system, or some such similar device that initiates concurrent execution. Interrupt-driven invocations were discussed earlier in Section 6.4.1.

Once invoked, the process A executes (perhaps concurrently with B) completely and reaches the join, where it enters a dormant or waiting state. While waiting for B to complete, A may be activated again and again. Once both A and B are at the join simultaneously, however, A becomes inactive (ineligible), and the program again enters a sequential mode. An arbitrary number of concurrent processes, such as B, may appear between the fork and join, and any number of modules, such as A, may also appear.

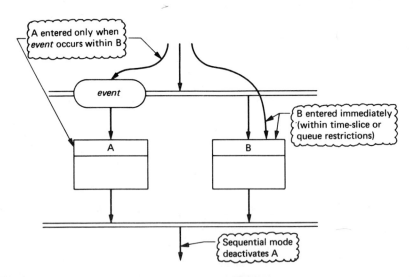

Figure 6-30. Event-actuated concurrent structure (A does not execute until invoked while B is executing)

Any one of the processes can invoke any of those available for invocation (such processes may even be concurrent with themselves, if programmed to be reentrant).

A slight variant of the join-philosophy applies when no modules of the type labeled "B" in Figure 6-30 appear. In this case, depicted in Figure 6-31, when an event-actuated process reaches the join, it enters the dormant or waiting state until all of the other processes also reach the join, at which time, the processes merge into sequential flow again without disabling any of the functions. This convention fosters nested refinement of concurrent service tasks, as shown in Figure 6-32. Using the convention, one may proceed with a top-down design, knowing that certain concurrent functions (such as A and B in the figure) will be invoked within a process (such as D) without specifying how those functions will be configured until a later refinement. The concurrent functions, shown enclosed in a "dashed box" on the chart, in such cases would appear as a single striped module at the upper level, to be expanded into more detailed submodules at a later, more appropriate design phase. However, there must be an early recognition that a concurrent mode of operation is to take place; hence, major structural decisions tend to percolate to the top level in such designs.

When the event invoking the initiation of a concurrent process shown at an earlier design level is an executive service request (ESR) of the operating system, the invocation appears much the same as an ordinary subroutine call. Moreover, to the program that invokes the service, the

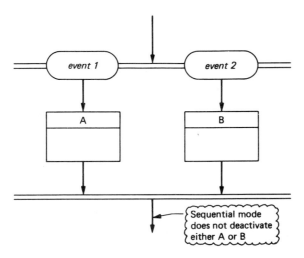

Figure 6-31. Concurrent configuration establishing processes A and B for invocation without deactivation

function is in many ways indistinguishable from one performed by a subroutine. The only visible difference in logic is usually a need for synchronization (see Section 6.1.5). For this reason, such invocations can appear on a chart, as shown in Figure 6-33; horizontally or vertically striped, as appropriate, with an appropriate cross-reference identifier, X. When the ESR invokes a simple operating system function, neither the stripes nor the cross-reference may be necessary.

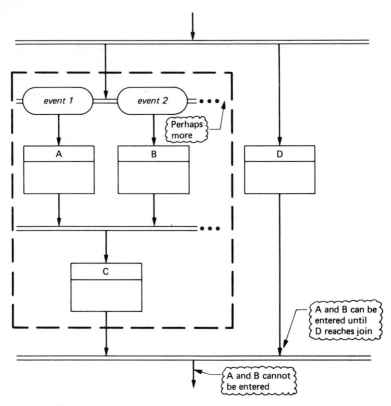

Figure 6-32. Nesting of event-actuated processes within a concurrent structure

6.5.3 Paranormal Departures to Invoked Concurrent Processes

Whenever a subprogram X declares internally that a concurrent process A is to be invocable while in the remainder of X, as well as during a subsequent process B, the paranormal concurrent departure from X is of the invocable variety (and perhaps conditional as well). Figure 6-34 illustrates a notation for declaring such program structures when the departure is unconditional; the addition of a decision symbol extends this notation to cover a conditionally invocable paranormal process.

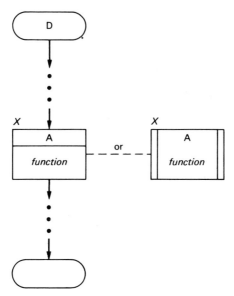

Figure 6-33. The invocation of a programmable event-driven concurrent process A within module D (see Figure 6-32) when *event 1* is a programmable executive service request

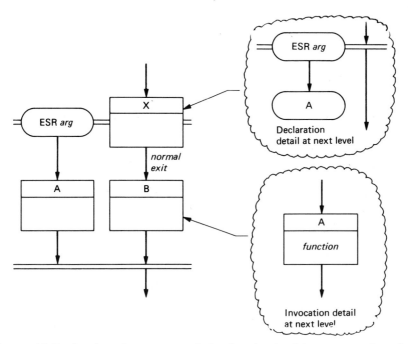

Figure 6-34. Declaration of a paranormal structured entry into concurrent mode within X to execute process A whenever invoked in remainder of X, or within B by a programmable executive service request (ESR)

6.5.4 Concurrent Structure Design Options

The choice of which fork-join discipline should be followed in designing a program very often depends heavily on, or is dictated by, the intended programming language or operating system services available to implement the concurrent structures discussed so far.

If, as a programming standard, the code must be made to correspond modularly, on a one-for-one basis, to the flowcharted design, then some of the structures shown may not be available in some implementation languages. For example, if an operating system dictates that concurrent portions of a program be registered as separately compiled segments and be invoked by executive service request events, then there is no way that the code for such processes can appear adjacent, as might be depicted on a strict fork-join flowchart. If, however, concurrent processes can be coded in adjacency, as in Concurrent PASCAL [45], then the code can be arranged so as to match the flowchart modularly.

On the other hand, if implementation standards do not require exact modular correspondence between flowcharts and code, then conventions can be adopted so as to allow wider, less restrictive use of concurrent structures, yet retain strict logical consistency between code and flowcharts. However, in such cases, the code corresponding to adjacent functions on a given flowchart may appear segmented among many program segments, and the design-to-code cross-referencing problem is more acute.

Further discussion relative to such coding conventions and restrictions will be delayed until the next chapter and Chapter 13.

6.6 SUMMARY

In this chapter, I have tried to indicate some of the inherent difficulties in concurrent, real-time programs and, thereby, the greater need for a structured approach in developing these programs. Real-time multiprograms and concurrent processes have many of the same attendant problems; to avert many of these, I have imposed the requirement for consistency—repeatable results even when errors are present—a position that necessitates synchronization of processes accessing common resources. In all but the simplest situations, synchronization must be gained by way of higher-level arbitration, often at considerable overhead.

As was the case in the previous chapter, and for the same reasons, I have presented the material using flowcharts as illustrations, rather than giving examples in a programming language. Having now determined the control-logic characteristics of structured programs—real-time and concurrent, as well as non-real-time—as flowchart topologies, I am in a position to define corresponding code structures. I do so in the next chapter.

Problems for Chapter 6

6-1 Prove that the program in Figure 6-21 is consistent.

6-2 A set of numbers $\{X_n\}$ stored on a computer file represent samples of a function $X(t)$ for $t = n\Delta t$, $n = 0,1,\ldots,N$. A computer program is to "filter" these by the algorithm $y_n = (\Delta t)X_n + e^{-2\Delta t}y_{n-1}$ and to plot these as samples of the resultant output process $y(t)$. Develop a flowcharted program in which file reading, computations, and plotting can be concurrent.

6-3 A computer system has resources $R_1,\ldots,R_n$ shared among concurrent processes $P_1,\ldots,P_m$. Design and flowchart an arbiter to assign resources to process in deadlock-free sets. Prove that there will be no deadlocks using such an arbiter.

6-4 A real-time process $X(t)$ is sampled by an analog/digital converter once per millisecond and processed by the numerical algorithm in Problem 6-2. Floating-point arithmetic operations are to be used, but these are supplied in the form of subroutines that cannot be used inside interrupt routines. Once every second the filtered function is plotted on a cathode ray tube display. Assume 1-millisecond and 1-second interrupts initiate reading and display subroutines. Flowchart such a program using the real-time programming structures of Section 6.4.1. Prove your program is consistent and correct. What are the timing requirements for the three program parts, and what are the interrupt priorities?

VII. CONTROL-RESTRICTIVE INSTRUCTIONS FOR STRUCTURED PROGRAMMING (CRISP)

The purpose of a higher-level programming language has historically been to simplify the expression of algorithms or subprogram functions created by an important class of problems. The flexibility and productivity of such languages are gauged by the ease with which, and the degree to which programmers may vary the composition and execution of programs [47]. The widely diverse classes of problems have, over the years, led to the development of an exceedingly large number of languages [48], both wide-application (general-purpose) and restricted-application (special-purpose). There is no doubt that standardization is needed, but defining a "standard language" is probably only feasible within a distinct problem class.

The characteristics sought in a standard language, however, are noble: the language should be capable of solving problems over a wide range of applicability, and should contribute to the solution of those problems large measures of stability, maintainability, readability (or self-documentation), understandability, and machine (or installation) independence. Furthermore, it should lend itself as much as possible to program production tools, automatic design methods, easy assessment of correctness, easy or automated verification and testing, and easy or automated quality assurance

217

measures. To be acceptable, as a *minimum* requirement, a standard computer language must not hinder the programming process. On the contrary, the purpose of a standard is to help.

The principles set forth in this chapter do not attempt to specify a standard programming language, but instead, provide a *programming language standard*—that is, a disciplined *way* of programming to achieve the goals of the preceding paragraph.

In the current chapter, I present a language control-structure concept that will be used throughout the rest of the monograph. The notes here are not meant to provide a programming manual in the sense that the reader will necessarily be able to write his own programs. Hopefully, however, the concept comes across to the extent that the programs I write are understandable to the point that their correctness is intuitive, if not rigorous.

7.1 THE CRISP CONCEPT

In block-structured programming languages, such as PASCAL, ALGOL and PL/I, structured programs are GOTO-free. Structured programming, however, can be extended to almost any language, and should not be characterized simply by the absence of GOTOs, but rather by the presence of an organized control-logic discipline. The use of a language having structured control-logic instructions facilitates the process.

Program control-logic is specified in the remainder of this chapter by a set of Control-Restrictive Instructions for Structured Programming, called CRISP, augmenting an arbitrary programming language. Programmers construct code using statements from the arbitrary language, such as FORTRAN, BASIC, or assembly language, except for statements governing the program control-logic (branching, looping, etc.); such control is accomplished by using a CRISP statement instead.

The CRISP control structures are precisely those found in the two preceding chapters. The CRISP concept thus extends the advantages of structured programming [49] to those languages which most fit a particular problem.

CRISP preempts all control statements from the base language and substitutes a set of statements that will force programs to be structured; that is, any program written in CRISP is automatically structured without the need for GOTOs. "GOTO-less" structured programming is currently available in some other languages, such as BLISS [50], IFTRAN [51], and SIMPL-X [52]; special limited preprocessors for FORTRAN, such as

SFTRAN [53], are also now available. These do not, however, have a common control syntax.

The strength of CRISP, as opposed to these other structured programming languages lies in the fact that *only* the control statements are preempted. Given an operating CRISP preprocessor for the base language most suitable for the problem at hand, the programmer may proceed to solve the problem in the language he wants, and is already familiar with. If he is called upon to solve another problem in another familiar language, then he again finds the same set of control-logic statements by which to organize that problem in the other language.

7.1.1 Elements of CRISP Statements

A CRISP statement begins with a reserved word or symbol identifying the type of structure, or a module within a structure, or the end of a structure. Because the CRISP statements are keyword-actuated, it is necessary that all non-control statements in the base language not begin with these keywords. Otherwise, alternate CRISP keywords must be chosen. More detailed restrictions appear in Appendix G.

Additionally, CRISP statements may contain strings that are part of the base language or are other CRISP statements. For example, in the CRISP structure shown in Figure 7-1 below, the substring denoted by c is a condition string, which will be substituted directly into a conditional statement in the base language to produce code having the structure shown in Figure 7-1. The strings s_i are either base language statements or other nested CRISP constructions.

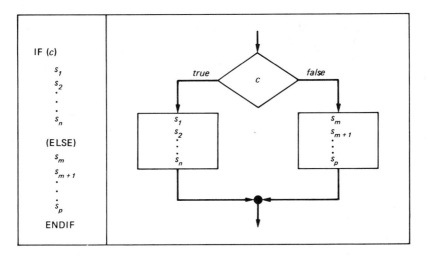

Figure 7-1. The CRISP IFTHENELSE structure

The complete superset of CRISP constructions is given in Appendix G, along with their flowchart equivalents. (Not all of these will apply to a given base language.) Each such program structure will be here referred to as a CRISP-*block* (not to be confused with the definition of a block in block-structured languages such as ALGOL and PL/I); subdivisions of blocks into constituent parts will be referred to as *clauses*. Blocks and clauses are typed by their initiating key-words, as for example, an IF-block, or an ELSE-clause. In some cases, block names may need further description, such as may be desirable to contrast a LOOP-block from a LOOPFOR-block.

The CRISP syntax given here and in Appendix G has had the benefit of a considerable amount of cosmetic evaluation, both from my students as well as from colleagues. Probably the most profound such influence came as a result of my participation in the Language Standards Working Group of the Jet Propulsion Laboratory Committee on Modern Programming. CRISP very strongly resembles the control structures adopted by that working group.

The IF-block shown in Figure 7-1 is the canonic "IFTHENELSE" structure used in Chapter 5. CRISP also has a single-line (IFTHEN) form with no ELSE-clause,

IF (*c*) *s*

The single-line IF form is signalled by the presence of the statement *s* on the same line as the IF-clause.

The IFTHENELSE structure in CRISP is only a special form of the more generalized selection structure depicted in Figure 7-2 below. Within this generalized IF-block, only the case consisting of statements corresponding to the first-encountered true condition c_i gets executed. The ELSE-clause is always optional.

CRISP also provides for another type of multi-valued decision structure, the CASE-block shown in Figure 7-3. The symbol *i* in the figure denotes an index variable in the base language; *j* and *k* are integers. A special CRISP internal flag, OUTCOME, can also be tested by the CASE-block (a description of the OUTCOME feature appears in the following Section 7.1.2).

Iteration in CRISP programs occurs within LOOP-blocks, which take the three forms shown in Figure 7-4. CRISP also permits, in addition to the forms shown, the use of: LOOP UNTIL (*c*), which means LOOP WHILE (NOT *c*); and REPEAT UNLESS (*c*), which means REPEAT IF (NOT *c*). Various options for indexed loops (LOOP FOR...) also exist, and are described in Appendix G.

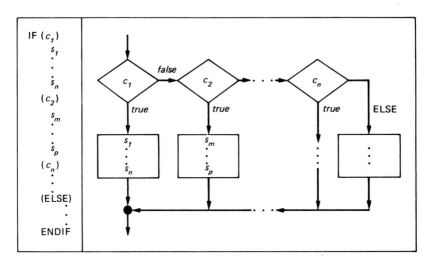

Figure 7-2. The generalized IF-block; the ELSE-clause is optional

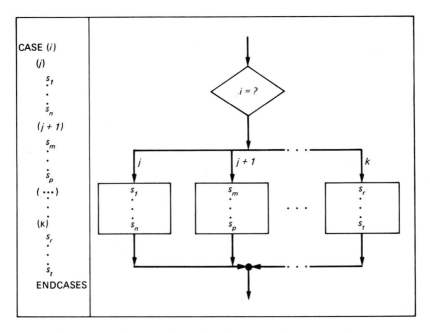

Figure 7-3. The CASE-block (an ELSE-clause may also appear after case k)

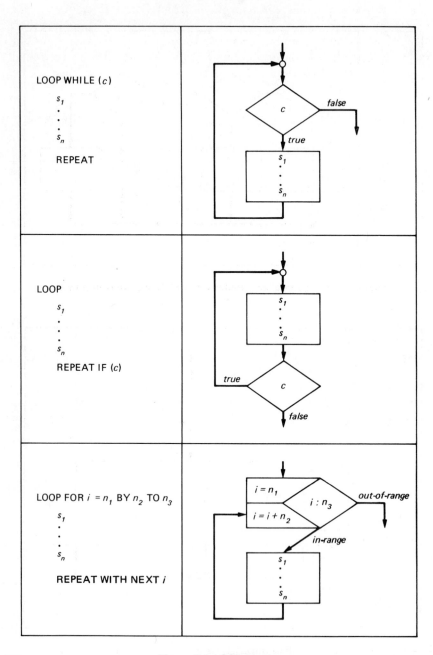

Figure 7-4. LOOP-blocks

CRISP structures can conceptually be iterated and nested to any level desired to produce the intended program. Indentations and annotations for readability, which I shall discuss later, however, will tend to limit the amount of nesting within blocks, because the listing tends to crowd toward the right-hand edge of the page. Rather than contend with this continued crowding, the user naturally finds himself inventing procedures to be substituted, linked, or called (and programmed later). As a result, CRISP program, subprograms, and subroutines generally fit on one page each (but link to procedures on other pages).

As Mills [12] points out, segmentation of program listings to a prescribed size, such that each segment enters only at the top and exits (normally) at the bottom, is a major asset in coping with program complexity.

CRISP makes allowance for up to three distinct types of procedure calls within a program. The first takes the form

DO p

which links the current block to the procedure named p in a

TO p
  .
  .
  .
  ENDTO

block. In some CRISP processors, it is conceivable that the entire procedure named p could be substituted into the object code for the DO p statement in the source code. Arguments may conceivably be passed in the calling string p, but generally, all parameters are considered as global.

The second procedure call is

CALL f

which creates a subroutine linkage to a named procedure f declared in a

SUBROUTINE: f
  .
  .
  .
  ENDSUBROUTINE

block. Subroutine arguments may be passed in the normal way between the CALL and the SUBROUTINE definition. Such subroutine blocks translate into the normal subroutine-defining mechanisms in the base language.

Functions, when permitted in the target language, are the third form of procedure call, and are identified by block declarations of the form

FUNCTION: *f*

.

.

.

ENDFUNCTION *answer*

The *answer* string is an optional device that may be required in some base languages to return the function value. Functions are defined, invoked and linked in the usual base-language mode.

The main program is identified as the block

PROGRAM: *name*

.

.

.

ENDPROGRAM

Within a program, the SYSTEM directive releases the control of execution to the operating system; STOP, to the operator. Again, both of these options may not be available in an arbitrary target language. ENDPROGRAM signals one of these actions as the normal exit consequence.

7.1.2 Module Terminations

As discussed in Chapter 5, there are times when module exits other than the normal structured exit are needed for program efficiency and clarity. These may take the form of responses to pathological or abnormal events, in which case, they are *abnormal terminations*. Sometimes, however, the event leading to a desired immediate non-normal (non-structured) exit is one that is expected. For example, it is a typical practice to input data until an end-of-file indication signals the program to begin processing in a new mode. I have called these non-structured exits from a module *paranormal* terminations.

CRISP restricts a module to having only one normal (structured) exit statement per module. However, the top-down development of program modules having multiple exits may necessitate inserting several non-structured exit statements into the module and CRISP, therefore, allows them. However, these can sometimes create difficulty in isolating errors or in performing subsequent actions unless there is some way of telling *which* exit of the multiplicity was actuated.

Paranormal exits are signalled by EXIT *n* within TO...ENDTO, by RETURN *n* within SUBROUTINE:...ENDSUBROUTINE, and by LEAVE *n* within LOOP...REPEAT. The integer *n* identifies the value given to the special CRISP flag variable, OUTCOME, upon exit; OUTCOME is always equal to 0 when the exit is normal or when *n* is omitted. OUTCOME is not altered if all EXITs omit *n*.

The OUTCOME flag is accessible only by using the CASE-structure, as, for example,

```
CASE (OUTCOME)
    (1) <*NORMAL*>
      .
      .
      .
    (2) <*END-OF-FILE*>
      .
      .
      .
    (3) <*FILE ERROR*>
      .
      .
      .
    ENDCASES
```

Because there is only one OUTCOME flag, care must be taken to locate OUTCOME tests immediately after the block having the paranormal exits, before another such structure destroys the value.

Other paranormal exits necessitated by error or other conditional traps are accommodated by the CRISP AT-block shown in Figure 7-5. If any of the trap events $t_1,...,t_n$ occurs in the statements $s_1,...,s_n$, then immediate transfer takes place to the indicated place corresponding to that trap. If none occurs, then the NORMAL-case clause executes.

The CRISP directive ABORT *l* terminates any activity abnormally and transfers control to the recovery procedure labeled *l* defined within its AT-block. Any label exclusive of commas may be used, including the name of a trap identifier; however, no ABORT-label may appear in more than one AT-block.

7.1.3 Module Exit Conventions

A top-down program may be written, as I indicated earlier, in a format whereby each module has its entry at the top and a normal (structured) exit at the bottom. Any exits in between are either calls to modular procedures

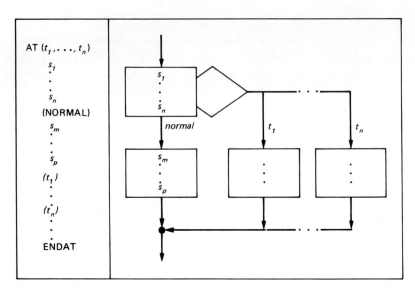

Figure 7-5. The AT-block

(usually, but not always farther down in the code), or extra-normal transfers to points within modules at previous design levels (usually higher up in the code).

Calls can be classified by the data-space state upon initiation of the called procedure. For example, subroutine calls will pass the return address and optional arguments to the subroutine procedure, often in a stack configuration. Coding for the normal exit (in the subroutine case, RETURN) reconfigures the data space for proper resumption of program execution. The same consideration must be given to extra-normal exits. (In the subroutine case, these exits must also unstack return addresses and arguments.)

Abnormal terminations may transfer back through an arbitrary number of levels, all at once, to a recovery procedure. Paranormal exits may likewise transfer back through a number of levels, but only one flowchart level at a time (although in an optimized object code listing, this could appear as a single jump).

Just as it facilitates flowchart readability and understandability to identify normal, paranormal, and abnormal exits separately (but consistently), it is likewise the case with the code corresponding to these exits. Many base languages may not have separate statements for all the cases and some may not even allow all of those given in Table 7-1 below to be implemented. CRISP syntax, however, does contain provisions for them. Table 7-1 summarizes the syntactic conventions.

Table 7-1. Striped module exit conventions

Type	Meaning
SYSTEM, ENDPROGRAM	Program termination, return control to system.
STOP	Program termination, return control to operator.
ENDTO	Subprogram normal termination. Control transfers back to invoking module at preceding level.
ENDSUBROUTINE, ENDFUNCTION	Subroutine and function normal terminations. Control returns to calling module.
EXIT n	Subprogram paranormal exit. Sets OUTCOME $= n$ and transfers control back to invoking module.
ABORT l	Abnormal exit to module labeled l in an AT-block earlier in program; l must be unique.
RETURN n	Subroutine and function paranormal exits. Sets OUTCOME $= n$ and transfers control back to invoking module.

7.2 A CRISP PREPROCESSOR

A source-program consists of a mixture of CRISP and base-language code, which can then be translated into executable instructions for a given computer system. The translator may take the form of a compiler, by which the source statements are translated directly into executable form. But rewriting or modifying an existing compiler to accommodate CRISP can be averted by implementing the translation via a CRISP preprocessor.

Such a CRISP preprocessor accesses sequential source records, written in CRISP or base-language syntax, and replaces the control-logic statements by target-language statements that perform the equivalent action.

7.2.1 Operational Modes

The hypothetical CRISP preprocessor I am using tutorially in this text operates in a number of modes, and I will describe aspects of each in turn.

The main mode is the *translation* mode, which outputs base language statements. The second and third modes are edit modes: *update* and *annotation*. The update mode is a text-editor that permits insertions, deletions, and alterations of CRISP programs. The annotation mode indents CRISP blocks and supplies them with flowlines and their Dewey-decimal reference and cross-reference numbers (see Section 5.1.3.2).

The processor allows comments to appear anywhere in a source program, within target-language statements, as well as within CRISP control statements, and to be indicated by surrounding the comment string with "<*" and "*>", as, for example, <*comment*>. The *comment* may then contain any string of characters except "*>". CRISP comments do not continue automatically on the next line if the final "*>" is omitted; comments must be continued in the same manner as other statements.

The strings "<*" and "*>" naturally, must not be valid constructs in the base language statements. If either is, alternate comment delimiters, such as (*...*), or [*...*], or /*...*/, may be substituted as a convention for implementing CRISP in that base language.

CRISP statements may be continued on several lines by terminating each unfinished line with "&". Base-language statements (also continued using a final "&") are continued only if permitted within the base language syntax.

7.2.2 Macro Processing

The hypothetical CRISP processor has a minimal, but useful, compile-time text-macro capability. Base languages having better macro handlers may, therefore, choose not to have this particular feature implemented. There are two directives; the first is the *macro definition*, one form of which is

%*template* MEANS *base string*%END

which declares that occurrences of the second type %*source string* that match %*template* will be replaced, both in CRISP control statements, as well as in target statements, by *base string*. An instance of the type %*source string* is an instance of a *macro call*. The *base string* may extend over many lines, defining a procedure and forming a block of text to be transferred. The end of a defining macro is signaled by %END.

The macro template may also contain formal parameters to be transmitted into the target string; these are signaled by the occurrence of the parameter marker in the template. Whenever a % occurs in an input source line, a scan of the remainder of the line begins, much the same as in the STAGE2 macro processor [54]. When a match occurs between the input string calling macro and a macro template, the *base string* corresponding to that template is evaluated with the actual parameters resulting from the template match. The result of this evaluation replaces the matched source string in the output.

Correspondences between actual and formal parameters are set up during template matching. The template is a sequence of fixed strings separated by parameter markers (%), or "holes". When the matching process is complete, each parameter marker corresponds to some substring of the input line and the fixed strings exactly match the other substrings of the line. The *i*-parameter string gets inserted into the target string wherever occurrences of %*i* appear in *base string*.

Macro definitions and calls may be used anywhere in the CRISP source code; in particular, a call can precede the macro definition. Macro definitions may contain macro calls, but not other macro definitions.

7.2.3 Example of the Use of Macro Capability

The following is an example of the use of the macro capability. Somewhere in a CRISP program, there is a definition module,

```
%RANDOM ARRAY MEANS A%END
%FILL %(%:%) MEANS
 DIM %1(%2:%3)
 LOOP FOR DUM=%2 TO %3
   %1(DUM)=RANDOM
   REPEAT WITH NEXT DUM%END
```

The appearance elswhere in the program of the call

```
%FILL %RANDOM ARRAY(1:50)
```

produces first the intermediate statements

```
DIM %RANDOM ARRAY(1:50)
LOOP FOR DUM=1 TO 50
   %RANDOM ARRAY(DUM)=RANDOM
   REPEAT WITH NEXT DUM
```

which are then rescanned for CRISP control statements and possible further translations. In this particular case, there is further macro action, leading to the final CRISP code:

```
DIM A(1:50)
LOOP FOR DUM=1 TO 50
   A(DUM)=RANDOM
   REPEAT WITH NEXT DUM
```

7.2.4 Other Compile-Time Features

Perhaps the most unique of the compile-time features is what may be termed a "compile-time" edit statement:

REQUIRE AT *d*: *s*

This statement causes the statement *s* to be inserted in the object code immediately before the code for statement *d*, numbered in the Dewey-decimal fashion. Its purpose is to permit truly top-down development and readability of programs. For example, suppose a DO *p* appears inside a loop. At the time the DO *p* statement was written, the programmer envisioned a certain, *definite function* would be performed by an as-yet *undefined algorithm*. However, in programming *p* at the next level, he may discover that, to program the intended function efficiently, an unforeseen variable needs to be declared and given an initial value back at an earlier program level, outside the loop.

But the program development up to this point was not concerned with this value. It has only just become important. Furthermore, the declaration and initialization of a *new* variable does not in any way alter the correctness assessment of the program up to that point (except perhaps in timing, if critical). Hence, it makes sense to associate the statement initializing a procedure *with* that procedure, rather than back at the previous level. Otherwise, it threatens readability and understanding, both in the previous module ("what is *this* doing here?") as well as the one needing it ("where on earth did I initialize that variable, and what to?").

Every data structure need not be declared using a REQUIRE statement, some are naturally passed on to procedures as data on which they are to operate. Use of the REQUIRE, however, can enhance readability when local structures need remote initializations.

Each module statement can also automatically be given a number by the CRISP processor in its annotation mode, and each flowline is assigned a special module-execution counter as a compile-time option to record the number of times that that particular path has been executed when the program runs. The execution count display prints upon execution of the CRISP directive

DISPLAY THRU LEVEL *n*

The value *n* is the level of hierarchical nesting within the program as determined by the decimal count in the Dewey-decimal statement identifier.

This path-execution-count capability is invaluable in program testing, for one may readily identify which paths have been executed and which have not. Moreover, because of the program structure, it is possible to design and provide input data to exercise these paths (See Chapter 9).

For fully verified programs, the overhead setting up and incrementing these counters can be removed by prefixing the source program by the CRISP directive

CANCEL MODULE COUNT

Selected portions of a program may have their module counters enabled and disabled by using the directive

ENABLE MODULE COUNT

with the CANCEL directive above.

7.3 CRISP CODING

I have not yet addressed how the CRISP structures stand in relation to the readability of the code, the fifth criterion in Chapter 5 for a set of control structures. Obviously, there are times when the coded procedure corresponding to a striped-module of a flowchart might need to appear directly in-line for speed efficiency, rather than having a coded call to the procedure. Using canonic structures, this presents no readability problem, but in multi-exit structures, there is likely to be a problem in identifying the connectivity of the code. Moreover, if it were deemed objectionable in Chapter 5 to replace flowcharts for striped multi-exit modules in a 2-dimensional medium, it seems to me even more objectionable to allow substitution of multi-exit code for procedure calls in the viewable source program, a linear medium.

For these reasons, all the CRISP blocks conform to simple control-connectivity conventions. Coded procedures representing flowchart striped modules may have paranormal exits, to be sure; however, the code for a TO...ENDTO module cannot be inserted at the previous level to replace the DO... statement because the EXIT *n* statements would have nothing to connect to. (Instead, such statements would attempt to exit the higher-level module.)

Thus, the CRISP constructions automatically fall in step with all the structural criteria stated in Section 5.5.1. There is a one-to-one correspondence between structured flowcharts and CRISP code. For these reasons, flowcharts can be coded into CRISP almost directly, and the code can be matched, or verified, with the design by a reader very quickly. Moreover, if errors are found and corrected, these can be transferred back into the design documentation immediately.

7.3.1 CRISP Module Numbering Method

Each CRISP block corresponds to a flowchart structure containing nodes and flowlines, and each CRISP statement either corresponds to a node or a flowline.

Comparing flowchart structures and their CRISP code structures, such as is illustrated in Figure 7-6, one finds that when "IFTHENELSE" configurations are drawn with *true* to the left of *false*, and when multiple decision branches always are drawn in case-order left to right, then the *code statements corresponding to numbered flowchart boxes (Section 5.1.3.2) always appear in the program in sequential numeric order from the top-down.*

The CRISP processor can therefore easily simulate the preorder traverse of flowchart nodes and annotate certain lines of the code with appropriate numbers. This annotation for statements within procedure blocks takes the form

. *n*   *statement*

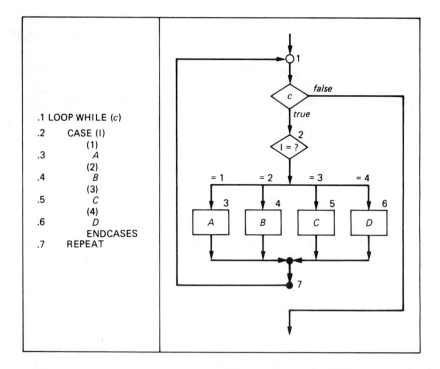

Figure 7-6. A preorder traverse of flowchart nodes makes CRISP code modules appear in numeric order in the listing

The *statement* can either be CRISP or target language code. The *.n*, flush with the left margin for easy identification, is the number assigned by the preorder traverse. Module numbers for procedure-definition statements are the Dewey-decimal reference numbers assigned earlier in the program; they appear flush at the right-hand margin, as

TO *name*   MOD# *d*

Thus a statement *.n* within a procedure having Dewey-decimal number *d* is uniquely identified as the Dewey-decimal *d.n*.

Statements that invoke procedures (DO and CALL) may have module numbers of the form *.n/Ai*, which signals that module *n* of the current procedure calls the *i*-th subroutine of a class with alphanumeric designation *A*.

7.3.2 Indentation and Annotation

Although the syntax does not require it, the program structured hierarchy should be displayed by indenting the lines of code, such as shown in the syntax table in Appendix G. Examples in this monograph are indented according to the following rule:

If a block contains only one clause (such as a LOOP-block), then indent statements comprising that clause by a prespecified number of spaces beyond the block header (the LOOP). If a block contains more than one clause (such as the CASE-block), then indent 3 spaces past the block header (CASE) to the clause header (the case label), and each line of the clause another 2 spaces beyond the header. Certain blocks do not have a separate clause header within the block, such as the IF-THEN block. For consistency, these are indented just as though they were multiple-module blocks.

Programs indented this way are almost as easy to read as flowcharts, because the block type is identifiable by its header, which protrudes from the body of the block, and the beginning of each module within the block stands out in the same way. Successive indentations occur for block structures within modules.

The CRISP processor supplies the necessary indentation automatically on the listing and, in addition, annotates the code with flowlines and, on option, module numbers as shown in the following example. The base language used in this example is an abbreviated form of English; the use of such expressions is discussed in Section 7.4.

procedure: post-order_traverse_of_a_binary_tree

```
        <* This procedure performs a post-order walk of a tree
        <* represented as follows:  each node of "tree" is
        <* composed of 3 (or more) fields.  The first is called
        <* "value" (and may be actually more than one field);
        <* the next is called "son", and contains a pointer to
        <* the leftmost descendant of the current node; the last
        <* is called "brother", and contains a pointer to the
        <* current node's next sibling (having the same parent
        <* node) to the right.  The procedure makes use of a stack
        <* to keep place in the walk.  The notation "p.q" denotes
        <* the value of the q-field of the tree node pointed to by p.
```

```
 .1     empty_stack
 .2     push pointer_to_root_of_tree on stack
 .3     let visited = false <*the tree-walk flag*>
 .4     loop while (stack_not_empty)
 .5     ↑   let current_node = top_of_stack
 .6     ↑   if (not visited and current_node.son = nil)
 .7     ↑   :     push current_node.son on stack
        ↑   :->(else) <*node is a leaf or has been visited*>
 .8     ↑   :     do process_this_node <*for intended application*>
 .9     ↑   :     if (current_node.brother = nil)
.10     ↑   :     :   let top_of_stack = current_node.brother, &
        ↑   :     :       visited = false
        ↑   :     :->(else) <*no brothers*>
.11     ↑   :     :   pop_the_stack <*discard the node*>
.12     ↑   :     :   let visited = true <*we are now backing up*>
        ↑   :     :..endif
        ↑   :..endif
       <<<repeat
```

endprocedure

7.3.3 Some Examples of CRISP Coding

In this section, I shall present a few short programs and subroutines to illustrate what CRISP programs look like. The reader may note that the code is rather sparsely annotated, and is not suitable as stand-alone finished documentation. But I have three reasons for the formats given. First, I want to illustrate the readability of bare CRISP code; second, I want to display the various CRISP structures themselves rather than to formally document the program; and third, the designs are existing, proven algorithms that I have only adapted into CRISP format. I do, however, provide separate accompanying explanatory design and analysis narrative to aid the reader in digesting the solution methods.

7.3.3.1 Example of Bubble-Sort Program

The program presented in Section 7.3.2 rearranges and prints in increasing order a set of numbers input from a terminal, according to the "bubble-sort" algorithm [31].

Algorithm: Scanning the input list from top to bottom, interchange consecutive pairs that are not in increasing order. When the bottom of the list is reached, reduce the list size by one (the bottom of the list is in sort) and repeat.

Analysis: This sorting program goes through $N(N-1)/2$ comparisons to sort any input array; the number of exchanges can range from 0 to the maximum, the number of comparisons. On random data, the average number of exchanges is $N(N-1)/4$.

Program: The algorithm appears in the program in the form of two nested LOOP FOR...REPEAT loops, which are readily seen to embody the algorithm correctly. The base language in this example is MBASIC [55], which permits dynamic dimensioning of arrays by the DIM statement, exchange of variable values by the = = operator, and free-form input (integer, decimal, or exponential notation) by the # format. MBASIC also permits modifier constructions which reduce the number of lines of code; but for clarity I have not used them here.

Illustrated in the program are the CRISP structures LOOP FOR ...TO...REPEAT and IF...ENDIF, and the use of the text macros to clarify and annotate the code so that the code actually executes the annotation. The CRISP preprocessor automatically adds the flowline and module number annotations to the output listing.

```
PROGRAM: BUBBLE-SORT                                              MOD#  1
    < * SORT IN-PLACE AND PRINT A SET OF NUMBERS
    < * INPUT FROM A TERMINAL*>


.1   INPUT USING %PROMPTING MESSAGE AND FREE-FORM INPUT: N
.2   DIM %ARRAY TO HOLD NUMBERS
.3   PRINT 'ENTER NUMBERS TO BE SORTED:
.4   INPUT USING %FREE FORM: %ENTIRE ARRAY


.5   LOOP FOR J=N BY -1 TO 2 <*DROP OFF J-TH ELEMENT EACH CYCLE*>
.6   ↑  LOOP FOR I=1 TO J-1 <*BUBBLE LARGEST ELEMENT TO ELEMENT J*>
.7   ↑  ↑   IF (%ELEMENTS I AND I+1 OUT OF ORDER)
.8   ↑  ↑   :    %EXCHANGE VALUES
     ↑  ↑   :..ENDIF
     ↑  ◄◄◄REPEAT WITH NEXT I
     ◄◄◄REPEAT WITH NEXT J


.9   PRINT \'SORTED VALUES:'\%ENTIRE ARRAY; <*BACKSLASH GIVES
        <*CARRIAGE RETURN AND SEMICOLON CONTROLS SPACING WHILE
        <*ARRAY IS BEING PRINTED*>
     ENDPROG


<*MACRO DEFINITIONS:*>
%PROMPTING MESSAGE AND FREE-FORM INPUT MEANS
  %'HOW MANY NUMBERS TO BE SORTED? #'%END
%ARRAY TO HOLD NUMBERS MEANS A(N)%END
%FREE FORM MEANS '(#)'%END
%ENTIRE ARRAY MEANS A%END
%ELEMENTS I AND I+1 OUT OF ORDER MEANS A(I)>A(I+1)%END
%EXCHANGE VALUES MEANS A(I)==A(I+1)%END
```

7.3.3.2 Example of Shuttle-Interchange Sorting Subprogram

The following subprogram rearranges in-place and in increasing order a set of numbers contained in an array A(N), according to the "shuttle-interchange" sort algorithm [56].

Algorithm: Scanning the input array from top to bottom, interchange consecutive pairs that are not in increasing order; when an interchange occurs, hold that location and repeat the process from this location backwards until consecutive pairs are found in order. Then jump back to the saved location and continue the process onward.

Analysis: The shuttle-interchange sort algorithm is very similar to the bubble-sort algorithm given in the previous example. There are, however, some significant differences.

If the data is already in sort, there is only one pass through it, or $N-1$ comparisons with no interchanges; if the data is sorted in reverse order, there is an interchange and backup involving $I-1$ interchanges at each of the $N-1$ steps on I, for a total of $N(N-1)/2$ exchanges. For random data, one may expect about $N(N-1)/4$ comparisons and exchanges. Therefore, shuttle-interchange sorting is more efficient than bubble sorting, especially for nearly sorted data, where it is better by a factor of about $N/2$ in the number of comparisons.

Program: The program is slightly more complicated than the mere bubble sort; it illustrates the use of CRISP structures LOOP FOR...UNTIL ... REPEAT and IF...ENDIF. The interchange action in the program can be seen to take place when A(I) and A(I + 1) are detected to be out of order; then the backup begins if I>1 when A(I−1) and A(I) are out of order; and the backup, which exchanges A(K) and A(K + 1), continues until K = 1 or until A(K) and A(K + 1) are no longer out of order, as detected by the setting of the structure flag, SORTED. The listing also illustrates that macro definitions may occur anywhere; in this case, within the first LOOP FOR-block and at the end of the program.

A flowchart of the program appears in Figure 9-6 of Chapter 9 to illustrate how tests can be generated to verify that the algorithm is correct.

```
TO SHUTTLE-SORT ARRAY A
      <*SORT IN-PLACE A SET OF NUMBERS CONTAINED IN
      <*ARRAY A(N) UPON ENTRY*>

. 1   LOOP FOR I=1 TO N-1
      ↑   %OUT OF ORDER AT %,% MEANS A(%1)>A(%2)%END
      ↑   %EXCHANGE VALUE AT %,% MEANS A(%1)==A(%2)%END
. 2   ↑   IF (%OUT OF ORDER AT I,I+1)
. 3   ↑   :     %EXCHANGE VALUES AT I,I+1
. 4   ↑   :     IF (I>1) <*NOT FIRST ELEMENT IN ARRAY*>
. 5   ↑   :     :   IF (%OUT OF ORDER AT I-1,I)
. 6   ↑   :     :   :   SORTED=%FALSE<*INITIALIZE BACKUP FLAG*>
. 7   ↑   :     :   :   LOOP FOR K=I-1 BY -1 UNTIL (SORTED=%TRUE)
. 8   ↑   :     :   :   ↑   %EXCHANGE VALUES AT K,K+1
. 9   ↑   :     :   :   ↑   IF (K=1) <*BACKED UP TO FIRST ELEMENT*>
.10   ↑   :     :   :   ↑   :   SORTED=%TRUE <*END BACKUP*>
.11   ↑   :     :   :   ↑   :->(NOT %OUT OF ORDER AT K-1,K)
.12   ↑   :     :   :   ↑   :   SORTED=%TRUE<*END BACKUP*>
      ↑   :     :   :   ↑   :..ENDIF
      ↑   :     :   :   ←←←REPEAT WITH NEXT K
      ↑   :     :   :..ENDIF
      ↑   :     :..ENDIF
      ↑   :..ENDIF
      ←←←REPEAT WITH NEXT I
      ENDTO

%TRUE MEANS 1%END <*MBASIC LOGIC CONVENTIONS*>
%FALSE MEANS 0%END
```

7.3.3.3 Example of a Program to Sort a Short File

Quite often, the items to be sorted will appear on a disk file rather than being input from a terminal. The program in this example accesses a user-specified file of numbers of unknown size, sorts them using the shuttle-interchange subroutine lifted from previous example, and then refiles them in a user-specified output file.

Program: Numbers are read into an array; maximum size may not exceed a predetermined maximum, %MAXFIL. Numbers on the file are assumed to be readable in free-form by MBASIC.

The program illustrates the AT...ENDAT interrupt-handling structure and the use of EXIT *n* to direct control to the alternate procedure of an OUTCOME-block.

```
PROGRAM: FILESORT
    <*SORT A USER-SPECIFIED INPUT FILE*>
    %MAXFIL MEANS 10000%END <*MAXIMUM ASSUMED CAPABILITY*>
    DIM A(100) <*INITIAL TRIAL SIZE FOR ARRAY*>
    STRING INFIL:50,OUTFIL:50 <*FILE NAMES, 50 CHARS EACH*>
    INPUT USING <*PROMPTING MESSAGE AND FREE FORM:*>&
        'ENTER INPUT FILE NAME: #OUTPUT FILE NAME: #':INFIL,OUTFIL
    OPEN INFIL FOR INPUT AS FILE 1
    OPEN OUTFIL FOR OUTPUT AS FILE 2
    DO INPUT FROM FILE TO ARRAY A <*SET N TO SIZE*>
    CASE(OUTCOME)
    :->(0)<*NORMAL,SO NO ACTION REQUIRED*>
    :->(1)<*NOT ALL OF FILE EXAMINED*>
    :       PRINT 'FILE TOO LARGE, AT LEAST %MAXFIL ITEMS'
    :..ENDCASES
    DO SHUTTLE-SORT ARRAY A
    WRITE ON 1:A<*ONE ITEM PER RECORD IN FREE-FORM FORMAT*>
    PRINT 'SORTING COMPLETE. NUMBER OF ITEMS=':N
    ENDPROGRAM <*STOP AND CLOSE BOTH FILES*>

TO INPUT FROM FILE TO ARRAY A
    %END-OF-FILE MEANS ENDFILE(1)%END
    <*INITIALIZE FOR ARRAY INPUT*> J=1,N=100
    AT (%END-OF-FILE)
    :       LOOP FOR I=1 TO %MAXFIL
    :    ↑  INPUT FROM 1:A(I) <*FREE-FORM INPUT*>
    :    ↑  IF (J=100) <*A IS FULL*>
    :    ↑  :   J=0,N=N+100 <*RESET J AND NEW ARRAY SIZE*>
    :    ↑  :   IF (N>%MAXFIL) N=%MAXFIL
    :    ↑  :   DIM A(N) <*REDIMENSION ARRAY*>
    :    ↑  :..ENDIF
    :    ↑  J=J+1 <*COUNT NUMBER OF ITEMS SINCE A REDIMENSIONED*>·
    :    ←←←REPEAT WITH NEXT I
    :    :->(NORMAL) <*MAXIMUM NUMBER READ INTO A*>
    :<-------EXIT 2
    :    :->(%END-OF-FILE) <*LESS THAN MAXIMUM NUMBER READ IN*>
    :    :   N=I-1 <*RECORD THE NUMBER ACTUALLY READ IN*>
    :    :..ENDAT
    :<--ENDTO
```

7.3.3.4 Example of Concurrent Input/Output Program

This is Brinch Hansen's "Readers and Writers" problem [42]. There are two kinds of concurrent processes, called "readers" and "writers" which access a common data base. All readers can access the base simultaneously, but writers must have exclusive use; when a writer is ready to write, he should be given permission to do so as soon as possible, maintaining program consistency.

Program: The solution below illustrates the use of FORK...JOIN to enclose concurrent procedures READER and WRITER. Mutually exclusive use of the data base is gained via AWAIT, REQUEST, and RELEASE arbitration discussed in Chapter 6; the arbitration, however, only encompasses two storage locations that record, respectively, the number of currently active readers and the number of currently active writers. WRITING executes only when all currently active readers have finished; only one writer at a time is active, others (readers and writers alike) are locked out because AWAIT has placed both activity indicators in critical regions. READING executes when no writers are active and with no variables in critical regions; hence, readers may execute concurrently.

The functions AWAIT, REQUEST, and RELEASE are not part of the CRISP language specification (in Appendix G); they are assumed to exist or have been programmed into the base language as privileged instructions, as discussed in Chapter 6.

```
PROGRAM:
    %ACTIVE WRITERS MEANS ACTWTR%END
    %ACTIVE READERS MEANS ACTRD%END
    %INCREMENT(%)  MEANS %1=%1+1%END
    %DECREMENT(%)  MEANS %1=%1-1%END
     . . .
    %ACTIVE READERS,%ACTIVE WRITERS=0
    FORK n
    : : ->(1)<*PROCEDURE:READER*>
    : :        . . .
    : :        . . .
    : :     AWAIT %ACTIVE WRITERS=0,
    : :     :   CRITICAL ON (%ACTIVE WRITERS,%ACTIVE READERS)
    : :     :   %INCREMENT(%ACTIVE READERS)
    : :     :..RELEASE(%ACTIVE WRITERS,%ACTIVE READERS)
    : :     DO READING
    : :     REQUEST(%ACTIVE READERS)
    : :     :   %DECREMENT(%ACTIVE READERS)
    : :     :..RELEASE(%ACTIVE READERS)
    : :       . . .
    : :       . . .
    : :
    : :->(2)<*PROCEDURE:WRITER 1*>
    : :       . . .
    : :       . . .
    : :     REQUEST(%ACTIVE WRITERS)
    : :     :   %INCREMENT(%ACTIVE WRITERS)
    : :     :..RELEASE(%ACTIVE WRITERS)
    : :     AWAIT %ACTIVE READERS=0,
    : :     :   CRITICAL ON (%ACTIVE WRITERS,%ACTIVE READERS)
    : :     :   DO WRITING
    : :     :   %DECREMENT(%ACTIVE WRITERS)
    : :     :..RELEASE(%ACTIVE WRITERS,%ACTIVE READERS)
    : :       . . .
    : :       . . .
    : :->(...)
    : :       . . .
    : :       . . .
    : :..JOIN
       . . .
    ENDPROGRAM
```

7.4 CRISP AS A PROCEDURE-DESIGN LANGUAGE

It is certainly no more difficult to write structured-program code than it is to draw a flowchart when both contain approximately the same level of detail. Some may argue, since the code listings have to be produced anyway, that supplying further documentation in the form of flowcharts is then a duplication of effort. Moreover, maintaining consistency between human-drafted flowcharts and code listings during an iterative development cycle can be a very time-consuming task, even if such iteration is minimal.

Furthermore, it can be argued that structured code is more rigorous than a flowchart. For one thing, it is written in a programming language whose syntax and semantics are well defined. For another, the structured code is part of the operating program, no translation being necessary (with its attendant possibility of introducing error). Structured code contains no unconditional branches and no statement labels to branch to. The logic flow of each program always proceeds linearly from beginning to end. Because there is straight line logic, flowcharts tend not to be needed for understanding.

Nevertheless, structured code, even with annotated flowlines (as in the CRISP examples above), is somewhat less graphic than a flowchart, and the rationale and functional specification of program modules may be a little less understandable in code annotations than the narrative that properly accompanies a flowchart.

In the foregoing discussion, I oriented the CRISP concept toward a compilable programming base language; the output of a CRISP processor in such cases would be, of course, executable code. However, the use of CRISP control structures superimposed on English as a base language can also be a very useful tool during the procedural design phases of development, not only to the designer himself, but to any readers, as well. The statement of Mills' algorithm in Section 5.4 was, in fact, a description using constructions much like CRISP, superimposed on regular technical English. The procedure shown in Section 7.3.2 is another such case. Neither description, as it stands, is compilable, but using macros as indicated (Section 7.3.3), this need not always be the case.

The use of terse English phrases to describe concepts to be expounded upon more fully at later levels, imbedded in the CRISP control-logic structures, is much like the IBM technique referred to as "PIDGIN" and what others have called a "structured design language". I hesitate to label this technique using the CRISP control structures CRISP-PIDGIN for obvious reasons.

As another example of the use of structured English as a program procedure-design language (PDL), let me suppose that one wishes to describe a simple CRISP preprocessor design for an undisclosed target language. The level-1 specification might appear listed as

```
PROGRAM:  CRISP PREPROCESSOR WITHOUT MACRO HANDLING
    INPUT CONTROL CODES
    INITIALIZE WORKSPACE
    LOOP WHILE (SOURCE DECK NOT EMPTY)
    ↑    INPUT SOURCE IMAGE INTO BUFFER
    ↑    DETERMINE STATEMENT TYPE AND PARAMETERS
    ↑    GENERATE TARGET CODE
    ←←←REPEAT
    END PROGRAM
```

Each of the subspecifications has been given a unique, descriptive name for reference purposes, by which refinements can be located at the next design level. Each subspecification can then be expanded into any needed detail at successive subsequent levels. For example, the next level of design for the DETERMINE... subspecification might appear as

```
TO DETERMINE STATEMENT TYPE AND PARAMETERS
    INITIALIZE POINTERS TO FIRST CHARACTER IN BUFFER
        AND ROOT OF TEMPLATE GRAPH
    LOOP WHILE (INPUT POINTER NOT AT END OF INPUT BUFFER)
    ↑    IF (INPUT CHARACTER MATCHES TEMPLATE NODE CHARACTER)
    ↑    :      ADVANCE INPUT POINTER AND GRAPH POINTER
    ↑    :->(ELSE)
    ↑    :      IF (THERE IS ALTERNATE TEMPLATE NODE)
    ↑    :      :    EXECUTE GRAPH NODE ACTION CODE FOR CURRENT NODE
    ↑    :      :    SET GRAPH POINTER TO ALTERNATE NODE
    ↑    :      :->(ELSE)
    ↑    :      :    SET STATEMENT TYPE TO "UNRECOGNIZED"
    ↑    :      :    EXIT UNRECOGNIZED
    ↑    :      :..ENDIF
    ↑    :..ENDIF
    ↑    IF (INPUT BUFFER EXHAUSTED AND GRAPH NODE IS LEAF)
    ↑    :      SET STATEMENT TYPE TO LEAF NUMBER
    ↑    :..ENDIF
    ←←←REPEAT
    EXIT NORMAL
    ENDTO
```

The reader may note at once that such CRISP-PDL procedural descriptions, being devoid of non-procedural explanations, may not always reveal everything that someone, other than the originator, needs in order to understand how the program works. In the procedure above, for example, the "template graph" data structure has not been described (it is in Chapter 12), and the reader may stumble about without such information. Besides descriptions of data structures, the reader may also need to have other forms of rationale provided to explain why things are being done as they are, or what the significance of a particular step is. As a documentation tool, the technique does much to emphasize human readability, but it is not the whole answer.

Nevertheless, as a design tool, CRISP-PDL has permitted the designer to state the algorithms he is developing in a structured, procedural, and very readable way before any code has been generated. Such a tool allows him to write down several alternative procedures for evaluation, correctness assessment, etc., before they get committed into flowcharts, formalized documentation, and code.

Changes in the design during this time do not cost in coding, debugging, or extra documentation. Many adherents to the use of structured English thus advise, "Don't code until you can't think of anything else to do!", as a means of saving costs.

Once the CRISP-PDL descriptions are firm enough to flowchart and code, these processes can take place fairly rapidly by persons having quite a lower level of technical skill, and perhaps even aided by the computer (see Chapter 17). Once the design is done, implementation can be more of a production-type job; it is easier to schedule, since design-creativity is the commodity that comes in uncertain chunks.

7.5 DESIGN DOCUMENTATION IN CRISP

While CRISP alone goes a long way toward illustrating *what* a program does very graphically as a self-documented product, it may not go quite far enough in communicating all the *whys* necessary for a reader to review and understand the program, unless properly annotated.

The code listing for a program is the only exact representation of what is executed by the computer. No matter what is written in memos, discussed at meetings, inserted into design documents, or attached to the code in the form of comments, the machine will read and execute only what is coded. Everything else is surrogate.

Nevertheless, I tend to believe that, as long as human beings are reading it, a program is not well structured unless it is accompanied by well-structured narrative—however irrelevant this may be to the abstract theory of program verification (see Chapter 9). In Chapter 17, I discuss provisions whereby the program listing can contain all the information necessary to document the program design. Narrative can be carried entirely in the form of readable and relevant comments using the same clear, concise prose as good technical writing. Design flowcharts, as well as flowcharts of the executable code, can be drafted automatically from the listings. Automated auditing of the design and code against the program specification, each for conformity with project standards, can also be achieved to a certain extent.

Designing procedure specifications in CRISP and providing relevant narrative, from which flowcharts or narrative descriptions of the program can automatically emanate, should still precede the introduction of executable code, in keeping with the top-down development philosophy of earlier chapters. Module interface specifications can be done directly in code, so that there is less opportunity for misunderstanding and error. There is then also no programming toward hypothetical or temporary interfaces; every interface is defined at the proper logical point in the project, and used as a fully specified reference from there on.

The CRISP code structures I have been discussing, together with the capability for macro extensibility and comment annotations, abet the concept of phased concurrency in design, coding, testing, and documentation. The documentation principle I expect to be in effect is that documentation will be certified at the end of each development phase by some form of audit before the next phase takes place. That is, for example, the design phase of a module may not end until that module is fully documented and audited.

The surest way of assuring that a design at a given point *can* be coded is to *do* the coding. The first such opportunity occurs in the top-down approach when the very first part of the structured design has been made. To ascertain that there are no errors, the program can then be *run*.

To be sure, the embryo program will not perform all, or perhaps any, of its specified tasks at this primitive level of the design. However, it can produce evidence that the program sequences through its stated subfunctions in the proper order in response to controlled stimuli, and that variables advertised to be passed to, or obtained from, a subfunction are actually accessed in the correct manner. It does all this by substituting simplified dummy segments of code (stubs) for the as-yet-uncoded subfunctions to verify the correct sequencing of subfunctions and to validate all the interfaces of the program at the current state of design.

These principles are largely based on techniques put forth by Mills [57] who developed them as a means of implementing and testing programs, with reliability in mind. Besides being a check on the design and documentation, another advantage is that the central logic of the system is tested most, since it is run every time a new subsystem replaces one of the dummy stubs. System integration problems are almost entirely eliminated, because when a newly coded module is tested, it is integrated with all the already defined parts of the system.

The reason for phased concurrency and auditing is that it is just too costly to produce possibly incorrect software, including documentation, with the view that it can be corrected later. Catching all corrections in documentation at a later time is a very risky, time consuming job. Concurrent coding and testing are aimed at revealing design and documentation errors at the earliest possible stages, before they can influence the remainder of the emerging program.

7.6 SUMMARY

In this chapter, I have introduced a set of statements to aid in creating structured programs in an arbitrary base language. Algorithms may initially be stated in a CRISP-PDL format, which leads, through a series of refinements, into compilable code. In the absence of a CRISP processor, the control structures may be translated into the base language through a simple discipline using conditionals and "GOTOs". If these constructs are coded in a consistent fashion, the programmer soon realizes that he is playing the role of a macro processor. General-purpose macro translators, such as STAGE2 [54], can place most of the CRISP capability within the access of programmers in a very short time and with very little effort on their part.

Indenting CRISP code and addition of annotating "flowlines" turns a source listing into a two-dimensional, flowchart-like display of the program. The potential for program readability using CRISP code is, therefore, very high. In Chapter 17, I demonstrate that the CRISP code is also suitable for machine generation of actual flowcharts. Use of CRISP-like constructs not only then provides the opportunity for top-down concurrent design, coding, and testing, but it also provides a common, highly visible repository for all the documentation relative to these, namely, the source listing. These characteristics are very important ones in raising project productivity, as I discuss in Chapter 10.

I realize that I have not discussed the use of many of the features of CRISP such as DISPLAY, REQUIRE, ABORT, etc., in very much detail. I have tried to relate the reasons why these have been put into the syntax, however. Hopefully, the reader will gain a better appreciation for some of the features as the monograph continues.

I have not developed language structures in this chapter for specifying abstract data types beyond those facilities inherent in the base language upon which CRISP is imposed. I did express, in Chapter 4, the view that the design of an algorithm cannot usually be separated from the design of the data structure upon which it operates. And thus, since I have given structural topologies for program control flow in CRISP, it would seem that I have forgotten here about the other half of the problem.

That accusation is largely true. If CRISP were ever to evolve into a modern programming language, the facilities for abstract data definition would have to be included. However, as long as it is intended merely for use as a structuring preprocessor for existing unstructured languages, very little can be done to include abstract data declarations and operations capabilities into CRISP. When used as a program design language to format text, however, CRISP supports abstract data definitions as well as any language now extant; the programmer, in fact, is free to introduce any syntax for constructing data structure specifications within comprehension.

Further discussion on data structure description languages and their implementation into a modern programming language may be found in Chapter 17. A useful bibliography of papers concerning data description language features has been compiled by Tennent [58].

Problems for Chapter 7

7-1 Program the flowcharts produced from Problems 5-1 and 5-3 in CRISP. Assume that A, B, C, etc., are names for the modules shown, and that a, b, c, etc., are condition strings valid in the target language.

7-2 Program the skills-inventory problem (see Problems 4-3 and 5-6) using CRISP structures. Annotate the code with the appropriate flowchart box numbers.

7-3 Design, flowchart, and then code using CRISP syntax the first three or four tiers of a complete CRISP preprocessor. Indicate which parts of the design are dependent on the implementing language, which are dependent on the target language, and which are independent of either of these.

7-4 Program the flowcharts produced by Problems 6-2 and 6-4 in concurrent and real-time CRISP structures, respectively.

7-5 Write a CRISP-FORTRAN subroutine to solve an $N \times N$ set of linear equations using the Gauss elimination technique.

VIII. DECISION TABLES AS PROGRAMMING AIDS

Although flowcharts are a widely accepted means of describing the logic of a computer program being developed, they have several significant disadvantages during program specification and early design. These disadvantages should encourage one to seek alternate methods for stating the pertinent aspects of a problem. *Decision Tables* (also called *Decision Logic Tables*) provide such an alternative. First, some of the disadvantages of flowcharting during the initial parts of program development can be listed [59]:

- Although flowcharts are often very appropriate for describing scientific or mathematical algorithms where the logic is predefined and where each box can represent a certain amount of computation, flowcharts are very often not appropriate for describing problems in systems programming, business data processing, or information retrieval, where actions in response to a long sequence of logical decisions must be made.

- Flowcharts for programs with intricate logical structures tend to become lengthy, involved, and difficult to follow.

- Flowcharting requires that one define his problem and develop his computer program in the same operation.

Decision tables tend to overcome these disadvantages, while providing some advantages, as well. They are, therefore, another useful tool that can contribute to the success of a software development project. This chapter exposes some of the salient features of decision tables and their use.

8.1 DECISION TABLE TYPES

A decision table [60] is a tabular display of the pertinent logical aspects of a programming problem, showing all relevant conditions, relationships, and actions to be taken under each set of circumstances. Used in programming design, decision tables separate program control logic from program computing functions, to allow each program path to be explicitly defined. The use of decision tables is not restricted, however, only to computer programming. In general, they can be used anywhere a complicated logical situation must be described.

8.1.1 Decision Table Format

The normal decision table representation has four separate parts in a specific format, as shown in Figure 8-1: The *condition stub*, the *condition entries*, the *action stub*, and the *action entries*.

Condition Stub	Condition Entry
Action Stub	Action Entry

Figure 8-1. Skeleton form of a decision table

The condition stub is a list of all the relevant conditions, usually posed as questions, upon which resulting actions are to be based. Normal decision table theory does not require any order to the conditions, but certain programming aspects make an order more appealing and readable.

The condition entries are columns ("rules") in which sets of pertinent answers are given to the conditions. In the simplest decision tables, rules contain only logical *true/false* or *yes/no* entries; however, they often display other answer types, as well.

The action stub is a list of all possible actions that may be taken in response to the various sets of conditions. These need not be in any order, but for ease in understanding, a natural order may result.

The action entries are columns associated with the condition entry columns. They contain indicators to identify which of the actions are to be performed, and the sequence in which the various actions are to be taken when a given rule is satisfied.

A decision table thus presents the sets of condition entries and their related sets of action entries as a set of vertical *rules* represented side-by-side. Whereas flowcharts depict decision processes serially, the decision logic tables represent the same processes in parallel.

8.1.2 Limited-Entry Decision Tables

Limited-entry decision tables (LEDTs) are the most widely used type and, in fact, most of the theoretical results apply only to these "LEDTs". They are readily identified by the fact that the condition entries are restricted to "Y", "N", or are immaterial (represented "-"). Other notations are often used: "T", "F", and blank for "Y", "N", and "-", respectively, etc. If only one action per rule appears, the action entries contain only the character "X" to indicate which particular action is to be taken.

As an example of how to use a limited-entry decision table, consider the following problem: Having reached this point in the monograph, the reader undoubtedly faces a number of uncertainties and wonders what to do next. His quandary can be solved by preparing a decision table, such as the one shown in Figure 8-2.

READERS QUANDRY		1	2	3	4	5	6	7	8
1.	Is the reader tired?	Y	Y	Y	Y	N	N	N	N
2.	Is the reader interested?	Y	Y	N	N	Y	Y	N	N
3.	Is the reader confused?	Y	N	Y	N	Y	N	Y	N
1.	Reread first part of chapter	X				X			
2.	Continue reading chapter		X				X		
3.	Skip to next chapter							X	X
4.	Stop reading and rest			X	X				

Figure 8-2. Limited-entry decision table: "The Reader's Quandary"

Here, various pertinent conditions and a set of actions that could be invoked are listed. The table recommends one of four actions for each of the eight sets of circumstances involving three decisions to be made.

The table recommends the reader "Stop reading and rest" (Action 4) whenever he is tired and uninterested, regardless of whether he is confused or not; he may "Skip to next chapter" if he is not tired, but not interested, regardless of his state of confusion. When situations of this type occur, the "don't care" response, indicated by "-", is useful, as shown in Figure 8-3.

Despite the possibility that the recommendations given may not be the same as those that would be chosen by someone else, the table in Figure 8-3 is too simple to be effective. For one thing, there is an implied looping back to the beginning of the chapter when the reader is confused. If rereading does not clear up his confusion, but he insists on following the table's advice, then he ultimately tires or becomes uninterested. Consequently, he stops to rest or skips the rest of the chapter and, in either case, never reads to this point. (I may assume, therefore, that either you are not confused, or you don't take advice.)

Since I obviously want this chapter read, either the first part of the chapter should be fixed so there can be no confusion after rereading, or else I should supply another condition, so as to allow the reader to proceed in the text, hoping his confusion will be alleviated later. Such a condition is added in Figure 8-4.

QUANDRY REDUCED	1	2	3	4
1. Is the reader tired?	–	–	Y	N
2. Is the reader interested?	Y	Y	N	N
3. Is the reader confused?	Y	N	–	–
1. Reread first part of chapter	X			
2. Continue reading chapter		X		
3. Skip to next chapter				X
4. Stop reading and rest			X	

Figure 8-3. "The Reader's Quandary" with reduced rules

QUANDRY REDEFINED	1	2	3	4	5
1. Is the reader tired?	–	–	–	Y	N
2. Is the reader interested?	Y	Y	Y	N	N
3. Is the reader confused?	Y	Y	N	–	–
4. Is this the second reading?	N	Y	–	–	–
1. Reread first part of chapter	X				
2. Continue reading chapter		X	X		
3. Skip to next chapter					X
4. Stop reading and rest				X	

Figure 8-4. "The Reader's Quandary," redefined

The addition of condition 4 permits the reader to continue, if interested, after the second reading of the material, confused or not.

Several of the advantages of decision tables have been illustrated in the foregoing example:

- Logic is stated precisely and compactly.

- The logic is easy to understand and the relationships among the various aspects of the problem are readily visualized.

- Decision tables lend themselves easily to update and change.

8.1.3 Extended- and Mixed-Entry Decision Tables

Another type of entry used in the condition entry stub is the *extended entry*. Here the answer to the condition is not expressed as a logical true/ false, but is whatever value is required to answer the condition:

What color is the house?	White	Yellow	Pink	Other

It can readily be seen that an extended-entry question is equivalent to several yes-no questions asking if each of the possible entries is true. For example, the above extended entry can be represented as the following limited entries:

Is the house white?	Yes	No	No	No
Is the house yellow?	No	Yes	No	No
Is the house pink?	No	No	Yes	No

Features characteristic of both limited-entry tables and extended-entry decision tables (EEDTs) may be combined into a single table called a *mixed-entry table*. In any one horizontal row, however, entries are limited to one of the two types, exclusively. Mixed-entry decision tables (MEDTs) have one major advantage. Conditions that can be appropriately expressed by binary values (i.e., Y or N) may be represented in that fashion, such as conditions that are defined by relational expressions.

8.2 ADDITIONAL ASPECTS OF DECISION TABLES

In this section, I discuss some additional aspects of decision tables as an aid in developing them. These aspects include the reduction of entries by combining rules or by a single rule covering multiple entries, and the testing of decision tables.

8.2.1 Simplification of Decision Tables

If two or more rules have the same action sequence and if their rule entries are logically similar, the two rules may often be combined into one rule. For example, two LEDT rules having identical actions and differ only in the entries for one condition may be combined by substituting a "don't-care" entry for that condition:

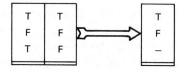

Similarly, don't-care entries may logically contain other, more explicit LEDT entries:

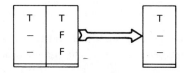

The complete rules for combining LEDT entries having identical actions are identical to those for combining terms in Boolian expressions used in logical design. This type of reduction is not always as straightforward for EEDTs or MEDTs, and in many cases such tables must be converted to their LEDT counterparts before processing can be attempted. I refer the interested reader to the literature [61,62] for further details concerning reduction of tables.

8.2.2 The ELSE-Rule in Decision Tables

Each of the condition entries in all of the decision tables discussed so far contains explicit answers to explicit questions. Questions may be asked in any order, arbitrarily, with the same action(s) taken in each case. All possible sets of answers appear in condition entries (although some answers may be immaterial). Matching a given array of answers with those in the condition events can likewise be done in any order.

In many cases, however, a designer may want to specify explicitly only a relatively few condition entries with their corresponding actions, under the implicit understanding that all unspecified situations are to be handled alike as another single rule. He does this by stating the explicit rules in the normal way, and then adds an extra column of action entries to be performed in the event that none of the explicitly defined rules is satisfied. This rule is called the *ELSE-rule*.

A conversion of the problem in Figure 8-4 to the ELSE-rule format appears in Figure 8-5.

QUANDRY WITH ELSE RULE		1	2	3	ELSE
1.	Is the reader tired?	–	Y	N	
2.	Is the reader interested?	Y	N	N	
3.	Is the reader confused?	Y	–	–	
4.	Is this the second reading?	N	–	–	
1.	Reread first part of chapter	X			
2.	Continue reading chapter				X
3.	Skip to next chapter			X	
4.	Stop reading and rest		X		

Figure 8-5. "The Reader's Quandary" in ELSE-rule format

Using the ELSE-rule avoids exhaustive enumeration of all the immaterial answers to a set of conditions for which the actions are all the same anyway. Since all sets of answers are not enumerated, a given array of answers must be checked against those appearing in the explicit rules first, before deciding to take the ELSE actions. There is therefore now an implied order by which one goes about deciding whether to apply one of the explicit rules, or else, the ELSE rule. The procedure for searching through the table to see which rule applies to a given array of answers is called a *sequential testing procedure* (or *STP*), and is the subject of the next section.

8.2.3 Sequential Testing Procedures

In executing a decision table as if it were a program, there is an implicit order in testing the conditions to find the valid condition entry, and, thereby, the action to take. A *sequential testing procedure* (STP) is an algorithm for processing the upper half of a decision table, to determine which rule is to be activated.

One simple STP is the following: Starting at the first condition and first rule, perform the condition test and compare the result to the entry ("don't-cares" do not have to be tested). If the result matches the entry, go on to the next condition test and the next lower entry. If the result does not match the entry, step back to the first condition and the next entry column (rule). When all of the condition tests satisfy a rule, then all the actions for that rule should be done in the order stated. However, if no entry column satisfies the condition tests, then do the actions for the ELSE-rule.

8.3 APPLICATION OF DECISION TABLES

When the logical conditions stated in a decision table can efficiently be the same as those tested by a program, then that table reveals much about the program design, as well. It doesn't reveal everything, of course. A flowchart and program written directly from a decision table would seldom be very efficient. For one thing, specifications of data processing generally state the global effect of operations, rather than the sequencing and intermediate operations that compositely build that global effect.

Nevertheless, a flowchart drawn from a decision table may form a good starting point for the program design. In fact, the design process may take the form of a series of refinements of the specification decision tables into design tables. I give an example of this later in this chapter.

Obviously, any proper program can be represented by one or more decision tables, because proper programs have an equivalent structured form. The program organizations allowed by structured programming may be easily implemented in decision table format, and these structures are sufficient to code any program.

8.3.1 Decision Tables as Programmable Algorithms

Decision tables are an entirely different way of thinking about an algorithm. The advantage is not so apparent on smaller problems, and, in fact, decision tables may seem, at first, to be an awkward way of representing a small problem. However, when decision tables are used to analyze a larger problem, they allow one to cope with one rule at a time, independently of the other rules. They also tend to show when, or what will happen when, rules have been omitted unintentionally.

The structure 'IF c THEN f ELSE g' is simply represented by the table (Figure 8-6):

IF ... THEN ... ELSE	1	2
Is c true?	Y	N
Perform f	X	
Perform g		X

Figure 8-6. If...THEN...ELSE decision table

Similarly, the structure 'WHILE c DO f is simply represented as the table (Figure 8-7):

WHILE ... DO		1	2
1.	Is c true?	Y	N
1.	Perform f	1	
2.	Repeat table	2	
3.	Continue on		X

Figure 8-7. WHILE...DO...decision table

Action 2 (Repeat) causes the condition entries to be reevaluated and subsequent action taken according to the activated rule; the numbers occurring in the first action entry indicate the sequence in which the actions are to be performed. (Since only one action occurs for the second rule, an "X" is sufficient to mark it.) Action 3 (Continue on) causes cessation of the action for this table.

Normally, the flow of a program represented by the chart would carry on to the next structure in order. Often, it is useful to designate actions to connect decision tables:

n	Perform table t next	X	

In this way, decision tables can reflect the hierarchic nature of the specification or design process. Tables can also be kept to a reasonable size by relegating certain actions to subtables, as indicated above.

8.3.2 Example: The Sieve of Eratosthenes

This example illustrates how a decision table can be used to define a program; in this case, the program generates the first 300 prime numbers.

The prime-number generator works merely by setting the first prime equal to 2, and then considering each odd number N, trying to divide it by the primes discovered so far. In trying to find prime divisors, we need try only primes already found up to $N^{1/2}$ as divisors. (If N is not prime, it must have a factor less than or equal to $N^{1/2}$. This fact is easily demonstrated by supposing the contrary were true, namely, that $N = ab$ where a and b both exceed $N^{1/2}$. But we would then have $N = ab > N$, which is impossible.)

The following table (Figure 8-8) describes the program:

SIEVE OF ERATOSTHENES	1	2	3	4	ELSE
1. First pass?	T	F	F	F	
2. K < 300?	–	T	T	T	
3. N/TABLE(I) an integer?	–	T	F	–	
4. TABLE(I) > SQRT(N)?	–	–	F	T	
1. Set N = 2	1				
2. Set N = 3	6				
3. Set K = 1	2				
4. Set I = 1	3	1		4	
5. Set TABLE(K) = N	4			3	
6. Set K = K + 1				2	
7. Set N = N + 2		2		5	
8. Set I = I + 1			1		
9. Print N	5			1	
10. Repeat this table	7	3	2	6	
11. Terminate					X

Figure 8-8. The Sieve of Eratosthenes

The first pass (Rule 1) prints the first prime (2) and inserts it in the table at index $K = 1$. On future passes, whenever an N is considered and is divisible by a prime (Rule 2), it is discarded. When it is not divisible by the Ith prime but $N^{1/2}$ is greater than the Ith prime (Rule 3), the next prime divisor is tried. Then (Rule 4), when I has sequenced to that point in the table of primes where $N^{1/2}$ is less than the Ith prime, then N is judged to be prime, and is printed. Ultimately, when 300 entries into the table have been made, the ELSE-rule terminates the program.

The table in Figure 8-8 serves to illustrate that decision tables have the advantage that each program path (i.e., rule) is specifically enumerated and defined independently from all other rules. If a modification needs to be made to the actions for any rule, it can be made with assurance that the actions for other rules are not changed.

8.3.3 Translating Specifications to Computer Programs

The use of decision tables to specify a program function has several distinct advantages, among which are that it forces a clear problem statement, and it defines completely at the top hierarchic level those decisions to be implemented. Moreover, as a technique, it is not inconsistent with the concepts introduced in Chapter 3, detailing program characteristics in hierarchic specification units. Decision tables lend themselves to hierarchic decomposition quite conveniently, as was illustrated in Figure 8-6.

Earlier in this chapter (Section 8.3.1), I indicated that decision tables form a good starting point for beginning the design process. The tables depict algorithms whose global effects have been stated explicitly and concisely. Therefore, turning these into flowcharts or coded procedures in a series of refinements (in the interests of efficiency) assures program correctness with respect to matching actual program response to specified response.

Also, sequential testing procedures ultimately lead to the decision trees generated when an LEDT is converted to a flowchart or computer program. Translation of decision tables to programs can be done manually or with the aid of special computer programs developed for this purpose or for simulating the execution of the table [63,64,65]. The translation can be oriented toward minimizing either the amount of memory used or the speed required to decide which rule is in effect.

Several enhancements can be used to speed up computer processing substantially. One simple and obvious enhancement is to save the result of the condition tests as a set of flags as they are performed, so that they need not be redone when one rule is not satisfied and the testing starts again at the top. This saves re-executing the condition tests for each column (rule).

A second enhancement is equivalent to arranging the table so that the most heavily used rules appear first in the columns. These rules can be determined by simulating the execution, keeping a running count of rules satisfied during execution.

Dynamic simulation enables self-adaptive optimization as follows: When a rule is satisfied, compare its count with that belonging to the rule (if any) on the left; if it is less, switch the rules.

If *a priori* statistics are available, they can be used to determine the STP directly, as will be outlined later in this chapter.

There are many manual and automatic ways [66,67] that decision tables can be turned directly into computer programs. Programming in CRISP, however, is almost as automatic a first translation as could be hoped. For example, the Reader's Quandary (Figure 8-4) merely becomes the following:

Assume that flags TIRED, INTERESTED, CONFUSED, and SECOND TIME reflect the state of the conditions, and that the actions are REREAD, CONTINUE, SKIP, and STOP; then the CRISP embodiment of the Reader's Quandary (in which condition 2 is tested first, then 3, 4, and finally 1) is the short program:

```
IF (INTERESTED)
:    IF (CONFUSED)
:    :    IF (NOT SECOND TIME)
:    :    :    DO REREAD CHAPTER
:    :    : ->(ELSE)
:    :    :    DO CONTINUE READING
:    :    :..ENDIF
:    : ->(ELSE)
:    :    DO CONTINUE READING
:    :..ENDIF
: ->(ELSE)
:    IF (TIRED)
:    :    DO STOP READING
:    : ->(ELSE)
:    :    DO SKIP TO NEXT CHAPTER
:    :..ENDIF
:..ENDIF
```

By this example one can see that programs derived from decision tables are inherently structured and modular. Aside from not being quite so compact as the table, the program is perhaps just as straightforward and readable, however.

But the same table could have been coded by testing condition 1 first, then 2, 3, and 4 in order. The result then would have been a much longer program, as follows:

```
IF (TIRED)
:    IF (INTERESTED)
:    :    IF (CONFUSED)
:    :    :    IF (SECOND TIME)
:    :    :    :    DO CONTINUE READING
:    :    :    :->(ELSE)
:    :    :    :    DO REREAD CHAPTER
:    :    :    :..ENDIF
:    :    :->(ELSE)
:    :    :    DO CONTINUE READING
:    :    :..ENDIF
:    :->(ELSE)
:    :    DO STOP READING
:    :..ENDIF
:->(ELSE)
:    IF (INTERESTED)
:    :    IF (CONFUSED)
:    :    :    IF (SECOND TIME)
:    :    :    :    DO CONTINUE READING
:    :    :    :->(ELSE)
:    :    :    :    DO REREAD CHAPTER
:    :    :    :..ENDIF
:    :    :->(ELSE)
:    :    :    DO CONTINUE READING
:    :    :..ENDIF
:    :->(ELSE)
:    :    DO SKIP TO NEXT CHAPTER
:    :..ENDIF
:..ENDIF
```

The order in which the tests are made thus can affect the program size and speed, sometimes to a large extent. The reason why the second program above is more complicated than the first is directly traceable to the fact that, even though only 2 of the 5 rules requires a test of condition 1, nevertheless, this test was conducted first. As a result, condition 2 had to be repeated in each leg of the first IFTHENELSE structure.

The first version of the program tested condition 2 first; but then, because condition 1 had "-" for every 'Y' answer, testing that condition could be omitted from the THEN branch. Similarly, testing condition 3 and 4 are superfluous to the ELSE branch, and so on.

8.3.4 Conversion of LEDT to Computer Program

Several algorithms have been put forth for the automatic conversion of LEDTs into computer programs, with the aim of minimizing storage requirements, execution time, or compiling time. The following procedure based on Pollack [68] converts an unambiguous LEDT into a flowchart:

   a. Select one row of the original LEDT by a suitable criterion C (to be discussed later). The condition in that row becomes the first comparison of the flowchart.

   b. Decompose the table into two subtables having one less row—either subtable may perhaps only contain one action—and associate each subtable with a branch of the flowchart decision. That is, one subtable consists of all the remaining conditions and the set of rules for which the condition selected in (a) above is true; the other is similar, except that the condition answers are false.

   c. If a subtable has more than one action, select one of its rows by criterion C and attach the condition for that row to the proper branch of the previously selected condition producing that subtable.

   d. Continue (b) and (c) above on each subtable until each rule of the original LEDT or the ELSE-rule is represented in a branch of a condition (or until a subtable indicates that the original table contained redundant or contradictory rules).

The criterion C above can, among other things, check for redundancy or contradiction among rules. If, at any stage, two rule columns exist without containing at least one Y,N pair in some row, redundancy or contradiction exists. Such a condition, for example, exists in the table shown in Figure 8-9:

Condition	1	2
c_1	Y	–
c_2	N	N

Figure 8-9. Redundant or contradictory rules

If the actions for rules 1 and 2 are the same, the rules are redundant and one can be eliminated; if the actions are the different, the rules are contradictory, and the table is in error.

By choice of the proper criterion C, Pollack and others [66–70] had hoped to produce flowcharts that would minimize either the memory space occupied by the decision process or the time required to make the decision. But none of these criteria *always* achieved its intended purpose, nor indeed, *can any one-pass criterion ever be found which will.* The reason for this is that the algorithm has no provision for *backing up* to select a different flowchart, even if a suitable criterion *could detect* that it is now producing a suboptimum flowchart.

In 1966 and 1967 Reinwald and Soland [64] gave algorithms that *do* produce optimum flowcharts, minimizing either execution time, or storage, or any increasing cost function of the two. The algorithm is essentially the same as that given above, except the criterion keeps track of a cost metric; whenever this metric for a partial flowchart exceeds a certain bound, the procedure backs up to consider alternate flowcharts.

To explain the coming criteria, it is useful to rearrange and augment the decision table so that it appears as in the example shown in Figure 8-10.

AUG-MENTED LEDT	Rule								Time Cost, (μsec/ decision)	Storage Cost, (cells/ decision)
	1	2	3	4	5	6	7	8		
	Probability									
Conditions	0.10	0.15	0.25	0.20	0.05	0.05	0.05	0.15		
c_1	Y	Y	N	Y	N	N	N	Y	50	30
c_2	Y	Y	Y	N	Y	N	N	N	68	75
c_3	Y	N	Y	N	N	Y	N	Y	25	18
Actions	A_1			A_2			A_3			

Figure 8-10. Example of LEDT showing rule relative frequencies and execution-speed and memory costs

In this table, the rules have been grouped together wherever they have the same action (A_i). What these actions are, and what the actual conditions are, have been suppressed. The table appears in its *full form*, without "don't-cares". Tables having indifferent entries, as I have said, are sometimes useful as an aid to problem specification and for simplification of the table into a more manageable, understandable form. The table in its reduced form is acceptable by some of the various criteria used in the Pollack procedure.

But rules can often be combined in many different ways to produce "don't-cares", which may lead to different non-equivalent "minimal cost" results in the procedure. I shall instead, for the treatment here, parallel the Reinwald-Soland technique, starting with the unreduced table, and proceed to define flowchart cost metrics for minimization.

The LEDT in Figure 8-10 has some elements not present in previous tables: the probabilities (relative frequencies) with which each of the rules occurs, and the costs, both in execution speed and memory occupancy, associated with making tests of the conditions. The figures I have put into this table are entirely hypothetical.

Notationally, I shall represent the table in a skeleton form by a row vector **p**, whose elements p_r are the 2^n rule probabilities, and column n-vectors x_r, **t**, and **s**. The column vector x_r contains the Y, N results of tests of conditions for the rth rule; **t** is the time-cost vector; and **s** is the storage-cost vector. In Figure 8-9, for example, $n = 3$ and

$$\mathbf{x_3} = \begin{bmatrix} N \\ Y \\ Y \end{bmatrix}, \quad \mathbf{t} = \begin{bmatrix} 50 \\ 68 \\ 25 \end{bmatrix}, \quad \mathbf{s} = \begin{bmatrix} 30 \\ 75 \\ 18 \end{bmatrix},$$

$$\mathbf{p} = (.10,.15,.25,.20,.05,.05,.05,.15)$$

The component of x_r corresponding to condition c will be denoted as x_{cr}; for t, as t_c; and for s, as s_c. For example, $x_{2,3} = Y$, $t_1 = 50$, $s_3 = 18$.

As a further notational convention, I will refer to the events $c_i = Y$ and $c_i = N$ merely as i and $\bar{i}$, respectively. I shall also refer to k-tuples of such events in the notation,

$$\mathbf{e} = (e_1, e_2, \cdots, e_k)$$

The entire set of rules satisfying an event set **e** will be denoted R(**e**). In the example above,

$$R = \{1,2,3,4,5,6,7,8\}$$

$$R(\bar{2},3) = \{6,8\}$$

The former of these reflects that the set of rules is not restricted; the latter contains only rules 6 and 8, since both have $\mathbf{e} = (\bar{2},3)$, that is, $c_2 = N$ and $c_3 = Y$.

Two functions are needed to define the flowchart decision-time metric. The first is the *don't-care discriminant*,

$$D_c(r_1,r_2) \triangleq \begin{cases} 1 & \text{If rules } r_1 \text{ and } r_2 \text{ agree except at} \\ & \text{condition c (i.e., } x_{cr_1} \neq x_{cr_2}\text{), and} \\ & \text{both lead to the same action, } A_j \\ 0 & \text{Otherwise} \end{cases}$$

The symbol "$\triangleq$" means "equals by definition".

Reinwald and Soland have shown that the expected *extra* time contributed to the execution of a flowchart, caused by making a test of condition c next after the outcomes of events $(e_1,\ldots,e_k) = e$ are known (having already been tested by the flowchart), is given by the second function,

$$\Delta T_c(e) = t_c \sum_{R(e)} (p_{r_i} + p_{r_j}) D_c(r_i, r_j)$$

where the sum extends over all pairs of rules $r_i < r_j$ satisfying e. The condition c, of course, is not included anywhere in e.

The formula for $\Delta T_c(e)$ is somewhat intuitive; it says that, once the decisions reflected by e have been made, the expected time loss incurred by testing condition c is the time t_c required to test c, times the probability that the actual rule in effect has c as a "don't-care" condition.

Reinwald and Soland have further proved for a given LEDT, that the average total decision time T for any flowchart which tests condition c first cannot be smaller than a computable *lower bound* T_c:

$$T_c = \sum_{k=1}^{n} t_k - \sum_{k=1}^{n} \Delta T_k + \Delta T_c$$

and, therefore, that the average decision time T of any flowchart equivalent to the given LEDT cannot be made smaller than a value T_0, given by

$$T \geq T_0 \triangleq \sum_{k=1}^{n} t_k - \sum_{k=1}^{n} \Delta T_k + \min_{c} \Delta T_c$$

Another pair of functions will produce the storage-cost metric for a flowchart; the first of these is the *utility discriminant*,

$$U_c(e) \triangleq \begin{cases} 1 & \text{If a rule } r_1 \text{ exists in } R(e) \\ & \text{such that } D_c(r_1, r_2) = 0 \text{ for} \\ & \text{every other rule } r_2 \text{ in } R(e) \\ 0 & \text{Otherwise} \end{cases}$$

This function reflects the utility of a condition c with regard to whether some rule in that subtable conditioned on the events e actually requires a test of condition c.

Reinwald and Soland have then shown that the *additional* storage cost incurred due to testing condition c, conditioned on the prior-tested events e, is given by the second function,

$$\Delta S_c(e) = s_c \left[1 - U_c(e)\right] + \sum s_k U_k(e,c) \, U_k(e,\bar{c})$$

The sum on k extends over all conditions in (e,c). Again, c does not appear anywhere in e.

This formula, too, is somewhat intuitive, in that it states (in its first term) that a test of an irrelevant condition c uses up s_c storage locations needlessly, and (second term), that since $U_k(e,c) \, U_k(e,\bar{c})$ equals one only if condition k is relevant in both the subtables conditioned by (e,c) and by (e,$\bar{c}$), there will be an expenditure of an additional s_k storage locations for each remaining condition k, since condition k must then appear in both branches of the flowchart beyond c. At each subsequent point at which a condition k is relevant in both subtables, an additional cost of s_k is again incurred.

There is a lower bound on the amount of storage S used by a program equivalent to a given LEDT; if the program tests condition c first, this lower bound is

$$S_c = \sum_{k=1}^{n} s_k U_k + \Delta S_c$$

Thus, the decision-storage required by any program equivalent to an LEDT cannot be smaller than a lower bound S_0, given by

$$S \geq S_0 = \sum_{k=1}^{n} s_k U_k + \min \Delta S_c$$

This lower bound, however, is rarely achieved.

8.3.5 Criteria for the Pollack Procedure

Even though I have repeatedly stated that the Pollack procedure does not always produce the optimum result, nevertheless, it is a simple algorithm. Large LEDTs are very unwieldy anyway, so simple procedures can provide a means for achieving a fairly good program, even if not optimum.

Since the Reinwald-Soland functions, which I have called ΔT_c and ΔS_c above, are direct measures of the extra time and storage required as the consequence of a decision c, they make excellent metrics for minimization. The criteria given by Pollack [68], Press [66], Shwayder [69], etc., are somewhat similar.

8.3.5.1 Criteria

For the Pollack procedure, a criterion that will tend to reduce the expected execution time of the flowchart is thus the following:

Criterion C1 (Reduced Execution Time)—Compute the metric ΔT_c for each condition c in the subtable remaining for consideration. Choose that c for which ΔT_c is a minimum value.

One can readily see that, if a flowchart exists which actually achieves the lower bound, then that optimum flowchart will be found by the Pollack procedure using criterion C1 above, except possibly in cases where two or more conditions at a certain stage of the development have equal values of ΔT_c, least among all remaining ΔT_c. Then there is a possibility that the wrong condition may be chosen at that stage. The converse, unfortunately, is not true, flowcharts found by the Pollack procedure are not always optimum.

A criterion for the Pollack procedure that will tend to reduce the storage occupancy is the following:

Criterion C2 (Reduced Storage Occupancy)—Compute the metric ΔS_c for each condition in the subtable remaining for consideration. Choose that c for which ΔS_c is a minimum value.

The two criteria can be combined into one criterion by the introduction of a suitable cost function, which I will denote by $\$(\Delta T_c,\Delta S_c)$. The only restriction on $\$(x,y)$ is that it be an *increasing* function, nondecreasing in each argument.

Criterion C3 (Reduced Cost)—Compute ΔT_c, ΔS_c, and the metric $\$(\Delta T_c,\Delta S_c)$ for each condition in the subtable remaining for consideration. Choose that c for which $\$(\Delta T_c,\Delta S_c)$ is a minimum.

8.3.5.2 Examples

The following two examples illustrate the minimization of execution time and storage allocation by the Pollack procedure using Criterion C1 and C2, respectively.

a) *Example*: Flowchart for Figure 8-10 "minimizing" execution time by the Pollack procedure (Criterion C1).

First, the values for ΔT_c are:

$$\Delta T_1 = 50\,(.10 + .25 + .20 + .05) = 30$$

$$\Delta T_2 = 68\,(.05 + .05) = 6.8$$

$$\Delta T_3 = 25\,(.10 + .15 + .05 + .05) = 8.75$$

Since ΔT_2 is least, condition 2 is chosen first. The two remaining subtables with c_2 excluded are:

$c_2 = Y$	1	2	3	5	Cost
	0.10	0.15	0.25	0.05	
c_1	Y	Y	N	N	50
c_3	Y	N	Y	N	25
	A_1		A_2		

$c_2 = N$	4	6	7	8	Cost
	0.20	0.05	0.05	0.15	
c_1	Y	N	N	Y	50
c_3	N	Y	N	Y	25
	A_2		A_3		

At this second stage, one can verify that

$$\Delta T_1(2) = 50\,(.35) = 17.5 \qquad \Delta T_1(\bar{2}) = 50\,(.25) = 12.5$$

$$\Delta T_3(2) = 25\,(.25) = 6.25 \qquad \Delta T_3(\bar{2}) = 25\,(.10) = 2.5$$

Therefore, condition 3 is to be tested on each branch of condition 2; these now result in the four subtables:

$c_2 = Y, c_3 = Y$	1	3	Cost
	0.10	0.25	
c_1	Y	N	50
	A_1		

$c_2 = Y, c_3 = N$	2	5	Cost
	0.15	0.05	
c_1	Y	N	50
	A_1	A_2	

$c_2 = N, c_3 = Y$	6	8	Cost
	0.05	0.15	
c_1	N	Y	50
	A_2	A_3	

$c_2 = N, c_3 = N$	4	7	Cost
	0.20	0.05	
c_1	Y	N	50
	A_2		

The rules in the first and last subtables all belong to one action, and, therefore, need not be tested. The resulting flowchart appears in Figure 8-11.

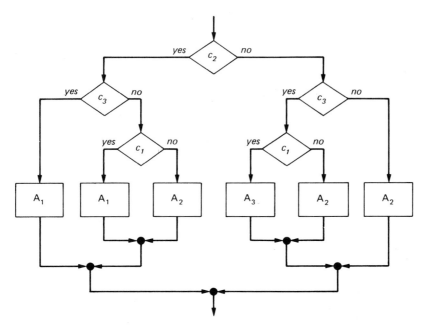

Figure 8-11. Flowchart resulting from decision table in Figure 8-10 by Pollack's procedure using criterion C1 (average decision time is 113; storage used is 171)

In this case, the Pollack procedure has produced the actual optimum flowchart, even though the average execution time slightly exceeds the lower bound $T_0 = 143 - 45.55 + 6.8 = 104.25$.

b) *Example*: Flowchart for Figure 8-10 "minimizing" storage allocation by the Pollack procedure (Criterion C2).

First, the values for ΔS_c are:

$$\Delta S_1 = 30\,(1 - 1) + 75 \cdot 1 \cdot 1 + 18 \cdot 1 \cdot 1 = 93$$

$$\Delta S_2 = 75\,(1 - 1) + 30 \cdot 1 \cdot 1 + 18 \cdot 1 \cdot 1 = 48$$

$$\Delta S_3 = 18\,(1 - 1) + 30 \cdot 1 \cdot 1 + 75 \cdot 1 \cdot 1 = 105$$

Hence, as in the last example, condition 2 is to be tested first; the two subtables are the same as in the previous example, except the costs are now 30 and 18 cells, rather than 50 and 25 μsecs. Next,

$$\Delta S_1(2) = 0 \qquad \Delta S_1(\bar{2}) = 0$$

$$\Delta S_3(2) = 0 \qquad \Delta S_3(\bar{2}) = 0$$

Thus, the extra storage incurred by either conditions is zero on both branches, so either condition can be chosen for either branch; let us say condition 1 for event 2 and condition 3 for event 2. The four subtables that remain are:

$c_2 = Y, c_1 = Y$	1	2	Cost
c_3	Y	N	18
	A_1		

$c_2 = Y, c_1 = N$	3	5	Cost
c_3	Y	N	18
	A_1	A_2	

$c_2 = N, c_3 = Y$	6	8	Cost
c_1	N	Y	30
	A_2	A_3	

$c_2 = N, c_3 = N$	4	7	Cost
c_1	Y	N	30
	A_2		

Again, the rules in the first and last subtables all belong to one action and, therefore, need not be tested. The resulting flowchart appears as shown in Figure 8-12. The chart is undoubtedly optimum, since the minimum additional storage cost decision was chosen at first step, and the remainder had no additional storage costs.

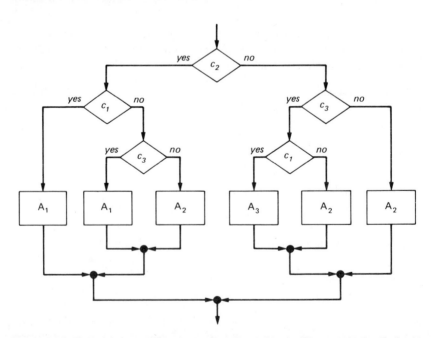

Figure 8-12. Flowchart resulting from decision table in Figure 8-10 by Pollack's procedure using criterion C2 (storage used is 171, the same as is used in Figure 8-11, but the average decision time is 124.25)

Unfortunately, such an easy indicator of optimality (zero additional cost at each step) appears only rarely in processing an LEDT; the lower bound on storage is $S_0 = 171$, achieved by the optimum. The chart in Figure 8-11 achieves both the optimum average execution time and storage costs.

By way of comparison, the chart shown in Figure 8-13 has an average decision time of 134.25 and a storage requirement of 216, more than either of the two previous charts.

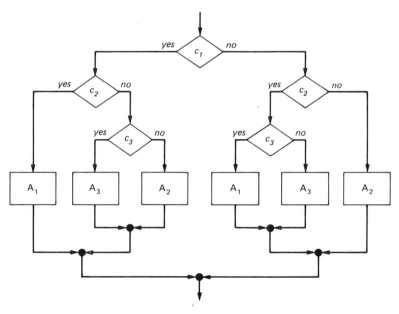

Figure 8-13. A non-optimum flowchart equivalent to decision table in Figure 8-10 (average decision time is 134.25; storage cost is 216)

8.4 THE USE OF DECISION TABLES IN PROGRAMMING

As was stated earlier, decision tables provide a way of differentiating between conditions and actions; specifically, all conditions are tested before any of the actions are performed. When programming without the aid of decision tables, one generally intermixes the two, following an impulse to "act as soon as you know you must" [64]. Frequently, one delays the execution of an action implied by a subset of conditions already tested, by setting a flag to remember the test outcome for later reference (a good example is the setting of a loop structure flag). None of the previously stated minimum-cost procedures allows for such intermixing of condition tests and actions, or the use of flags to delay execution of an action.

However, minimum cost techniques very often lead to more efficient programs; the development of algorithms incorporating these features is thus desirable, and probably feasible. The fact that decision tables tend to become unwieldy when there are more than half a dozen conditions is, in many ways, an advantage, because it is almost always symptomatic of poor program organization. It encourages the programmer to reexamine the problem, break it into smaller, more manageable modules wherein each module finds its expression in a single table.

8.4.1 The Reinwald-Soland Procedure

The procedure developed by Reinwald and Soland is essentially the same as the Pollack procedure, with two significant differences. First, a *cumulative* metric is maintained for the entire flowchart, up to its current state, whereas the previous procedures only examined, and then discarded, the *incremental* costs. And second, the procedure can backtrack to a previously-considered stage in the flowchart development (one that was rejected at that time because its metric was too great) whenever it ascertains that the metric at the current stage has exceeded the metric at the previous stage. I shall not elaborate on the algorithm in any greater detail; the interested reader, however, may consult the references [64].

8.4.2 Testing the ELSE-Rule

Very often, the reduction procedure leading to an optimum flowchart leads to subtables that correspond to only one single action, but in which some conditions remain untested and not explicitly indifferent. For example, suppose the decomposition process has, at a particular stage, resulted in the (hypothetical) partial tables below:

$c_1 = Y$	1	2
	0.25	0.25
c_2	Y	Y
c_3	Y	N
	A_1	

$c_1 = N$	3	4
	0.1	0.1
c_3	Y	N
	A_2	A_3

Condition c_3 in the leftmost table is immaterial; however, c_2 is given as an explicit condition, which must be Y before action A_1 is to be invoked. But what action is to be taken in the event the answer to c_2 is N? It depends. If $c_1 = Y$, $c_2 = N$ is a *possible* event, then the action to be taken is contained in the action entry of the ELSE-rule, in which case a test of c_2 must be made. However, if $c_1 = Y$, $c_2 = N$ is *not* a possible event, then c_2 need not be tested. If the event *is* possible, but highly improbable, there may arise concern as to what course should *properly* be taken in the program design: incur the extra expense to test the condition(s), or leave out the test(s) and run the risk of encountering the unlikely event(s).

The design decision, of course, is mitigated by the *seriousness* of omitting the test, compared with the *cost* of making it. For example, if omission of a test merely causes momentary erroneous data once in a great while, there is a great temptation to leave it out, in the interest of "efficiency". But if not testing that very unlikely event can blow the program, obliterate or falsify a great body of data, cause physical hazards, etc., then most certainly the test will be made, whatever the cost.

In keeping with the goal of this monograph—correct programs—design standards should require that the ELSE-rule be tested completely, except on a case-by-case basis where it can be *shown* that the likelihood of an untested ELSE-event is extremely low and the consequences of not testing that event are clear and justifiable. The program documentation should carry the rationale for each such exception.

8.4.3 Extensions to Mixed- and Extended-Entry Tables

The procedures given in the preceding sections of this chapter for turning decision tables into flowcharts (i.e., programs) are restricted to tables with binary branchings. With minor revisions, these can be generalized to tables in which multiple branching is permitted.

One obvious way of doing this is to convert all non-binary decisions to binary decisions, and proceed as in the previous sections. Depending on *how* multiple-branch decisions can be implemented in the target computer language, such a procedure may not be so inefficient as it may seem at first. Many multiple decisions are, in reality, merely cascaded binary decisions anyway.

In general, however, one can preassign a cost to each outcome of each decision. Previously, I considered these to be the same for Y and N answers (but they needn't have been), and collected these in the rightmost column(s) of the LEDT. If the costs of a test depend on the outcome, then these can be inserted, as shown below, into the table adjacent to the corresponding outcome. If a_j is an *answer* to rule j:

EXTENSIONS	1	2	• • •	r
c_i	a_1, t_{i1}	a_2, t_{i2}	• • •	a_r, t_{ir}

Decomposition of the table takes place just as it did previously, except there will now be a subtable associated with each answer a_j to the chosen condition.

The procedures for minimizing costs are the same as given previously, except, instead of associating a cost with each condition (say t_i corresponding to condition i), now a cost is associated with each answer to each condition, as t_{ij} corresponds to the j*th* answer to condition i.

8.4.4 An Example of the Use of Decision Tables in Programming: A Card Cross-Reference Program

The following example demonstrates the use of decision tables from the conceptual stages of program specification to the development of a computer program.

Problem: A program in source-language form exists on a set of cards. Another program, to be written, reads these cards and identifies the variable and label names on each card according to specified control data input. It then prints, adjacent to each pre-specified variable (or to every variable in lexicographic order when no variables are specified in the control data), the card number on which that variable appears within a specified card-number range (or the entire program when no range is given). Similarly, it prints for each specified label (or all labels, in lexicographic order when none are specified), the card number of all cards having a branch to that label within a second specified card-number range (or the entire program when no second range is given). The format of the control input is (*variable list*:*card-number range*;*label list*:*card-number range*). Nothing is to be printed if (;) is input; all variables and labels for all cards are printed if (:;:) or () is input. A specification such as (*v*) prints only for specified variables in the list *v* over the entire range; (:n_1-n_2) prints only for all variables over the specified card number range. Similarly, (;*l*) prints only for the specified labels in the list *l* over the entire range, and (:;n_1-n_2) prints only for all labels over the specified card-number range.

Analysis: The problem statement (i.e., requirement), while being rather long, is nevertheless, fairly vague, in that it only explicitly identifies actions for 7 events. A programmer, however, will readily identify the following set of logical conditions to be tested:

1. *v*-list given?
2. first ":" given?
3. *v*-range given?
4. ";" present?
5. *l*-list given?
6. second ":" given?
7. *l*-range given?

and actions to be taken:

1. print for selected variables

2. print for all variables

3. print for no variables

4. over selected range for variables

5. over entire range for variables

6. print for selected labels

7. print for all labels

8. print for no labels

9. over selected range for labels

10. over entire range for labels

11. print error message

Wishing to make a benevolent design, the programmer has himself added action 11, an ELSE-rule action. He also, upon study, sees that there are 5 printing formats for variables and 5 for labels, and thus that, to provide the flexibility for accommodating any combination of these, there must be 25 separate rules. Two inputs, ( ) and (:;:), yield the same action. He thus concludes that 27 rules, in all, are necessary.

On further study, and aided by the seven sample events, he fills out the program definition decision table shown in Figure 8-14. Let it be assumed that this table is then approved (by those writing the original problem statement). Now the design process begins. If the designer decides to flowchart using the Pollack procedure as a design prelude, he will find the need for 62 binary decisions (ELSE-rule completely tested)!

At this point, he seeks ways to simplify and reorganize the program definition without affecting the conditions and actions.

Reorganization: He recognizes that actions printing the variables and labels are very similar; independent tables such as those in Figures 8-15 and 8-16 can express these actions with simpler conditions. All 25 of the required actions are represented in the two tables; however, the null input, (), is improperly accounted for (neither table prints anything), and the ELSE-rule is incorrectly invoked. To eliminate a retest of the condition in which a null input might have occurred, Figure 8-15 introduces the setting of a flag.

CROSS-REFERENCING LEDT	1	2	3	4	5	6	7	8	9	10	11	12	13	14	15	16	17	18	19	20	21	22	23	24	25	26	ELSE
(explicit)	*									*					*			*	*			*	*		*	*	
Conditions:																											
1. v-list given?	Y	Y	Y	Y	Y	Y	Y	Y	Y	Y	N	N	N	N	N	N	N	N	N	N	N	N	N	N	N	N	
2. First ":" given?	Y	Y	Y	Y	Y	Y	—	—	—	Y	Y	Y	Y	Y	Y	Y	Y	Y	Y	Y	Y	Y	Y	Y	Y	Y	
3. v-range given?	Y	Y	Y	Y	Y	N	N	N	N	N	Y	Y	Y	Y	Y	N	N	N	N	N	N	N	N	N	N	N	
4. "," present?	Y	Y	Y	Y	N	Y	Y	Y	N	N	Y	Y	Y	Y	N	Y	Y	Y	Y	Y	Y	Y	Y	Y	Y	N	
5. ℓ-list given?	Y	—	N	N	N	Y	—	Y	N	N	Y	—	Y	N	N	Y	—	Y	N	Y	Y	—	Y	Y	N	N	
6. Second ":" given?	Y	—	Y	Y	Y	Y	—	Y	Y	N	Y	—	Y	Y	Y	Y	—	Y	Y	N	Y	—	Y	Y	Y	N	
7. ℓ-range given?	Y	N	Y	N	N	Y	N	Y	N	N	Y	N	Y	N	N	Y	N	Y	N	N	Y	N	Y	N	N	N	
Actions:																											
1. Print for given v	X	X	X	X	X	X	X	X	X	X																	
2. Print for all v											X	X	X	X	X	X	X	X	X								
3. Print for no v																				X	X	X	X	X	X	X	
4. Selected v-range	X	X	X	X	X						X	X	X	X	X												
5. Entire v-range						X	X	X	X	X						X	X	X	X								
6. Print for given ℓ	X	X				X	X				X	X				X	X			X	X						
7. Print for all ℓ			X	X									X	X								X	X				
8. Print for no ℓ					X			X	X	X					X									X	X		
9. Selected ℓ-range	X		X			X		X			X		X			X		X		X		X	X				
10. Entire ℓ-range		X					X					X			X		X		X		X				X	X	
11. Print error message																											X

Figure 8-14. LEDT for a Card Cross-Reference Program (rules indicated by * are explicit in problem definition, the remainder are inferred; no relative frequencies or decision costs have been provided)

VARIABLE REFERENCES	1	2	3	4	5	ELSE
1. *v*-list given?	Y	Y	N	N	N	
2. First ":" given?	Y	–	Y	Y	N	
3. *v*-range given?	Y	N	Y	N	N	
1. Print for given *v*	X	X				
2. Print for all *v*			X	X		
3. Print for no *v*					X	
4. Over selected *v*-range	X		X			
5. Over entire *v*-range			X	X		
11. Print error message and terminate abnormally						X
12. Set FLAG = 0	X	X	X	X		
13. Set FLAG = 1					X	
14. Perform table in Fig. 8-17	X	X	X	X	X	

Figure 8-15. Partial LEDT for the Card Cross-Reference Program, actions to print references to variables

LABEL REFERENCES	1	2	3	4	5	ELSE
5. *ℓ*-list given?	Y	Y	N	N	N	
6. Second ":" given?	Y	–	Y	Y	N	
7. *ℓ*-range given?	Y	N	Y	N	N	
6. Print for given *ℓ*	X	X				
7. Print for all *ℓ*			X	X		
8. Print for no *ℓ*					X	
9. Over selected *ℓ*-range	X		X			
10. Over entire *ℓ*-range			X	X		
11. Print error message						X

Figure 8-16. LEDT for the Card Cross-Reference Program, actions to print references to labels

The designer, however, recognizes from Figure 8-14 that, aside from the last two actions, the table in Figure 8-15 is always executed. Thus this table can be isolated as a separate action, prior to execution of Figure 8-16, which is to be executed then only when a semicolon is present. The table linking the two appears in Figure 8-17; the resulting flowchart appears as Figure 8-18. The total number of decision boxes has been reduced by this procedure to only 18 (tables in Figures 8-15 and 8-16 take 6 and 7,

VARIABLE AND LABEL REFERENCES	1	2	3	ELSE
4. Is ";" present?	Y	N	N	
5. *l*-list given?	–	N	N	
6. Second ":" given?	–	N	N	
7. *l*-range given?	–	N	N	
8. FLAG = 1?	–	Y	N	
15. Execute table in Fig. 8-16	X			
2. Print for all *v*		X		
5. Over entire *v*-range		X		
7. Print for all *l*		X		
10. Over entire *l*-range		X		
16. Do nothing, continue			X	
11. Print error message				X

Figure 8-17. LEDT for the Card Cross-Reference Program, linking tables in Figures 8-15 and 8-16

respectively). If logical connectives are permissible, then a further reduction occurs in the number of decisions, as shown by the CRISP-like procedure, ACTION, as follows:

> Note: The flowchart (Figure 8-18) and CRISP-like procedure are not the program to be written. Rather, they only show the required response to control data input insofar as actions to be taken are concerned.

```
PROCEDURE: ACTION <*DEFINITION OF CONTROL RESPONSE*>
    <*CONDITIONS %V-LIST, %COLON-1, %V-RANGE,
    <*%SEMICOLON, %L-LIST, %COLON-2, AND %L-RANGE, ARE ASSUMED
    <*TO BE SUPPLIED BY CALLING PROCEDURE*>&

    DO VPRINT <*PRINT VARIABLE REFERENCES*>
    IF (%SEMICOLON)
    :    DO LPRINT <*PRINT LABEL REFERENCES*>
    :->(ELSE)
    :    IF (%L-LIST OR %COLON-2 OR %L-RANGE)
    :    :    CALL ERRMSG <*PRINT ERROR MESSAGE*>
    :    :->(ELSE)
    :    :    IF (FLAG=1)
    :    :    :    DO PRTALL <*PRINT ALL REFERENCES*>
    :    :    :..ENDIF
    :    :..ENDIF
    :..ENDIF
ENDPROCEDURE
```

```
PROCEDURE:   VPRINT <*PRINT VARIABLE REFERENCES*>
      FLAG=0
      IF (%V-LIST)
      :     IF (%COLON-1 AND %V-RANGE)
      :     :     DO ACTS25 <*ACTIONS 2 AND 5*>
      :     :->(ELSE)
      :     :     IF (NOT %V-RANGE)
      :     :     :     DO ACTS24 <*ACTIONS 2 AND 4*>
      :     :     :->(ELSE)
      :     :     :     CALL ERRMSG <*PRINT ERROR MESSAGE*>
      :     :     :     ABORT
      :     :     :..ENDIF
      :     :..ENDIF
      :->(ELSE)
      :     IF (%COLON-1)
      :     :     IF (%V-RANGE)
      :     :     :     DO ACTS15 <*ACTIONS 1 AND 5*>
      :     :     :->(ELSE)
      :     :     :     DO ACTS 14 <*ACTIONS 1 AND 4*>
      :     :     :..ENDIF
      :     :->(ELSE)
      :     :     IF (%V-RANGE)
      :     :     :     CALL ERRMSG <*PRINT ERROR MESSAGE*>
      :     :     :     ABORT
      :     :     :->(ELSE)
      :     :     :     DO ACTS36 <*ACTIONS 3 AND 6*>
      :     :     :     FLAG=1
      :     :     :..ENDIF
      :     :..ENDIF
      :..ENDIF
      ENDPROCEDURE

PROCEDURE:   LPRINT <*PRINT LABEL REFERENCES*>
      :
      :
      ENDPROCEDURE
```

The subprogram LPRINT (to print label references) is very similar to VPRINT, and so, for prevention of further ennui, it is omitted here.

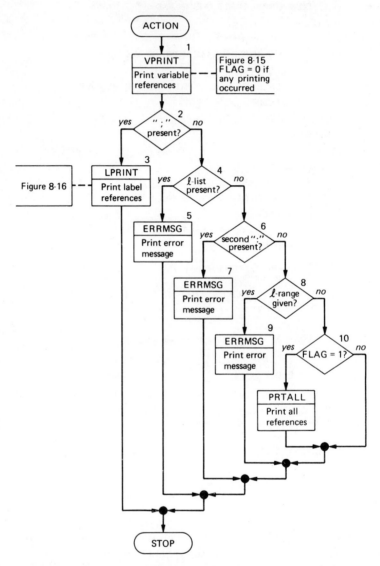

Figure 8-18. Flowchart for Example 8.4.4, Card Cross-Reference Program (decision logic follows table in Figure 8-17; this is a program definition flowchart, not a program design flowchart)

It is worth pointing out that the original table (Figure 8-14) and the simplified program are not strictly equivalent. The former would have dismissed the input (:) as an error; the latter treats it as being equivalent to (:;), printing all variable references throughout the program. Discrepancies of this type necessarily must be identified and shown not to be in conflict with the original problem statement. In this case, it is not, and in fact, leads to a more forgiving input specification (which still should, I would think, require approval by the proper authority, before continuing).

At this point, the designer has a correct algorithm insofar as its response to input *control data* is concerned. However, he has not yet imbedded his algorithm into a program that will efficiently accumulate the input data upon which the algorithm is to operate, and that will efficiently print the specified results. How the input is to be accumulated into a form suitable for the algorithm to access and how the output printing is to be formatted was not given in the problem statement, but left as a design prerogative. Hence, the next design task is to define the needed data structures, accumulation algorithms, and printing formats, and then to refine the ACTION algorithm to interface these properly.

Let me suppose that the designer elects, as in Figure 8-19, to input the control data by a module CONTROL, which then parses it and thereupon sets the flags needed by the ACTION algorithm or terminates abnormally in an error message. If no semicolon appears, conditions 4, 6, and 8 of Figure 8-18 cannot be valid within the parsing algorithm, and may thus be omitted from ACTION. Moreover, items are to be accumulated, rather than printed, according to the ACTION specification. The designer thus renames the module ACCUMULATE. The accumulation module (Figure 8-20) iteratively reads the input data cards, examines them for labels and variable names, and stores them selectively into sorted, linked lists in accordance with the ACTION algorithm. Printing takes place after all cards have been processed by the module REPORT.

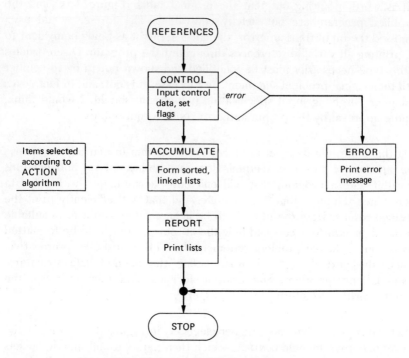

Figure 8-19. The entire REFERENCES program design

The reader may note that ELSE-rule checking has been relegated to the CONTROL module. Also, the EXTRACT module has been charged with retrieval of the card number; in case the cards have sequence numbers punched, these are merely extracted and used. However, if not, it must supply them by some other algorithm. (Another design prerogative subject to approval, since it affects the output definition.)

At this point, the designer feels he has his level-1 program designed, and he is reasonably sure it conforms to the problem statement. It is, in fact, somewhat better for two reasons: first, the design is more flexible with respect to control inputs, and second, this flexibility was achieved simply and efficiently.

The regular hierarchic design methods carry on from here.

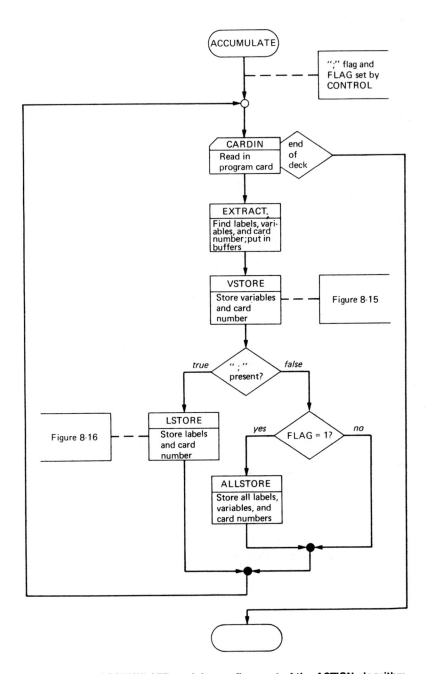

Figure 8-20. The ACCUMULATE module, a refinement of the ACTION algorithm

8.5 SUMMARY

This chapter has shown how decision tables can be used to develop and document a computer program from the top down, in modular hierarchy. Some characteristics of decision table usage worth summarizing before leaving the subject are listed below [59]:

- It forces a clear problem statement and shows where information is missing.

- It forces a complete logical description of the problem.

- It completely defines, at the top hierarchic level, those decisions to be implemented.

- It permits functional definitions and descriptions that are distinct from procedural content.

- It aids in translating a program definition into a working computer program.

- It permits development and orderly presentation of programs that are sometimes too complex for effective flowcharting.

- It modularizes the program by forcing a segmentation of the overall system into logically manageable tables.

- It is suitable for documentation, and for communication of the program operation between people.

- It assists in implementing program changes, and tends to identify consequences of any one change, even in a complex program.

- It is useful for presenting and communicating the program design to management for evaluation.

Standards for generating and using decision tables may be found in later chapters of this work. Format and documentation standards for decision tables are also discussed in Gray and Landon [20].

Problems for Chapter 8

8-1 Write a CRISP program to print the first N primes as illustrated in Figure 8-8.

8-2 Make appropriate assumptions for the frequencies, decision costs, and decision times for the card cross-reference decision table shown in Figure 8-16, and find a "minimal cost" STP by an appropriate Pollack procedure.

8-3 Make a decision table for the following simple elevator. The elevator goes between floors 1 and 2, the door can be open or closed, the button outside each door can initiate the "call" state, and the button inside only can activate (move) the elevator. The actions it can perform are: (1) close the door, (2) open the door, (3) go up, (4) go down, and (5) clear state of push buttons at current floor (inside and/or out). (Sets of actions, once started, go to completion before new conditions are tested.)

8-4 Design and flowchart a structured computer program to convert a given LEDT into a flowchart by the Pollack procedure with criterion C3 given in Section 8.3.5. (Hint: use recursive calls to a procedure that performs C3 on subtables.)

8-5 Design and flowchart a structured computer program to perform self-adaptive dynamic optimization of the sequential testing procedure for a limited-entry table-driven set of repetitive actions and decisions, as follows: Keep a running count of the rules executed; when a rule is satisfied, compare its count with that belonging to the rule (if any) on the left; and when it is less, switch the rules. Consider the feasibility of testing all conditions and setting flags before entering the STP, as opposed to testing each condition the first time it is required by the STP, and then only a flag each succeeding time.

8-6 Discuss the feasibility of the following LEDT implementation into a computer program: Test each of n conditions c_i, setting bit i of a computer word w equal to 1, if true, or to 0, if false. Then branch to the address contained in a 2^n-th element transfer-vector V, as indexed by the integer held in w, to initiate the actions invoked by the rule in effect.

8-7 Make an LEDT for the following problem. If a customer has placed an order that exceeds his credit limit, then send the order to the credit department. However, the order should always be accepted when it is one of our special customers; that is, one who does business with us regularly. Also, if the order is less than the minimum allowable shipping quantity, it should be rejected and sent to the shipping department manager. However, the system should be capable of receiving exceptions to this rule, as there will be cases when a customer will insist that his order be shipped, even though it is too small. In such cases, a special approval from the shipping department overrides the minimum-order requirement.

IX. ASSESSMENT OF PROGRAM CORRECTNESS

I have been harping about correctness of programs through eight chapters so far, without saying too much about exactly how that assessment is to be made. Since large programs cannot be fully demonstrated, either by rigorous, formal proofs or by exhaustive verification, these programs are almost certain to contain errors of one form or another. It is true that the modular, hierarchic decomposition of a program into functional subunits reduces complexity to a great extent, but probably not to the extent that concurrent, rigorous proofs of correctness are feasible.

What, then *can* be done to increase probable program correctness, or the "index of reliability", or "confidence level", as I called it in Chapter 5? At this writing, not enough; programs still require repairs, no matter how carefully they have been prepared, documented, coded, and tested. But there are some things that help, and that is what this chapter is about.

9.1 FORMAL PROOFS

The only known general method that can be applied to make a *formal* proof of correctness may now be stated as follows [71]:

For each flowchart flowline, make assertions which describe the current pertinent state of the program data space as the program traverses that flowline. For each process node, prove that if the incoming assertion is true, then the outgoing assertion is true; for each collecting node, prove that if any one of the incoming assertions is true, then the outgoing assertion is true; and for each branching node, prove that if the incoming assertion is true, then all of the outgoing assertions are true.

Proofs of termination are usually handled separately, but can often be decided by making the assertions contain a parameter that indicates convergence of the algorithm.

9.1.1 Proof of Program Behavior

I claimed in Section 5.1.4 that formal, rigorous correctness proofs are impractical, in that they are at least as complicated as the program they assert to be correct, and in that they are probably just as susceptible to error [38, 39, 40]. Nevertheless, the use of proof techniques does contribute to program correctness by forcing pr.grammers to express solutions to problems in two different ways: by an algorithm and by a proof of the algorithm. For this reason, I urge program designers to make such proofs to themselves or others—at least on an informal basis—as a reasonable assurance that the program will work before the design goes any further.

As an example of this technique, the program shown in Figure 9-1 (a modified version of that appearing in Knuth [71]) finds the greatest common divisor of two numbers N and M, input at a terminal, by Euclid's Algorithm. The needed assertions and a proof outline are given on the figure.

It is theoretically possible, and I shall discuss this in more detail a little later, to generate the required logical assertions on each program flowline in a well-defined formal way, all the way to the end. The proof of program correctness then comes down to verifying that the derived "end assertion" agrees with the program specification. The trouble with this formalized method is that it produces a logical assertion equivalent to the program function, but no general method exists for proving that a derived logical assertion matches the desired program function. That is why it is so useful to make intermediate, humanly easier-to-verify assertions along the way.

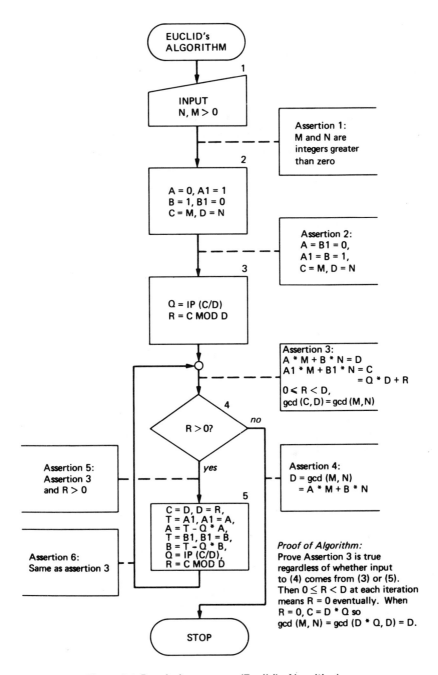

Figure 9-1. Proof of a program (Euclid's Algorithm)

9.1.1.1 Program Assertions

What kinds of assertions (also called *predicates*) are required for formal program verification? First and foremost, a program must have an *end assertion*. This is a statement (or set of statements) that defines what is meant by program (or subprogram) correctness. There may also be an *entry assertion*, which states initial conditions upon which the program operates. Other assertions along the way are theoretically not necessary, but practically, are very useful. Of particular utility are the assertions immediately following each loop collecting node; these are often referred to as *inductive assertions*. Figure 9-2 illustrates the various assertions above.

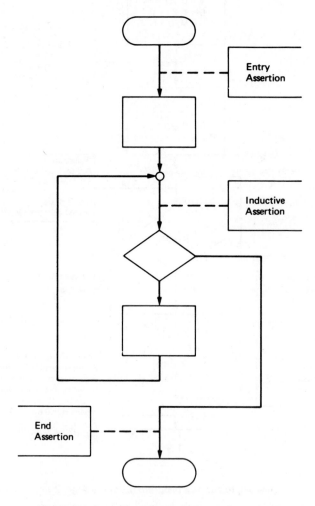

Figure 9-2. Assertions for formal program proofs

The inductive assertion of a loop, as well as all of the assertions supplied within that loop, must be invariant under the looping process. That is, each such assertion on a flowline must be true each time the program traverses that annotated flowline. Moreover, all assertions within a program (excluding the entry condition) must derive from the entry assertion in concert with the program operations.

In consideration of the method above, the "loop condition" in Mills' Correctness Theorem can be relaxed as follows: *the data space may be redefined dynamically so long as each of the assertions about the data space, on the loop-entry flowline and on the loop-iteration flowline, satisfy the inductive assertion on the flowline exiting this loop collecting node.*

The assertion at the entry to a proper program (perhaps the null statement) together with all the subsequent node operations define a set of formal assertions valid at all other points in the program. Such assertions are said to be *derived* assertions, as they result from purely formal logical manipulations; consequently, they reflect the exact behavior of the program at the given point. Other assertions may be attached to various points that specify the desired (correct) program behavior. These are called *invented assertions*. The correctness-proving problem comes down to the verification that the invented and derived assertions are compatible. The derived program function must *encompass* the desired function.

As an example, suppose that the desired response of a program is to output $\sin x$ whenever a positive value for x is input; $x < 0$ cannot occur, a physical constraint of the problem. A program whose derived response is $\sin x$, valid for negative as well as positive x, is compatible. But in the reverse situation (viz., when there is a desired response of $\sin x$ valid for positive, zero, and negative x, but the derived program response shows correctness only for positive x), there is incompatibility.

Figure 9-3 depicts a formal derivation of predicates (assertions) as a forward traversal of nodes. In part (a) of the figure, the program function F produces, in response to the assertion A_1, the compatible assertion A_2 ($\Rightarrow$ in the figure stands for "implies"). In part (b) of the figure, assertions A_2 and A_3 following the decision are compatible with the combined conditions stated in A_1 and those imposed by the outcomes of c. Finally in part (c) of the figure, the merging of two flowlines having assertions A_1 and A_2 into a single flowline produces a single predicate A_3 compatible with the two combined alternatives.

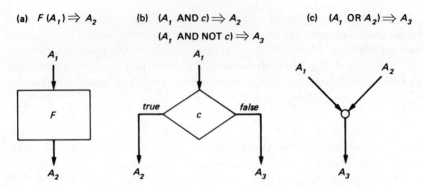

Figure 9-3. Forward derivation of assertions

9.1.1.2 Loop Correctness

Making a correctness proof for a loop is contingent on the formulation of the inductive assertion (the assertion on the outgoing flowline of the loop-collecting node). This assertion must be a true statement at every iteration.

If, as in Figure 9-4 below, A_1 is the assertion at the loop input, $A_2(n)$ is the assertion on the returning flowline (which may depend on the node-entry-number, n), then the outgoing inductive assertion $A_3(n)$ is the derived statement A_1 OR $A_2(n)$. Having recognized the possible dependence of the loop assertions on the number of iterations, I shall henceforth refer to $A_i(n)$ merely as A_i, unless a specific value is given to n.

One may start with an assertion inside a loop and derive assertions all the way around, until the same point is reached again; the two predicates, initial and derived, must then be compatible. Any predicate within the loop can be chosen, but the simplest to illustrate is A_3. In the WHILE c DO F configuration (Figure 9-4a), one may write, for example, the derived expression

$$A_1 \text{ OR } F(A_3 \text{ AND } c) \Rightarrow A_3$$

One may thus prove the correctness of a WHILE c DO F loop, for given A_1, A_5, F, and c, by finding an *invented* A_3 satisfying the two requirements:

$$A_1 \text{ OR } F(A_3 \text{ AND } c) \Rightarrow A_3$$

$$A_3 \text{ AND NOT } c \Rightarrow A_5$$

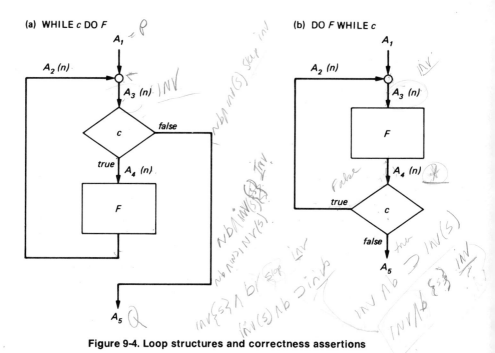

Figure 9-4. Loop structures and correctness assertions

A similar technique applies to the DO F WHILE c loop in Figure 9-4b:

$$A_1 \text{ OR } (F(A_3) \text{ AND } c) \Rightarrow A_3$$

$$F(A_3) \text{ AND NOT } c \Rightarrow A_5$$

The reader may verify for himself that the given inductive assertions for Euclid's Algorithm (Figure 9-1) do indeed satisfy these conditions.

A general method for proving that derived and invented forms of assertions are compatible is not presently known, although some work in this area has been reported [72]. At the present, proofs, if done at all, are done by humans, and these, as I have said, are just as susceptible to error as the program it "proves". However, the use of proof techniques will find many discrepancies in a design before the programming stage begins. Hence, while not perhaps producing a 100-percent error-free program, proofs (formal or informal) do increase the index of reliability measurably.

The increase in reliability, of course, depends on the expertise of the assessor. Rigorous, formal-logic proofs are not generally going to be forthcoming from the average programmer. But less formalized assurances that an algorithm behaves according to assertions supplied at various points are generally within his capabilities. Moreover, they take less time, and probably will be more productive in terms of correct modules delivered per day.

What I want to present here, then, is a discipline that draws upon formal correctness procedures, tempers them with practicality, and provides useful documentation of the program functioning as a by-product, as well.

9.1.1.3 Complexity of a Program

One measure of the complexity of a program is the length of its correctness proof: the more complicated a program is, the longer will be the argument required to understand the program and to show that it operates correctly. Even if "proof of correctness" is weakened to "assessment of correctness", or to "understanding", these shorter, more practical measures of complexity are probably still directly proportional to the former.

For a rigorous proof, a set of assertions, one per flowline, plus arguments to relate derived assertions to invented assertions, is sufficient. Each of the assertions is equivalent to an announcement of the program state (or change of state) as that flowline is traversed during execution. Hence, at best, the complexity of a program must be at least linearly related to its length.

If operations and program structure can be made simple enough that the logic and rationale for each program step are clear, then the arguments to relate invented and derived assertions are very short. The more significant portions of understanding are then devoted to discovering what each constituent of a program does, rather than to argue that each such constituent should appear as it does.

For structured programs, operations fall into a limited number of easily grasped program structure categories (sequence, IFTHENELSE, DO-WHILE, etc.). The constituent parts of the structure IF c THEN f ELSE g, for example, are c, f, g and the control structure, IFTHENELSE. The argument to understand the entire structure consists of verifying that the condition c does convincingly seem to partition the problem as it should, and that f and g are the proper functions to have been executed in each case.

Understanding the entire IF c THEN f ELSE g structure is thus really equivalent to understanding the distinct roles of each of its three separate components:

    a. Understand *c*.

    b. Understand *f*.

    c. Understand *g*.

since the **IFTHENELSE** structure is so simple as to be thoroughly understood already. That is, the complexity of this structure seems to be equal to the sum of the respective separate complexities of *c*, *f*, and *g*.

By induction then, understanding each component is linearly related to understanding its nested subcomponents, and so on down the line. For this reason, hierarchic, modular, structured programming holds the potential for developing programs which achieve a linear relationship between complexity and program length.

However, even a linear length-complexity relationship may be too much for programs or systems with tens or hundreds of thousands of instructions, unless the proportionality constant can be reduced to an acceptable figure by reduction of what will be required during development in the way of correctness assessments. Such reductions are the subject of investigation in the next section.

9.1.2 Proof of Control-Logic Correctness

The number of combinations of possible data inputs, and hence the number of corresponding computer states, is generally so great that only a relatively small number of them can ever be demonstrated. However, it is possible to check the control logic of a program in a reasonable time, either by making a correctness proof or by running a series of tests on the emerging program.

In connection with control logic analysis, the *complexity of control* may be defined as a measure of the length of the correctness assessment for the control logic of a program. Often such an assessment involves the calculation and measurement of the numbers of times each program flowline is traversed. Knuth [71] demonstrated that these numbers are governed by Kirchhoff's equations (for non-real-time proper programs, at least). There then always exists a set of flowlines which form a linear basis for the flowchart, in the sense that the number of times any other flowline is traversed during execution is a linear combination of the numbers for the basis set.

Robert McEliece pointed out, in an internal JPL working paper, that the control complexity of a program is therefore probably at least as great as the amount of work required to solve Kirchhoff's equations and verify the numbers in the program. For an arbitrary unstructured program, this effort can be as high as $O(n^3)$, where n is the number of nodes on the program flowchart. McEliece then also pointed out that for structured programs the basis flowlines can be found by inspection and thus that the solutions for the other flowlines can be written down immediately in terms of this basis set. In other words, the control complexity of a structured program is probably again only linearly related to the program length, $O(n)$.

In the remainder of this section, I present an analysis of what comprises a formal, mathematical proof of control-logic correctness. With this as a guide, I will then be able to define practical tests to be made in conjunction to the concurrent design and coding activities to lend reasonable assurance that program control-logic is valid.

A formal proof of control logic is much the same as a formal proof of the entire module function, but easier, as it need only be concerned with paths through the module.

Assertions (predicates) relative to logical control are merely statements defining the *conditions* that must be met for traversal along the corresponding flowlines. The proof of control-logical correctness of a top-down, structured, hierarchically-documented design thus consists of demonstrating that, for each module,

a. Each path segment (flowline) has an assertion relative to module control parameters.

b. Each assertion truly reflects the logical condition under which that path is traversed.

c. Each condition for traversal represents a circumstance that can occur (i.e., there are no untraversable flowlines).

d. Each such condition is decidable from documentation of the current module and its ancestor modules.

e. Once entered, module control eventually passes either to a normal or extra-normal termination.

Figure 9-5 shows an example of a control-logic correctness assessment of the Euclid's-algorithm program given earlier as Figure 9-1. Although each flowline in the chart can be assigned an assertion relative to control parameters (conditions), many of these assertions would merely duplicate actions in the function boxes, so they have been omitted, as have those functions that do not affect module control.

As the next step, the assertions have to be verified to show that each is a true and sufficient condition for traversal of the flowline (condition 2). I will

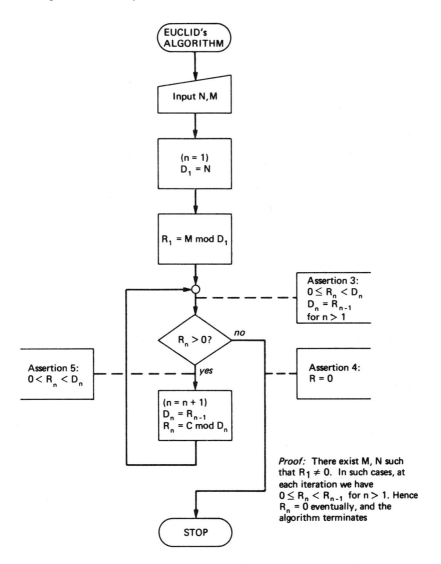

Figure 9-5. Assessment of control-logic correctness of Euclid's Algorithm (see Figure 9-1) (only the operations and assertions necessary for proof have been retained; values of R and D have been tagged with an integer (n) value denoting the iteration index at Assertion 3)

bypass the formal aspects of this issue, and rely on the reader's reasoning for assurance that the assertions given are true (i.e., an informal assessment).

Next must be found a set of conditions that together invoke every box on the chart (condition 3). In this case, it is clear that any given positive values of M and N produce either $R_1 = 0$ or $R_1 > 0$. All control is explicit and, therefore, decidable without outside reference (condition 4). Finally, the algorithm terminates (condition 5): if $R_1 = 0$, it terminates immediately; if $R_1 > 0$, the proof appearing in the figure may be applied.

As a first requirement, then, the control logic of a module will have to be documented to such a degree that it is *possible*, at any phase of design, to assess which submodules of the current module will be executed in any given set of circumstances.

9.2 COMPUTER-AIDED ASSESSMENT OF PROGRAM CORRECTNESS

Human fallibility and inability to cope with complexity in large programs, even with the benefits afforded by the top-down approach, dictate that there be some form of automatic checking of the design.

After one has become proficient in using a programming language, he might expect that he would no longer make any syntactic errors in writing programs. Yet this has amply been shown not to be the case. People still make such errors; fortunately, they are mostly caught by the compiler (or assembler) immediately. Some modern compilers now have the capability to process many of the global characteristics of a program for context, thereby catching many other errors that would not be noticed previously until that code was executed, if indeed the error were catastrophic enough to be classified as a failure.

The methods given so far have admonished the reader to take great care in each of the development activities, to be sure that what he is doing is correct before he proceeds. Unfortunately, just as compilers will always find syntax errors in freshly coded programs, there will always, with high probability, also be bugs in these programs, not locatable until actual execution of the code. At least, not until automatic program-provers come along.

But just as mathematicians generally do not undertake to prove a mathematical theorem correct until they are reasonably sure it is correct, neither should one undertake to execute a program until he is reasonably confident that it is also correct.

Checkout is the first step in program verification once coding has taken place. It is the validation of the program or a part of the program by the programmers themselves. It consists of compiling and assembling the code being checked until the listing contains no errors, and then running a series of tests to validate program integrity.

Debugging refers to fixing any uncovered errors or inconsistencies between the program specification and its actual operation.

Even if debugging is uninteresting and deplorable from the viewpoint of computer science, it nevertheless is a practical necessity in program production. Production systems that do not have automatic aids to permit software engineers to execute programs, wholly or partly, in a controlled, interrogative way doom program reliability and/or personnel productivity to abysmally low levels. I shall not discuss the kinds of debugging aids one should find in a good production system until Chapter 17. Worth mentioning, however, are some techniques that do contribute to hastening program checkout and that tend to be independent of the particular set of aids available on a given system.

9.2.1 Concurrent Design, Coding, and Checkout

Designing a program from the top down offers a great potential toward generation of initially correct programs. Concurrent coding provides a way of checking how a program actually operates to see if it matches the designer's intent, level by level through the program development process.

An unstriped submodule within a module can be coded as soon as the flowchart on which it appears (or its equivalent) is finished because unstriped modules represent specific, unambiguous functional statements concerning the action of that module. Moreover, the program can be run, provided each *striped* module is properly represented by a block of temporary code (*dummy stub*) that will act as though it were the actual code for the module, insofar as it produces a proper interface with the program at its current stage of completion.

Once a design has reached the stage that the coding of a number of modules (the current design phase) can begin, the design of the tests and dummy stubs for that phase can also begin. (Different dummy stubs may sometimes be required for different input sets.)

Of course, such stubs do not perform all that is necessary to make the program operate correctly for all possible inputs. Rather, stubs are intended to verify, by way of special test cases, that the operation is proper for the already coded part of the program. Recall that Mills' correctness theorem states that if the part already coded is absolutely correct, then it will still be absolutely correct after the rest of the program is coded, and need not be checked again.

In principle, the use of dummy stubs can reduce the amount of debugging and testing required during development to gain a certain level of confidence in the program. However, since absolute correctness is generally inaccessible, some rechecking may be necessary in practice. In addition, the amount of rework needed to correct an error is greatly reduced, because most errors are "nipped in the bud", caught before they are embedded in further levels.

By writing the code that calls the program stubs before the stubs themselves are developed, the interfaces between the calling and the called programs are defined completely so that no interface problems should be encountered later.

In a complete sense, "correct" means that the program takes the proper action for *all* inputs that may occur. In a practical sense, however, tests must be limited to representative cases. Certainly, extreme values and some non-valid data should be included as development-test-cases to assure that the program responds in the intended way at every phase of the design.

The test designer may elect, on occasion, to write test programs (*test drivers*) in which to imbed the current-phase design, or a part of it, or all of it plus some of the previously tested design. Such an extra effort is certainly in order when it is cumbersome, inefficient, or costly to compile, load, and run parts of a program with which modules at the current phase do not interface.

The principle of using the entire program as a test driver, however, has several advantages, among which are:

a. It tends to minimize the coding of special test drivers to the maximum extent possible.

b. It embeds modules in the same environment during testing that they will have later during operation.

c. It does not discard the driver-code after use (rather, it is the dummy stubs which are discarded after use).

d. It allows tests (run at one phase of the development) to be rerun at any subsequent phase, with consistent results.

I would like to emphasize again, that even though dummy stubs may provide test data to a module and its hierarchic ancestors, this data is not the actual data the program will access in final operation. It is data supplied to verify *logical control* and *data-space control* functions only. Therefore, testing a module having dummy stubs succeeds only in testing the control aspects of that module relative to any data emanating from the stubs. The data design is not verified until the actual data structures are accessed. Stub-tests may, however, by inference contribute to an assessment of the data structural and functional correctness of modules at the higher program tiers.

9.2.2 Validation of Control-Logic Correctness

The five criteria for a formal demonstration of control-logic correctness given in Section 9.1.2 above serve as guidelines for computer-aided demonstration of control-logic validity. The demonstration consists of devising sets of test data for a module to exercise each of its "flowlines", then executing that module with the test data as input, and, finally, verifying that the conditions stated for traversal of a given "flowline" are actually in effect. Additionally, module control must terminate as advertised.

Devising test data for a developing program is conceptually not difficult, and, in fact, can be computerized to some extent. The test designer merely identifies (perhaps with computer aid) each of the series of decisions along a path leading from the input test data to the "flowline" to be traversed, and then invents appropriate test data to invoke those decisions.

As deeper and deeper levels of a program are designed and coded, the test data can become hierarchically more and more refined, so as to invoke each of the paths within each of the modules that have replaced dummy stubs. That is, if a given test input caused the execution of a dummy stub, that same input will cause the module replacing that dummy to execute one of its paths; modifications of the input cause all its flowlines to be traversed.

9.2.3. Auditing and Verifying Functional Correctness

The second requirement needed to make a reasonable assessment of program correctness (the first was control-logic documentation) is that documentation should be carried to the level that permits an *audit* of a module algorithm against its stated function at the previous tier of the design. The purpose of such an audit is to ensure that everything assumed by the parent-level design actually appears within the module and that everything actually appearing in the module design is traceable back to the stated module function.

In designing and executing tests to validate control-logic correctness, one has simultaneously also designed the tests from which the functional audit can take place. The identification of a program path with a certain test input permits the assessor to tabulate what functions have been performed along that path. He can then assess whether their actions are being invoked in their "proper" sequence, even though some of them, at this stage of development, are as yet, only implemented as dummy stubs.

The job of tabulating the decisions necessary to cause the program to traverse a given path is algorithmic; in fact, programs such as FLOW, QUALIFIER, and PACE [73,74] generate optimal sets of test cases. The generation of data to invoke the test cases is likewise almost algorithmic, but generally requires human intervention to relate input processing to the predicates (program decisions) needed. The job of tabulating the functions performed along any path in response to test input can be purely automatic: counters and/or print statements (probes) inserted in each flowline will suffice. Then, the assessor must establish the correspondence of each input to its required output stated in the Software Functional Specification (SFS) and to the tabulated steps in the actual output of the tested program. While this is not perhaps automatic, it is nevertheless still at the audit level of complexity.

Human judgement and programming expertise, however, will generally be required to ascertain whether a given path tabulation is consistent with the program definition—that is, whether the output sequence of invoked functions operating on the input data do, in fact, represent the correct response of the program module at the current (incomplete) phase of development.

9.2.4 Example: Testing Module Control Paths

Problem: To generate sets of test data that will cause the shuttle-interchange sort program to traverse all program flowlines. Figure 9-6 displays a flowchart of the program coded in Example 7.3.3.2 (of Chapter 7). Some of the flowlines are explicitly numbered for reference in this example; others will be referenced by the numbers on the box they enter.

Analysis: To design these tests, one may choose each flowline in turn and ask first, "What is a composite set of conditions which must be true in order for this flowline to be processed?" In the example, to traverse flowline 8 (entering box 8), the conditions are $1 \leq I \leq N-1$, $A_I > A_{I+1}$, $I > 1$, $A_{I-1} > A_{I+1}$ (because A_I and A_{I+1} were exchanged in box 3), and SORTED = *false*.

The next question to be answered is, "What input data will cause this set of conditions?" In the example, the 3-element array $A = (3,2,1)$ satisfies these criteria for $I = 2$.

Usually, each data set tests a number of flowlines all at once. For example, the array $A = (3,2,1)$ causes traversal of flowlines 1,2,3 (and 4), 16, and 18 for $I = 1$; then flowlines 2, 3, (and 4), 5, 6 (and 7), 8 (and 9), 10, 14, and 18 for $I = 2$; and, finally, flowline 19 for $I = 3$. All that remains is to test

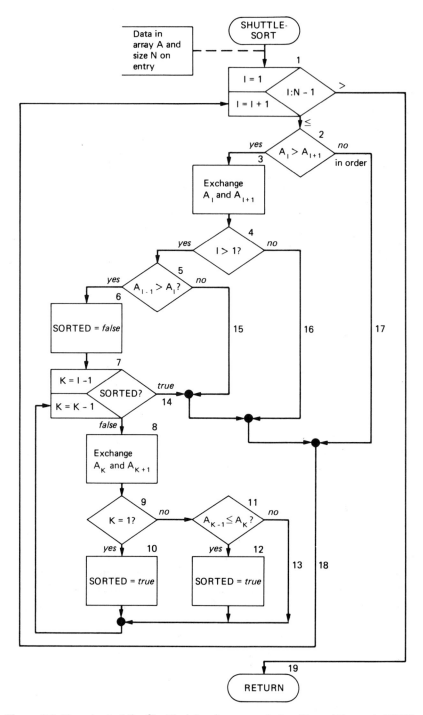

Figure 9-6. Flowchart of the Shuttle-Interchange sort algorithm of Example 7.3.3.2

flowlines 11, 12, 13, 15, and 17. The array $A = (1,5,4,3,2)$ fulfills this need. The composite array $A = (3,2,1,7,6,5,4)$ causes traversal of the whole program.

Although each flowline has now been tested, each path (i.e., valid combination of flowlines) through the program has not been tested. Hence, there may yet be errors in the program, but confidence that this is not the case is very high. Still, to be sure, it is wise to submit the program to the trivial (?) case $A = (1)$, and to as large a sample of random data as may be expected to appear in operation.

The simpler cases, such as $A = (1)$ and $A = (3,2,1,7,6,5,4)$, can be checked by hand (desk checking); however, to assure that the code matches the flowchart—or whatever medium served for desk checking—it is probably worthwhile also to submit the running program to the same examples used for desk checking.

9.2.5 Other Checkout Techniques

Another useful technique applies whenever the correctness of a module can be established based on an arbitrary value of a parameter, rather than the specific value it must have, as required by the overall program. For example, let me suppose that the overall program requires a buffer of, say, 20,000 words of memory, but the subprograms that access this buffer are programmed parametrically to accommodate a buffer of arbitrary size, B. It might then prove very costly to require the allocation of 20,000 words just to check out the access modules, when a smaller size of, say, 50 would do.

It was pointed out to me by B. Mulhall of the Jet Propulsion Laboratory that many numerical processes to be programmed are either inherently linear, or else have linear sub-parts (perhaps within some limited range of values). Conceptually then, each path through a program could be tagged as to whether it is supposed to produce a linear or nonlinear computation. Inspection of the specified algorithms would indicate the linearity of each such path (each path is a subfunction performed by the entire program).

If the program is a linear process, then the principle of *superposition* holds: If X is an input set resulting in the output data set Y, and if U is an input set resulting in the output set V, then processing X-U should output Y-V.

Even though a few such checks do not prove a program is linear, nevertheless, such tests are relatively easy to perform, and simple to check. Moreover, they increase confidence in using the program, especially when hand-computation of a calibration output set Y is difficult, error-prone, or lengthy.

Moreover, only one such calibration input/output pair is ever needed, say (X,Y). For any other input set U, one may define $W = U + X$; then if the output using U is V and using W is Z, the relationship $V - Z = Y$ should hold.

Code checkout may thus make use of simpler configurations or schemes to simulate facilities not yet available, as preliminary assurances of module integrity. Ultimately, however, the module must be tested in its actual environment. Programmers should thus be careful not to over-checkout their modules using oversimplified test cases.

On occasion, a programmer checking a program discovers that his job would greatly be simplified if he only had a certain debugging aid. On further consideration, he may find that such an aid can be made a general-purpose tool, to aid in many future developments, as well. So he begins developing the tool as a subdevelopment project within his current project.

The trouble with creating debugging tools is that it is the sort of thing a programmer can go wild over and lose his perspective, sometimes spending more time developing the tools than on developing the program. For this reason, it is probably best to develop such aids in small stages, with programmatic justification required for each enhancement. Otherwise, the effort can be very wasteful of project resources.

9.2.6 Prognosis for Success

In the design and coding of a program from the top down, the control logic has been made explicit, and it has been possible to test and verify that control logic with explicit, well-defined input data. On the other hand, data structures (other than control flags) and the functions which operate on them may have been verified more implicitly, since data may not actually get stored into these hierarchically defined structures until the very lowest operations in the hierarchy have been coded. There is, therefore, probably a larger chance for errors to occur in functions which operate on data hierarchies than there is in the functions which affect module control.

But even if data structures are perhaps more likely to be accessed incorrectly, or have the wrong information stored in them, nevertheless the module *control-logic* and *functional intent* will have been kept intact. What is most likely to go wrong, then, is that some of the data structures will be improperly interfaced, or some of the module correctness assessments based on assumptions not later fulfilled.

The first type of problem usually gets cleared up after a few tests are run and a *consistent* interface defined (and adhered to). A module whose function is correct but whose data accesses are found to be in error can be corrected at the detected level or modified at the later, exploded levels of that module as required, without upward side effects. With high likelihood, if such errors have not been permitted to remain unmended as the program develops, the program will be correct.

9.3 ASSESSING REAL-TIME PROGRAM CORRECTNESS

The structures introduced for real-time, concurrent programming (Chapter 6) and the concept of program consistency imposed as disciplines on program development separate the procedural correctness from proofs of timing correctness. Procedural correctness assessment of a real-time program is compatible with the formal and machine-aided assessments of correctness of non-real-time programs discussed previously. But formal proofs may be discounted from practicality for all but a select few, small programs.

The central problem then lies in selecting tests that infer probable correctness. Structured, consistent programming permits verification tests during development on a systematic basis. The principal difficulties in testing a multiprogram (presuming that the operating system makes consistency possible) will be in defining test data sets that cause all flowlines to be traversed, and then interpreting the "trace" of that program activity with respect to program-defined requirements.

Because concurrent processes can communicate data among themselves, the problem of defining input data sets to traverse each path segment at least once becomes more difficult. That is, each process not only depends on its owned input, but also on that shared with other processes; moreover, the data communicated between processes may be time-dependent, thus, harder to control.

Brinch Hansen [75] describes the testing methods used to validate the RC 4000 Monitor, which forms the nucleus of its multiprogramming system, multiplexing a single CPU among concurrent process and implementing the procedures that these processes may use to create other processes and send messages to them. In that case, the test stubs consisted of a hierarchy of simulated user processes selected to exercise a minimal set of Monitor functions that would give significant information about its handling of concurrent events. First, tests verified the multiplexer mechanism; then, the process communication procedures within multiplexed programs; next, all possible interactions between processes and peripheral devices of various types; and finally, the file system. As a result, the Monitor was virtually error-free within a few weeks.

One significant aspect of the Monitor program was that it was written *after* the testing philosophy had been specified. That is, the Monitor was designed with testability assigned a role of paramount importance. The *ways* that its processes *could* interact were designed in terms of the *tests* that could be performed to validate that interaction.

McCornock [76], for example, describes the development of a "synthetic environment" (which models the host computer, its operating system, and peripherals) to test real-time programs. Real-time process-control programs can be imbedded in this model and executed interpretively in parametric time (simulated real time) during the program development phase. This procedure separates out all the non-timing problems, and is capable of detecting many of the timing errors, as well. It further permits the majority of the program production to be accomplished using a computer with perhaps less than the full complement of peripherals or capabilities than the one in which the program will later be required to operate.

From the viewpoint of the software being executed, McCornock's synthetic environment is real. Devices are simulated, but the *actual program code* is executed, albeit in a controlled way. The program in its synthetic environment can even be run as a batch job, if desired. The testing speed of the program can thus be very high, because the rate of execution is not geared to peripheral speed, but to execution speed of the model environment. Control of the model resides in a set of data images stored on magnetic tape or punched cards. Changing operating modes, hardware characteristics, or "timing" of events is simple; evaluating their effect is made possible by the repeatability of the results.

But, in the end, the synthetic environment is still synthetic, and only a model of reality. The extent to which the model has validly simulated actuality has permitted program development to succeed to that extent. The final confirmation of correctness must come from the program operating in its true environment.

9.4 CONFIDENCE LIMITS FOR VERIFICATION TESTING

Correctness and reliability of software are crucial as practical matters for nearly all large programs and programming systems that are used on a continuing operational basis. Such programs are constantly being tested, as a part of normal operational usage, and errors continue to be uncovered long after the program has become operational, despite all precautions taken and all disciplines used during the development phase. Many postulate that no large system can ever be completely error-free.

Given a large program, its correctness is a matter of fact and not a matter of probability; the number of errors that a program contains is a fixed, although usually unknown, quantity.

However, the number of errors that can be found by testing tends to be a random variable, since it is very rare that all the possible responses of a program can ever be completely verified. Since any set of responses tested is in some sense a random sample of the entire set of all responses, the number of errors discovered during a test reflects on both the reliability of the program and the adequacy of testing.

Of course, if one sticks to exercising only the tried-and-proved cases, then one can be 100% sure that the program operates as it should (unless something has been tampered with in the meantime). But what of the untested cases? Is there any way to estimate the likelihood that a randomly chosen, untried case will perform correctly?

The answer is yes, although the reader may well appreciate that the accuracy in estimating or predicting a program's reliability from analyzing experience data is significantly influenced by how well the statistical model fits actuality; that is, how well the assumed error-effect and error-probing mechanisms mirror the actual errors and the way these are encountered by tests. The use of statistical inference techniques can, nevertheless, provide a worthwhile gauge of program correctness, and can help to define testing methods, test criteria and test procedures to demonstrate a program's reliability within a given confidence level.

The remainder of this section is devoted to one such technique that permits end-to-end verification that a program contains no more than a prescribed number of errors, subject to a quantifiable confidence factor.

9.4.1 Calibration of Testing Adequacy

Mills [77] transcribed Feller's theory of "Estimation of the Size of Animal Population by Recapture Data" [78] into software terms, and built upon it a simple, useful concept for designing and conducting tests, and inferring program reliability from the test results.

The model assumed by Mills is the following. The program to be tested is presumed to contain an unknown number of "indigenous" errors, which are the subject of investigation. Finding these, or at least estimating their number, is the object of "testing".

The method for estimating the number of indigenous errors consists of inserting a number of "calibration" errors covertly into the program before submitting the program to testing. Testing then reveals and locates a certain number of the errors, some of which are calibration errors (unknown to the testers at the time), and the remainder are indigenous. The calibration errors are then revealed.

If the insertion and testing are presumed to be unbiased (that is, so that errors of either kind are found without bias), then the theory states that the maximum likelihood estimator for the total number of errors in the program is given by the formula

$$\hat{e} = \frac{ic}{k}$$

in which the symbols represent:

$\hat{e}$ = the estimated number of indigenous errors

c = the number of calibration errors inserted

i = the number of indigenous errors found by the test

k = the number of calibration errors found by the test.

When k = c (all calibration errors are found by testing), then i (the number of indigenous errors found by testing) is the maximum likelihood estimate of how many there actually are. However, the estimate $\hat{e}$ is merely the most likely value for the total number of errors, based on the data; it does not reveal how confidently one can rely on that estimate. There is the possibility, since the actual number of errors in the program is still unknown, that errors, other than the ones that were found, are still lurking about, ready to pounce on an unsuspecting user.

Fortunately, Mills also gives a method for estimating the confidence that one can have in stating, "There are no more than E errors in the program", and, thereby, for specifying test criteria to validate such a statement, to within a given confidence level. The method forces testing to continue until a prescribed number, k, of the calibration errors are found, and then stops to examine the indigenous errors.

Let it be supposed that there are actually e errors in the program (but e is unknown). Confidence in the statement "no more than E errors exist" can be gauged as follows: If $i > E$, then, obviously, the hypothesis is false and would be rejected immediately; it warrants no confidence at all. But if $i \leq E$, then it is of concern whether other similar (random) tests would have produced $i > E$ (proving again that the hypothesis is false).

Thus, if $e > E$, then with calculable probability, the hypothesis, "no more than E errors exist", will be proved a lie by testing; no such statement would thus be made. The confidence one may take when such a statement can be made, therefore, is equal to this probability, that testing a program with any $e > E$ would find $i > E$, and prevent the lie from being told. Hence, the (pre-test) confidence factor is

$$\text{conf (``no more than E errors'')} = \min_{e > E} \ \text{Prob}\,\{i > E\}$$

Hereafter, I will refer to the left-hand side merely as "conf($\leq$ E)"; the minimum value is necessary (as a worst-case) because the actual value of e is unknown *a priori*. The numerical value for the confidence level when i errors are detected is given by

$$\text{conf}\,(\leq E) = \begin{cases} 0 & \text{for } i > E \\[2ex] \dfrac{\dbinom{c}{k-1}}{\dbinom{E+1+c}{E+k}} & \text{for } i \leq E \end{cases}$$

When testing continues until all of the calibration errors have been found (i.e., $k = c$), the formula reduces to

$$\text{conf}\,(\leq E) = \begin{cases} 0 & \text{if } i > E \\[2ex] \dfrac{c}{c+E+1} & \text{if } i \leq E \end{cases}$$

Figure 9-7 illustrates this confidence factor for c = k = 9, 19, and 99. As is shown, the confidence in a test with c = 9 that claims a program contains no errors is 90%; for the same test to validate that there are under 2 errors, the confidence drops to 75%.

Confidence in stating "≤ E" drops as E increases and as fewer calibration errors are used. These characteristics fit with intuition: The more calibration errors used and then found, the more thorough must be the testing to find them (and any indigenous errors, as well). The more indigenous errors a program is assumed to have, the less certain are tests to locate them all.

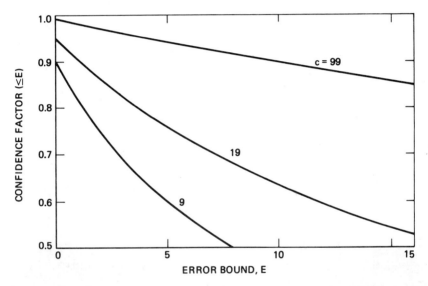

Figure 9-7. Pre-test confidence factor for cases in which all calibration errors are located by testing (c = k), as a function of presumed upper bound on number of errors

9.4.2 Test Monitoring

Testing by the method described above requires a test monitor and a test conductor. The monitor knows where the calibration errors are located and what they are. The test conductor knows neither of these things, although he may know the number that have been inserted.

As errors are located by the testing, they are presented to the monitor, who then reveals their type, calibration or indigenous, one by one. Testing ceases when either all calibration errors are found before E + 1 indigenous errors appear (a successful demonstration), or else when E + 1 indigenous errors are located before all c of the calibration errors appear (the demonstration fails).

Figures 9-8 and 9-9 illustrate two examples of a "test progress" chart; one of the programs passed its test, the other failed. Both programs were tested to demonstrate fewer than 7 errors, with 75% confidence (c = 21). Both figures also show maximum likelihood estimates for the total number of errors, calculated as each error was detected. As may be seen, the error estimator is subject to wide variations, especially during the early testing.

Although verifying, at a given confidence level, that a program is error-free is no less rigorous than demonstrating that a program has no more than an arbitrary higher number of errors, the amount of administrative work in preparing and monitoring the tests can be significantly less in the zero-error case. The number of calibration errors to be generated is less; the work of locating, cataloging, and, perhaps, repairing errors, is less (remember, most of the errors in the program during the test are calibration errors); and, if calibration errors are repaired as they are discovered, the costs in reassemblies or recompilations may become a significant cost factor. If not repaired, they may seriously hamper finding the others.

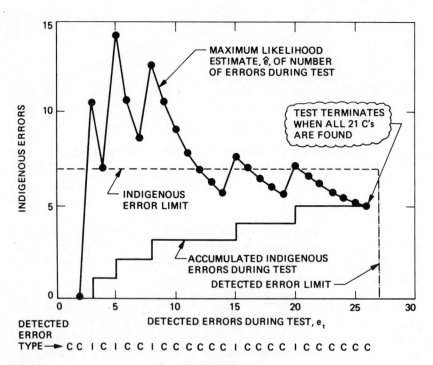

Figure 9-8. Test Progress Chart for a program to verify that it has fewer than 7 errors with 75% confidence level

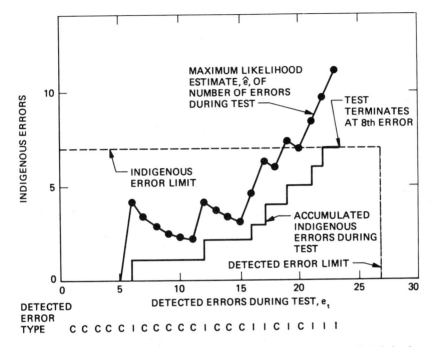

Figure 9-9. Test Progress Chart for a program that failed to show that it had no more than 7 errors (test designed for 75% confidence level)

9.4.3 Creating Effective Calibration Errors

The confidence-testing theory, which is being discussed here, depends on generating and insertng errors similar in nature to the errors (if any) that exist already in the program. Without knowing (or suspecting) what type of errors these may be, probably the best way is to insert errors at random.

There are many types of errors that this method does not apply to, because there are many ways to fix a program with errors (including rewriting the entire program so that it no longer resembles the original). However, for programs already highly reliable, one normally thinks of correcting errors by changing or adding a statement or a few statements. This, too, suggests that the idea of inserting errors randomly through the program will provide a useful model for testing. A procedure for doing this insertion is as follows:

> If there are c errors to be inserted, generate c random numbers and multiply each of these by the number of lines of code in the program. Then go into the program at these line numbers and alter the code (leave out the line, add a new line (or lines), misreference a variable, change a

constant, branch to the wrong label, make an array smaller or larger than it should be, clear a data cell, etc.) choosing the error type at random, as well.

It is not difficult to conceive of automatic algorithms for various programming languages to randomly introduce such errors but maintain correct syntax, for recompiling and testing. The error frequencies could be set to reflect actual experience in the given language at a given stage of development.

The highest confidence factor is achieved when testing continues until all c of the calibration errors are found. Testing to verify an assumed upper limit of errors, within a given level of confidence, can therefore be achieved by inserting and finding c calibration errors, where

$$c = \frac{(E + 1)\,\mathrm{conf}\,(\leq E)}{1 - \mathrm{conf}\,(\leq E)}$$

For example, to demonstrate with 90% confidence that there are no errors, only 9 calibration errors are required; to demonstrate with 99% confidence that there are no errors, 99 calibration errors are needed; to demonstrate with 75% confidence that there are no more than 200 errors, 603 calibration errors must be inserted.

The reader may well note that the number of calibration errors for insertion grows sharply as higher confidence levels are required and proportionately as a greater number of errors are supposed to exist. To verify with 90% confidence that a program is error-free only takes 9 calibration errors; to demonstrate with 75% confidence that a program contains no more than 5 errors, 18 calibration errors are required.

This does not mean, however, that it is easier to verify zero-error programs at 90% confidence than 18-error ones at 75% confidence. Quite the contrary. If a program has only 5 errors, it passes the latter test 100% of the time; it passes the former test less than 10% of the time.

Thus, to raise test confidence when only a fraction of the calibration errors are sought, it is necessary to raise the number of calibration errors inserted, and to find the appropriate percentage of these. There just isn't any way around thorough testing when a high confidence factor is at stake!

9.4.4 Post-Test Confidence Factors

Let me again assume that testing proceeds until the kth calibration error is detected, whereupon testing ceases, having uncovered $i = I$ indigenous errors. Knowing that there are at least I errors is more than was known before the test was run. This extra information can be used to refine the confidence estimate.

The post-test confidence factor for the statement, "there are no more than E errors if I-errors are found", is

$$\text{conf}\,(\leq E | I) = \min_{e > E}\ \text{Prob}\,\{i > I | e\}$$

and the formula for it is

$$\text{conf}\,(\leq E | I) = \sum_{i = I+1}^{E+1} \frac{\binom{E+1}{i}\binom{c}{k-1}}{\binom{E+c+1}{i+k-1}} \cdot \frac{c-k+1}{E+c+2-i-k}$$

As may be noted, the pre-test conf($\leq$ E) value is the same as the post-test conf($\leq$ E | E). For the case. k = c, there is a recursion formula to facilitate calculating the post-test confidence factor,

$$\text{conf}\,(\leq E + 1 | I) = \text{conf}\,(\leq E | I) + \left(\frac{c}{E+c+1}\right)[1 - \text{conf}\,(\leq E | I)]$$

Figure 9-10 illustrates the shape of the post-test confidence factor curves for the case k = c = 9 as a function of E for various values of I. As shown in the figure, if 2 indigenous errors are found by testing (I = 2), then there is at least 75% confidence that no more exist; there is 92% confidence that there are fewer than 4 errors, 97% confidence that there are fewer than 5 errors, etc. A test that finds no errors shows 90% confidence that there are no more; there is 98% confidence that there are fewer than 2 errors, 99% confidence that there are fewer than 3 errors, etc.

When testing fails to reveal all c of the calibration errors, stopping after the kth is found, then the effectiveness of the test is reduced, as is the confidence in the indigenous error bounds. The zero-error case takes a particularly simple form that illustrates the degradation very well:

$$\text{conf}\,(\text{no errors}) = \frac{k}{c+1}$$

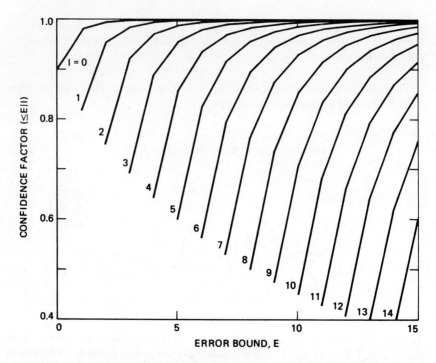

Figure 9-10. Post-test confidence factor for stating that a program has no more than E errors when I-values have been located by testing, for the case c = k = 9

Thus, if no errors have been detected when testing stops after finding 8 calibration errors of the 9 inserted, then the test confidence drops from the 90% expected; should testing have continued successfully to the detection of the 9th calibration error, to only 80%.

9.5 SUMMARY

The methods I have put forth in earlier chapters toward increasing program reliability are ones that encourage proper attention to detail in design by forcing a certain level of documentation and informal assurance of correctness along with the design before coding begins. Then coding has the opportunity to check the design as the program evolves, to the extent that, when the program is completed, every statement of code will have been executed at least once. (More than this, each flowline will have been traversed.) I have also mentioned a method for demonstrating program reliability based on confidence levels.

I realize that conditions and systems will vary from organization to organization and from project to project, making it perhaps impossible to establish a detailed standard correctness philosophy that will apply equally to every condition. Nevertheless, an overall methodology is not impossible, to identify and define candidate disciplines for software reliability calibration. There is a direct application of such methods in all software development projects, large and small—only the scopes and magnitudes of the efforts will change.

Problems for Chapter 9

9-1 Make a list, and discuss each item in the list, of techniques that can be used for debugging programs, but do not particularly depend on the set of aids available on a particular system. Discuss the aids you think should be available for debugging in a "standard software production system"

9-2 Draw a flowchart for the sieve of Eratosthenes (see Figure 8-8) and annotate it with assertions on each flowline. Prove each inductive assertion and then prove the end assertion in a rigorous, formal, mathematical way.

9-3 Write a set of dummy stubs for the CONTROL, REPORT, ERROR, CARDIN, EXTRACT, VSTORE, LSTORE, and ALLSTORE modules of the REFERENCES program shown in Figures 8-19 and 8-20. Design these to validate all control paths of the program by traversing every flowline at least once. Each module should print the module name and the value of control elements for that path. Then play the part of the computer and execute the program. From the output, assess whether the program is correct at this level of design by comparing the required behavior with the sequence of actions taken.

9-4 The subroutine SQRT shown below computes the square root of the incoming argument X and exits with $X^{1/2}$ in the A0 register. Attach control-logic assertions to each flowline that satisfy the criteria in Section 9.1.2. Prove rigorously that the algorithm terminates and that, on normal termination, A0 contains $X^{1/2}$.

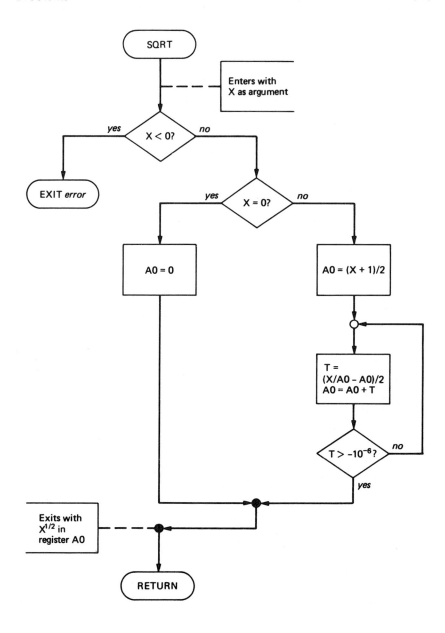

9-5 Design and flowchart (or code in CRISP) a program that will scan a CRISP source listing and then print the conditions for traversing each flowline. Comment on the utility of such a program for designing test data to validate other programs.

9-6 Devise tests that will validate the "Readers and Writers" program given in Example 7.3.3.4 (of Chapter 7).

9-7 The sequence of bits generated by the formula $a_{n+k} = a_{m+k} \oplus a_k$ is known to exhibit excellent random properties when n and m are properly chosen [79], n is the word size and "$\oplus$" is modulo 2 (exclusive or) addition. Starting with a word $w = (a_{n-1}, a_{n-2}, \ldots, a_0)$, the following procedure produces random words:

```
procedure: Random word w
.1   let register R=w <*the word from last time*>
.2   right-shift R by m bits, zero fill on left
.3   exclusive-or this R with w
.4   store result back in w
.5   left-shift R by n-m bits, zero fill on right
.6   exclusive-or this R with w
.7   store result back in w <* save for next time*>
end procedure.
```

Now the problem: prove that this algorithm produces as its next word the value $w = (a_{2n-1}, a_{2m-2}, \ldots, a_n)$ and thus, by induction, that each call of the procedure generates the next n bits in sequence.

9-8 Devise a test tree or set of test trees that cause every flowline of the CRISP-PDL post-order traverse program in Section 7.3.2 of Chapter 7 to be exercised. Then "run" the procedure on this test data with an appropriate dummy stub for "process this node". Be sure to include the PDL for the stub.

9-9 Rewrite the post-order traverse program to perform a pre-order walk. Test it and use the same PDL style as in Problem 9-8.

9-10 Compute the number of calibration errors needed in the post-order walk problem to build a 66.7% confidence level in the program. Insert this number of errors, of a subtle, minor nature, into the program and resubmit to the previous (all flowline) test. Did the test find all the calibration errors? If not, then how many?

X. PROJECT ORGANIZATION AND MANAGEMENT

For small, or perhaps even intermediate-sized programs, one person may be able to do all the design, coding, testing, and program maintenance tasks himself. But for larger programs he needs help. This chapter provides some guidelines toward the composition of a software development team, the roles of its members, their responsibilities, and the procedures they are to follow when developing a medium-to-large scale piece of software.

The approach parallels much of IBM's "Chief Programmer Team" or "CPT" concept [80], but is more flexible and tailored to the development procedures I have discussed up to this point. As in the Chief Programmer Team, the project organization I will describe separates the work of program development into specialized jobs, defines the relationships among specialists, and devises tools to permit these specialists to interface effectively. The project personnel work as members of a team rather than as individuals.

A definitive analysis of what constitutes good project organization and management practices is beyond the scope of this chapter. All I can hope to give are highlights, guidelines and examples of the kinds of things that need to be considered in developing top-down software effectively. I recommend to the reader interested in a more comprehensive treatment the work of TRW [81] contained in their Software Development and Configuration Management Manual.

10.1 SOFTWARE TEAM PRODUCTIVITY

An intelligent, hardworking programmer working by himself may be able to write a program of many thousands of lines of code in a relatively short time. Typically, such a person puts in many long hours, talks to very few of his co-workers, keeps very sketchy notes of his programs, but is very productive in actually producing lines of code. But as the size of a program grows, it becomes necessary at some point to add members to the development effort. Two equally capable programmers are usually not able to produce twice as much work as a single programmer. If a third programmer is added, he usually adds less to the overall output than was added by the second. As a result, a programmer working as a part of a team is less productive than if he were working by himself.

In the remainder of this section, I want to discuss this phenomena and propose organizational and programming guidelines to combat decreasing incremental productivity.

10.1.1 A Simple Model

The key to the insights I want to develop can be correlated with the following tremendously oversimplified analysis of a software team's productivity. Let me define *index of productivity* by the formula

$$P \triangleq \frac{L}{WT}$$

in which L represents the total number of lines of source code (excluding comment lines) delivered (i.e., *error free*) at the end of the project, W is the number of workers contributing to the product, and T is the average time each worker spent developing the software. The unit of this productivity index is lines/day.

For example, if 83,000 lines of source code were delivered in 22 months (477 working days) by an 11-man year effort (an average of 6 team members), then their team productivity was P = 29 lines/day. This is the figure published for IBM's New York Times project [82], the first to use the Chief-Programmer Team concept.

Let me apologize for the oversimplified measure of productivity by saying that I will use the measure only to provide some broad insights into why there are apt to be inherent difficulties with large projects, if improperly organized. It may be possible to refine the productivity model to account for such things as different levels of expertise, variation in salaries, etc., but I think the insights remain the same.

In the development effort, there are a number of software tasks to be performed, among which are:

    a. Design.

    b. Coding.

    c. Checkout.

    d. Documentation.

    e. Supervision.

    f. Acceptance testing.

    g. Quality Assurance.

There may be others, but these suffice for the argument to follow.

10.1.2 Task Separation

Let me first suppose (not seriously, however) that each of the seven software tasks above is undertaken by a single individual. There is then a complete separation of task areas within the project. This assignment means that the designer must design the equivalent of WP lines per day, the coder must code this many per day, the persons doing checkout and testing must test this many, the documentor must document all the design, coding, testing, etc., of WP lines per day, and the supervisor must oversee the activity of his team operating at this pace.

To match the New York Times Project's 29 lines per day, each of the seven members of the project I am describing must produce the equivalent of $7 \cdot 29 = 203$ *correct* lines per day.

But there is more to the story. In order for the project to run smoothly, it is necessary that each individual spend part of his time communicating with each of the other team members. For example, the designer must confer with the coder to resolve any questions the coder may have about the design; both of these must talk to the individual testing the code to give him the benefit of their experience with the program; each of these must talk to the documentor to assure that the documentation is proper and complete; and so on.

Thus each member may devote only a certain fraction of time to active production. The rest of the time is spent in necessary conference with teammates. Let me oversimplify again and suppose that the average time splits into

$$T = T_p + (W - 1) T_{np}$$

where T_p represents the average "productive" time, and T_{np} represents the average "non-productive" time each worker spends interfacing with each of the other team members. "Non-productive" time here does not mean non-useful or unnecessary—it means only that the individual is engaged in an activity other than active production in his task area.

The rate, or individual productivity level P_I that each team.member must sustain during his "productive" periods so that the team have overall productivity P, is given by

$$P_I = \frac{L}{T_p} = \frac{WP}{1 - (W - 1)(T_{np}/T)}$$

Obviously, as depicted in Figure 10-1, too many workers can spoil things! If the average time spent communicating ever reached the fraction,

$$\frac{T_{np}}{T} = \frac{1}{W - 1}$$

then the project is doomed! In order for these seven workers to output 29 lines per day, spending 5% of their time communicating with each other project member, each member must work at the rate of 290 lines of code per day!

10.1.3 Job Integration

Now let me suppose that *one* individual were to undertake the entire project and was capable of doing each of the seven tasks himself. The time spent in inter-task communication is then zero; all the material to be communicated is already in mind. This one individual, therefore, must design the equivalent of only P correct lines per day, code P lines per day, check out P lines per day, and so forth. All his time is productive. Intuitively, then, it might seem much more plausible to have one capable person do all seven tasks on 29 lines of code per day, rather than having seven people doing individual tasks at the rate of 290 lines per day each.

This is probably true if one person could undertake an entire large program and cope with its complexity; it would, however, take such a person about five times as long to complete the project as the seven-member team above (at a 5% non-productive index). Hence, let us try

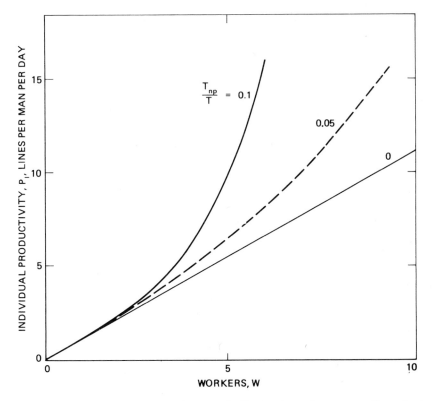

Figure 10-1. Individual productivity required to support an overall project productivity of P = 1 line/day, for non-productive time ratios of 5% and 10%

splitting the project among a number of such individuals to hasten things along.

Suppose that the program were to be segmented into W equally-sized modules, each within the human capability to cope with complexity, and let W workers be assigned, one per module, to perform all the needed tasks (design, coding, documentation, etc.). Each produces P_I lines per day, finished, correct code. As before, let L be the total number of lines of delivered code, and T be the average time each man spent in the project.

If each of the modules were to require the expenditure of non-productive interfacing time T_{np}, then the amount of code completed each day by the project is, on the average

$$\frac{L}{T} = P_I W \left[1 - (W - 1)(T_{np}/T) \right]$$

The figure in braces represents the loss in personnel efficiency due to non-productive interfacing time.

The amount of code that this project can produce per day has a maximum value, found to be (Figure 10-2)

$$\left(\frac{L}{T}\right)_{max} = P_I \left(\frac{1 + (T_{np}/T)}{2(T_{np}/T)}\right)\left[\frac{1 + (T_{np}/T)}{2}\right]$$

The figure in braces again represents the loss in personnel efficiency. This maximum production rate is achieved when the team size is

$$W = \frac{1 + (T_{np}/T)}{2(T_{np}/T)}$$

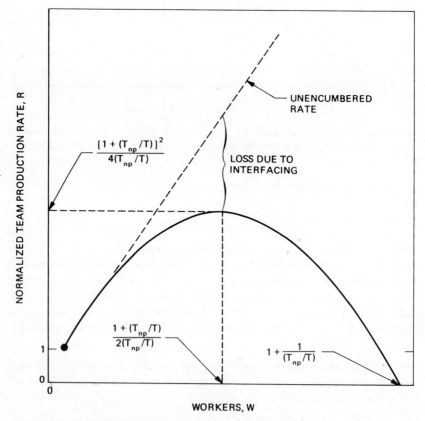

Figure 10-2. Normalized team production rate ($R \triangleq L/TP_I$) as a function of team size and non-productive time index

Notice that the efficiency of this team is never much better than 50% when producing at its maximum rate. For example, at a 5% non-productive index, the personnel efficiency is cut to 52.5%, and 10.5 people produce only 5.5 times as much code as one (ideal) individual. At a 10% non-productive index and 5.5 workers, the maximum rate is only 3 times as great as one individual.

If the New York Times team was of optimum size $(W = 6)$, then the 83,000 lines of code delivered in 22 months would have required an individual productivity index of $P_I = 53$ lines/day and would have had a non-productive time index of 9.1%.

Such a project hoping to deliver L lines within time T using W workers having individual integrated-task productivities P_I must keep their non-productive index within the bound

$$\frac{T_{np}}{T} < \frac{1 - (L/WTP_I)}{W - 1}$$

if there is to be success.

A six-member team attempting to deliver 83,000 lines of code in 22 months using workers skilled to the 35 lines/day level must find some way of limiting their inter-task non-productive-time index to 3.4%—less than 17 minutes a day per interface!

10.1.4 More on Modularity

To maximize productivity, one must reduce to the fullest possible extent all factors causing non-productive time. I used the illustration of seven people doing seven separate, strongly correlated tasks to show how non-productivity can escalate as a project grows in size, if organized along lines requiring human interfaces. The example in which team members performed integrated tasks, but spent non-productive time interfacing the modules, shows that their performance was no better.

In previous chapters, I propounded modularity as a means to combat complexity: modularization by functional segmentation into hierarchic levels having minimized program connections (in data, control, and services). I now add another dimension to modularity: modularization by organization of the program into hierarchic segments that minimize the interfaces required between project personnel. I can also quickly append another dimension: modularization into areas of personnel expertise.

Operating directly on these premises is the Chief Programmer Team concept, developed by IBM as a method to increase productivity in *production programs*; that is, those programs where "off-the-shelf" algorithms apply. Why it works can be argued on the basis that supervision, design, coding, and documentation are largely carried out by the Chief Programmer himself. Design is done mostly in code using "self-documenting" techniques (this merges much of the design, coding, and documentation processes into one activity, decreasing W). Interfaces with other programmers are directly defined in code as arguments passed to their module stubs. Complexity is controlled via structured programming and top-down development.

There are projects, however, that require more definite forms of documentation than descriptive variable names and fixed stub interfaces. Sometimes projects are too large for one person to manage effectively and still handle the Chief Programmer's role. There are company organizations where software management and design are performed in-house, while coding is done on contract (or vice-versa). To the extent that the concepts that pervade the Chief Programmer team are valid, they may be fitted to other organizational disciplines beneficially.

At some point as programs grow large, complexity exceeds the human ability to cope with it; when this happens, individuals spend more time floundering around than they do producing code or beneficially supporting its development. Assigning separate tasks to separate individuals invites, and, indeed, necessitates some non-productive time in the form of inter-task communication. Assigning too large a program segment to one person decreases productivity by fostering non-productive time of a different sort, namely, that needed to cope with program complexity.

10.1.5 Personnel Tradeoffs

The simplified models above leave many factors unaccounted for, and I caution the reader not to stretch their lessons too far. Individual capabilities, unequal salaries, and a host of other factors, [83], many very subjective, must be correctly modeled before an optimized approach to software development can be found.

Several factors are amenable to economic and engineering tradeoff studies, such as the cost benefits of assigning junior people, at lower salaries and skills, to tasks that necessarily raise T_{np}/T. Even though a decrease might occur in team productivity, there may nevertheless be a substantial cost savings in doing so. Junior personnel thus also become trained, increasing their company potential.

10.2 THE SOFTWARE DEVELOPMENT TEAM

The organization of the software development team I shall describe here owes its structure both to the top-down, concurrent design, documentation, coding, and testing concept and to the recognition that high capability for program development is a scarce commodity. Accordingly, the team organizes the work around senior-level professional specialists, in a disciplined, structured team environment.

A division of labor is not always necessary; when programs are small enough to be handled by one individual in a timely manner, then that should be the case. But when it is necessary to assign more personnel, their assignment should be into areas that take maximum advantage of their skills and minimize their non-productive time.

The CPT concept has hit on one way this can be done effectively: top-down, hierarchic, modular structured development. The Chief Programmer performs his activity top-down to a set stubs for completion by specialists. The function and interface for each stub is defined by the Chief Programmer directly in code, to minimize confusion and prevent others from programming to hypothetical interfaces.

A more generalized view of this concept is the division of team members into areas where necessary project documentation forms the personnel interface. I shall describe an example wherein the divisions fall between design, coding, and testing. Since each of these activities must produce documentation as a necessary part of its effort anyway, division into the three prescribed activities provides an opportunity to verify the adequacy of such documentation.

10.2.1 The Team Nucleus

The nucleus of the software development team consists of the Software Project Manager, a Chief Program Designer, a Lead Programmer, a Software Test Engineer, and the Interface Control Engineer. Other specialists may be assigned to this nucleus to aid in designing, coding, or testing modules, as directed by the Software Project Manager. The organization is charted as Figure 10-3.

The separate parts of the team (design, coding, testing) have somewhat different goals, and different requisite skills, as well. These parts interact in a closely-coordinated, interactive way, with checks and balances not only to increase overall productivity, but also to assure product reliability. I will describe this interaction in some detail later in the chapter.

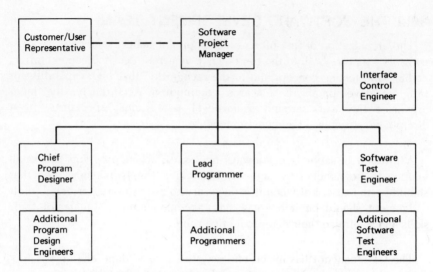

Figure 10-3. Software Development Project Organization

The project is also organized so that any or all of the major comprising efforts can be performed by contract personnel in the event that manpower or expertise in a given area is unavailable directly within the project-imbedded organization. The principal interfaces are indicated in Figure 10-4.

10.2.2 Team Qualifications

Software engineering, much like any other branch of engineering, requires specialized, well-trained, disciplined personnel—people skilled in the management, design, production, and quality assurance aspects of their trade. The organization I have described above defines a certain set of career specialties and a structure in which these specialties are interdependent, but not subordinate, one to the other.

The quality of the software produced is largely a function of the aptitude of the team nucleus. That's the way it should be in a project in which everything proceeds from the top downward. The best people must be placed at the top; competency at the bottom of an organization can't bail out incompetent people at the top because development will generally have been carried too far by the time the lower echelons get into the act.

10.2.3 The Software Project Manager

The Software Project Manager's role in the team is primarily one of technical management. He is there to define project priorities and milestones; to oversee and coordinate the activity of the design, coding, testing, and documentation efforts as the program evolves; to define design,

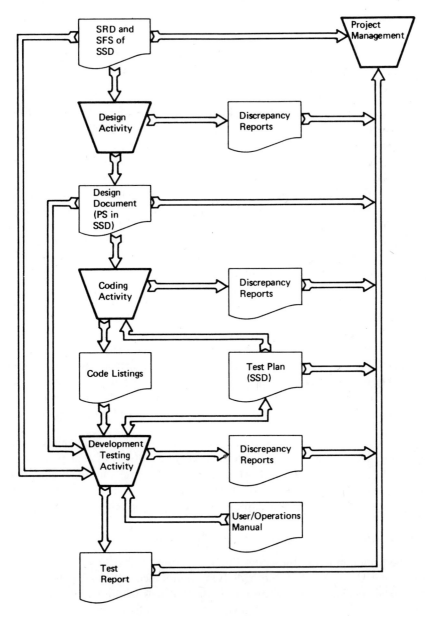

Figure 10-4. Primary Software Development Project interfaces are through necessary project documentation

coding, and testing phases; to allocate resources in the form of schedule, manpower, and computational facilities within his jurisdiction (or to obtain these from higher management should they fall outside his purview); to supervise development, including any redirections that may occur within the project lifetime, such as may occur due to a change in scope or due to some error in the design; to monitor the progress and productivity of the design team members; to review and approve the design, coding, and testing documentation; and to ensure that the program satisfies all requirements for delivery.

However, the Software Project Manager also takes an active part in the software development, technically. He does this, first of all, by supplying the preliminary design concepts to the team, and then by talking to the team members, giving them insights, solutions to problems, cautions to potential problems, and the like. He may also elect, in certain circumstances, to perform some of the technical tasks himself, such as devising program and module tests, or setting coding conventions, or designing some of the early-level modules. He is called on, finally, to assess and judge whether the performance of this team is technically correct and whether their output represents a feasible, efficient, and acceptable embodiment of the project technical goals.

To fulfill these functions, the Software Project Manager must be a highly competent individual, technically in the areas of software design, coding, and testing, as well as verbally for lucid and precise documentation, and administratively to motivate and lead the development team to a successful product. If he is not technically capable, he loses control over his team's productivity; if he does not express himself well, he may not be able to deliver clear enough instructions to get the job done in the most productive way; and if he is administratively ineffective, the project soon bogs down.

Every profession is characterized by highly creative individuals being involved directly in the first-line management functions of that profession. The job of Software Project Manager calls for such an individual. His managerial duties are set according to the structure and needs of the team, to maintain organizational discipline and high productivity.

10.2.4 The Chief Program Design Engineer

The principal job of the Chief Program Design Engineer is to design and document the program to be coded, in compliance with management and technical standards, and to enforce these standards within his design group. He also serves as the Project Manager's top consultant during the detailed functional specification and preliminary, conceptual design phases of the development.

He should be characterized as a highly creative individual, skilled both as a technical writer (for the documentation) as well as one extremely competent and productive in the area of program design. In practice, the Chief Program Designer designs and documents the earlier tiers, as well as other selected, critical phases of the program himself. He then defines program design-stub interfaces for others under his supervision to complete, and he reviews and incorporates the entire work of the design group into one unit.

10.2.5 Lead Programmer

The Lead Programmer's task is to translate the design from documentation into efficient code, to document that code in such a way that it can be audited for conformance to, and cross-referenced with, the design and project standards, and to enforce standards within his programming activity.

The lead programmer works very closely with the software design and testing activities; however, he reports directly to the Project Manager. The lead programmer should be very well versed in the system and environmental aspects of the host computer and thus provide the designers and testers with consultive feedback relative to design efficiencies and testing strategies.

The lead programmer and other members of his team supply dummy stubs as specified in the Software Test Plan, to be used for phase-testing the emerging program. The programmers are not responsible for the design of the stubs, but they are responsible for checking their code before it is delivered into the Software Development Library. Delivery into the library attests that, to the best of their knowledge, the code matches the design, adheres to coding standards, and operates within the test plan specifications.

If checkout uncovers any evidence that there is a program design error, then the program designer is notified; if there is any evidence of a test plan error, then the test engineer. In all cases the notification is written and logged into the project notebook. If checkout uncovers an error in a module belonging to a previous development phase, then a project descrepancy report is filed with the Project Manager for action.

10.2.6 Software Test Engineer

The software test activity has more project interfaces than any of the other activities, except project management. It is this activity that attests to program correctness. The activity is guided by the Software Test Engineer, who is responsible for the generation of the Software Test Plan, for the preparation of validation data by which the program will be verified, for the scheduling and supervision of acceptance tests, for the audit of all documentation and listings prior to delivery for correctness and conformity with standards, and for verifying that all the requirements for delivery of the program have been met. He reports all discrepancies noted during testing and auditing to the Project Manager for appropriate action. He impounds the results of all test runs in the project archives and maintains these archives in a form visible to other members of the team.

The test designer designs input to test all flowlines in modules of the phase currently to be tested and specifies what response all dummy stubs required must have. The test designer may do look-ahead test design, just as the program designer may do look-ahead module design.

In testing the program at the current phase, it is the job of the tester to *validate* the software, *not to debug it*. All failures are recorded in the test report and diagnostic material is given to the appropriate team member.

The Software Test Engineer is also the Project Manager's chief consultant during program definition, with regard to setting goals for testing and for designing testability into the software. The job calls for an individual capable of unwavering attention to meticulous detail. He also needs to have a background of working experience in software definition, design, and coding.

10.2.7 The Project Interface Control Engineer

The principal task of the Interface Control Engineer is to maintain the project personnel and program interfaces in a highly visible and controlled form. These interfaces are the various forms of documentation generated by the three project activities: the SDD, the SSD (which includes the Software Test Plan), code listings, etc. The Interface Control Engineer acts as custodian over all elements accepted into project control, whether it be documentation, coded program modules, dummy stubs, or test data. He alone is permitted to update or append approved elements to the Project Software Development Library (SDL) files and project-controlled documentation. All project documentation and elements of the SDL files are available to any requesting team member through the Interface Control Engineer. I shall discuss the SDL in greater detail a little later on.

The Interface Control Engineer also acts as the Project Manager's aide, taking charge of the project notebook, in which are recorded minutes of meetings, a log of detected discrepancies and their current disposition, a log of standards waivers and reasons for these, the current project schedule and all previous outdated project schedules, an up-to-date tier diagram (see Section 10.5.6), a log of factors causing schedule slippages, a log of changes made (and why) to elements after accepted into project control. A suggested outline for a project notebook appears in Appendix H.

The interface control task requires an individual with some software technical skill, but the main thrust of his background needs to be administrative. It is his ability to organize the custodianship of interfaces and to provide the Project Manager visibility into the current status of development that is his most important role in its effect on the team's performance and on the quality of the software produced.

10.2.8 The Customer/User Representative

For some reason, what a software design is supposed to do is subject to wide interpretation, even after previous agreement. It is important, therefore, to involve the customer or user organization in a formal way, so that it has had the opportunity to concur at earlier points than before final delivery. To give the development team free rein between requirements definition and operation is inviting trouble.

For this reason I have shown a customer/user representative as part of the development team. His involvement is meant to be real, in depth, and continuing throughout the project. He is there to aid in the generation of the functional definition (SFS), to participate in all reviews, and to observe and concur in the acceptance tests. He serves as the applications expert, to analyze the evolving program response to assure that it fulfills the technical objectives required for his application.

10.3 CONDUCT OF THE PROJECT

Now let me address the procedures and interactions among team members during program evolution. I will assume that the Project Manager has just defined a project *phase* as a certain portion of the program to be defined, designed, coded, tested, and documented as a project milestone before proceeding to the next phase. The scope of work in each area need not be uniform, but sized in the most meaningful way. For example, Phase 1 of the software definition activity may be very detailed, whereas Phase 1 of design, coding, and testing may only encompass the first few hierarchic tiers of the program. Portions of a given phase to be undertaken by separate individuals should probably be roughly the same complexity, however.

10.3.1 Work Breakdown Structures

Project phase-planning can be used as a viable method of allocating work keyed on priority of requirements. Such phases provide a medium for cross-referencing and auditing the design and implementation against program requirements and, thereby, also provide the tool for estimating schedules and costs for given, added, or deleted requirements. Monitoring phase status identifies the state of requirement fulfillment relative to the set of project priorities.

The project procedural discipline is shown in Figure 10-5. The diagram shows that definition must precede design, design precedes coding, coding takes place concurrently with test design. Design is based on definition, coding is based on design and definition, and so on. All design and coding of striped modules takes place in top-down hierarchic order within the scope of the defined phase. Coding begins only when the design has become well established and stable; developmental testing then can take place with the view of establishing correctness, not debugging the design.

Figure 10-5 does not show look-ahead efforts, nor does it apply to the earlier architectural design phase. Both are used to identify the key details and likely problems of the development and also to size the effort and permit the work breakdown structure to be formulated.

10.3.2 Joint Programmer-Reader Collaboration

A requirement levied in Chapter 9 to aid in assessment of program correctness was that documentation be carried to that detail which permits an audit of a module algorithm against its stated function at the previous level of the design. The purpose of such an audit is to ensure that everything assumed by the parent-level design actually appears within the module, that everything actually appearing in the module design is traceable back to the stated module function, and that design standards have been adhered to. Such an audit will decrease the possibility of oversight, prevent the augmentation or alteration of the design unilaterally at the later design stages without proper approval or integration of that augmentation in the design, and maintain a uniform, standardized design.

Notice that I have made no statement concerning the process of validating the module algorithm as part of the design audit. Rather, the auditing process is purely a "bookkeeping" job, something which keeps the design "honest". It can, and preferably should, be done by someone other than the designer himself, say a Quality Assurance representative. In a later chapter, I address the possibility of automated design auditing.

However, as in all good engineering practices, the design itself should be *verified*. Design verification, as it is meant here, is a careful examination of the design by someone skilled in design. Perhaps the best choice for this job is the designer's supervisor; at the least, it should be a peer or senior colleague. The purpose is to get corroborative concurrence that the design at the current level is correct (i.e., that it will do what it is supposed to do) and is "good" by whatever criteria have been established for the project.

The verification can take the form of a "structured walk-through", if desired. A *structured walk-through* is a generic name given to review or "paper tests" conducted with peers, supervisors, etc., to analyze the

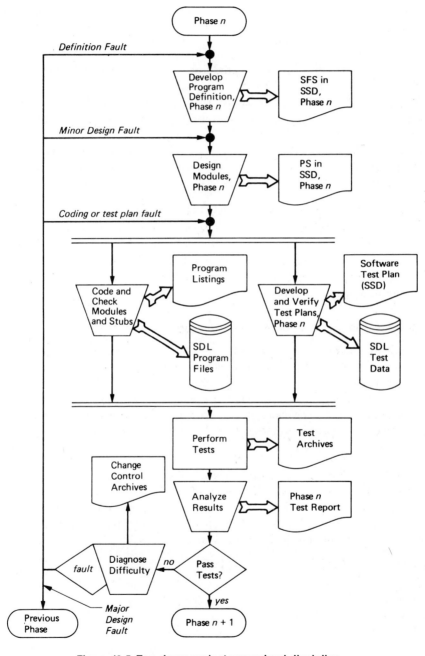

Figure 10-5. Top-down project procedural discipline

functional design, detect logic errors, develop test strategy, cross-educate team members, and motivate full team cooperation. The verification is meant to be a non-malicious collaborative procedure for probing and problem detection. Errors found at this level can easily be an order of magnitude cheaper to fix than at later times in the development.

The code should also be audited by someone other than the coder himself, say by his supervisor, or a Quality Assurance representative. The purpose of this audit is to assure that the code is, in fact, a direct translation of the design, that it is properly anotated, organized, etc., and that it is written in accordance with accepted standards pertaining to format, coding conventions, etc. National Information Systems, Inc. uses the procedure shown in Figure 10-6 to code the program from procedural specifications.

As with the other activities, verification of the test procedure, too, is in order: a non-malicious, but collaborative critical examination by a person or persons other than the test designer. Depending on circumstances, such an examination might will be performed by his supervisor, the Project Manager, the program designer, the coder, an intended user of the program, or a combination of these.

10.3.3 Concurrent Coding and Development Testing

Human fallibility and inability to cope with complexity in large programs, even with the benefits afforded by the top-down approach, dictate that there be some form of automatic checking of the design. The concurrent coding concept provides just what is needed for doing this task. It provides a way of checking how a program actually operates, to see if it matches the designer's intent, level by level through the program development process.

Once modules at a given phase have been successfully verified (corroborated and audited), the design documentation is inserted into the Software Specification Document, the code integrated into the previously verified program, the tests retained in the project test archives, and the results documented in The Software Test Report (STR).

But suppose a test fails. What then? There is an error somewhere—in the design, in the coding, in the dummy stubs, in the test data, or in the test procedure itself—and it must be fixed. This fix does not mean that those concerned put their heads together and patch the code until it seems to work. What happens is that, first, the cause of the failure is located. Then, if the error is one in coding, it is corrected and the tests rerun. Similarly, if the error is in the test, it is fixed, the test procedure reverified, and the test rerun. However, if the error is in the design, the designer must reconsider

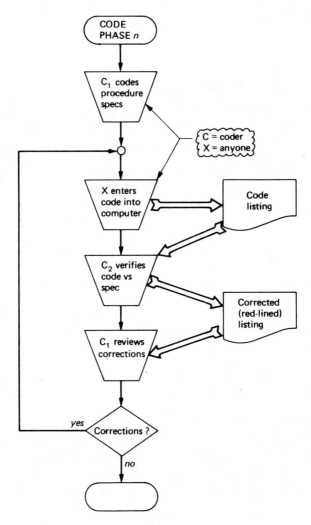

Figure 10-6. Joint coder-reader collaboration in coding the procedural specifications

his design and make whatever changes are required. If the changes he makes involve alterations at a previous phase, an appropriate return to that phase for coding and testing is in order.

10.3.4 Task Interfacing

I have defined project tasks that allow personnel to communicate with each other through *needed* documentation in a formal way. However, the documentation during this production need not be of publication quality. Formal, high-quality documentation is very costly and time-consuming to produce, and thereby gathers a lot of inertia. For this reason, designers and implementors loathe to make any but the easiest or least drastic changes; hence, premature formalized documentation has a tendency to "set things in concrete" before they really should be.

The Software Development Library, to be discussed in the next section, makes use of flexible, easily modifiable automatic documentation media to the maximum feasible extent to avoid the costs and inertia of hand maintenance. In many cases, however, hand-produced documentation is necessary and desirable. Many designers prefer to sketch their ideas, in the form of flow charts and to use these as interfacing documentation to coders. They have a tendency to work on an entire phase in one chunk, and then, when they feel it is appropriate, to release a whole sheaf of program modules all at once. If these have to be redrawn before a verifier or coder gets to them, then there is an unnecessary delay while the documentation is being brought up to quality. Several iterations of this process may be required to remove typographical errors and the like.

Therefore, while I have placed documentation in series between tasks, I by no means wish to have the redocumentation personel (typists, draftsmen, etc.) appear in series between tasks. In many cases, design sketches and handwritten notes can be given simultaneously to verifiers, coders, and redocumentors to avoid delays.

One such scheme, used by National Information Systems, Inc. on several of its projects, where required documentation consisted of template drawn, typed flow charts and typed narrative, is illustrated in Figure 10-7; the procedural discipline displayed is almost identical to that shown in Figures 10-5 and 10-4. The key feature of the procedure stressed by the figure is that designers and coders work generally from red-lined photostatic copies while any changes are being retyped. Another key feature of this procedure is that it keeps the documentation concurrent and accurate.

10.4 SOFTWARE PRODUCTION MANAGEMENT AND CONTROL

Inherent to efficient and successful program development is proper production management and control. The ability to maintain current status and configuration control of project documentation is a vital necessity for program management visibility.

10.4.1 The Software Development Library

The Software Development Library (SDL), Figure 10-8, is modeled after the chief programmer team Programming Support Library [84], and exists for the same purpose: to maintain the current status of the program and

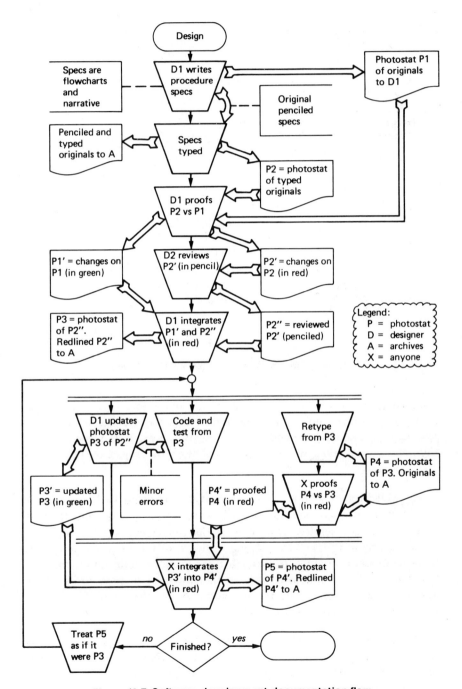

Figure 10-7. Software development documentation flow

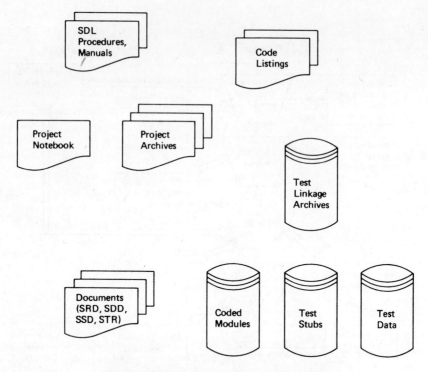

Figure 10-8. The Software Development Library

associated test stubs and test data in a public form, so that project personnel can work more effectively and with fewer errors, in a disciplined manner that encourages good engineering practices. It is responsible for the control, retention, storage, and distribution of project documentation and programs.

The SDL supports project management by providing visibility into the development process, and it supports the software development team by providing special services and configuration management. The SDL also serves an archiving function, keeping a record of the project history. The team members communicate through this visible medium rather than less tangible interfaces, and thereby have the potential to raise productivity. The SDL also provides a medium for enforcement of standards in all visible forms of the evolving product.

There are three parts of the SDL. The first is composed of the requirements, design definition, design, and test documentation (SRD, SDD, SSD, STR) accepted into the project under change control. Such documentation may not be altered without approval of the Project Manager (or his designate).

The second part of the SDL is composed of the actual developing program modules, test stubs, and test data. Programs are always kept at least in their symbolic (human readable) form, and possibly also in a compiled, executable form, as well. Modules accepted into project control may not be changed without approval of the Project Manager.

The third part of the library is a set of office and machine procedures and computer programs for filing, updating, and listing the program modules, dummy stubs, and test data during development. There may also be other special service programs and procedures, such as for running the program or parts of the program in a controlled environment during checkout, for generating and maintaining status reports, schedules, tier charts, or other management information, for documenting the program or tests, for accumulating development statistics, for automatic auditing of all documentation against format standards, and for automatic cross-referencing of definition requirements, design specifications and code listings.

Insofar as is practical, all elements of the SDL will be maintained in a machine readable form. Regardless of form, however, only the Interface Control Engineer is permitted to make any changes in the library elements, and if such changes pertain to elements under project configuration control, then, only under direction from the Project Manager. In larger projects the Interface Control Engineer may be assisted by a librarian with some secretarial skills, or by other personnel to aid in effecting the "public programming" practices.

Submissions to the SDL are made to the Interface Control Engineer in one of several ways: as "signed-off", completed new modules; as incremental, approved changes to existing modules, or reapproved versions of modules already extant in the SDL; or as "working level" elements, such as "look ahead" module designs, stubs, decision tables, etc.

The Interface Control Engineer also has the responsibility of all program "builds"; that is, the linking together of program elements (modules and dummy stubs) in preparation for testing, as requested by the Software Test Engineer, and as defined in the Software Test plan.

A full set of typical requirements for the SDL may be found in [84].

10.4.2 Software Configuration Management

The key to the success of the SDL is bound to its effectiveness as a design-control facility. The techniques for accepting and revising elements in the SDL should recognize that changes are of varying depth, such as:

- Changes that can be made (temporarily) on existing documentation without making it illegible or unintelligible.

- Additions that amplify, clarify, or augment existing documentation without making obsolete the present contents.

- Changes that are a whole or partial replacement for existing elements in the library.

Once placed under formal project configuration control, SDL elements will not be altered or modified in any way without proper documentation and approval (Figure 10-9).

During development it may not be necessary to have a rigidly documented request-analysis-response cycle for changes, unless those changes occur across program development phases (see Figure 10-5). When this is the case, it is probably important to document the change-control cycle rather carefully. Once the program or one of its documents is complete, and has been accepted into configuration control, certainly no change should be contemplated without the cycle.

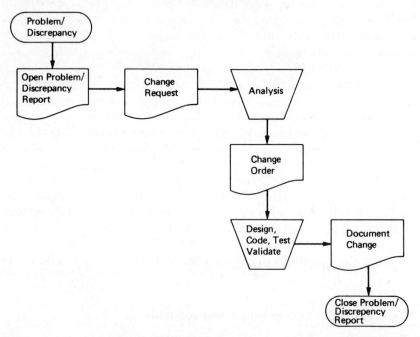

Figure 10-9. The change-control cycle in response to a problem or discrepancy affecting SDL elements under configuration control

The requirement for a formal change may be established by one of the following [85]:

- An open discrepancy or problem report.

- A request from the designer of an interfacing module.

- A change requested by the customer or design review board.

- A problem developed by changing an interfacing program module.

- A valid improvement in the functioning of a program module.

All changes during development must be authorized by, and then approved by the Project Manager.

Let me assume, for illustrative purposes, that the SSD will be typewritten documents with human-drafted graphics and flowcharts, and that the coding for program modules and dummy stubs lie in SDL computer files.

All original typewritten and drafted pages of documents accepted will be dated. Every striped module design will contain, probably on its flowchart, a signature block, such as:

Designed by	
Verified by	
Audited by	
Accepted by	

in which are entered corroborative testaments that the design is correct and adheres to design and documentation standards (or to specific waivers of these standards). Other document items, such as I/O formats, complex data structures, decision tables, core maps, etc., may exhibit similar sign-offs.

When all signatures have been affixed, the Interface Control Engineer enters the module design documentation into the SSD and logs that event into the project notebook. He also marks this event and enters any striped submodules of that module on the tier diagram (see Section 5.1.4).

Any changes to the SSD thereafter must be submitted in writing to the Project Manager as "red-lined" corrections or complete new modules, to which are attached the requirements and analysis of the change. Changes in the narrative of a clarifying or amplifying nature, when approved, cause redating of the affected pages; changes affecting the module more drastically require the reinitiation of the signature block procedure. The outdated items along with any attachments are retained in the project change-control archives.

Additions or changes in other project-controlled documents and in the code follow similar procedures.

The SDL should also possess copies of all "working level" program modules and documentation produced as a part of "look-ahead" efforts. These may be distributed by the Interface Control Engineer, but for information only. Other team members, therefore, must make no assumptions concerning the state of completion of working-level interfaces until they have been accepted into formal project configuration management control. Changes in working elements may be made at the discretion of the originating individual, but the Interface Control Engineer must be notified.

It is literally imperative, in the interests of maintaining management visibility into team activity and progress, to have regular submissions and updates of all "look-ahead" or other working-level material into the SDL. This fact has been recognized for some time by the CPT adherents [80], who observe and enforce its directive as a means to turn "private art into public practice". The surveillance of a constantly changing, evolving program is apt to be difficult without keeping all such data bases in computer files, to be accessed and updated in a controlled way. I shall discuss this automation in Chapter 17, A Standard Software Production System.

10.5 MANAGING THE SOFTWARE DEVELOPMENT

Managing a software development is largely keyed to defining major project milestones, planning work and allocating resources to achieve them in a timely manner, supervision of the team, monitoring its progress, and enforcing standards. Much of the Project Manager's ability to function effectively stems from his having visibility into the project, its capabilities and its working environment, as well as into the developing software, its problem areas, its state of completion, and its rate of progress. On this visibility is based any needed adjustments to the manpower plan, the financial plan, and the project schedule.

10.5.1 Planning

There is a definite distinction between *planning* activities and *doing* activities. Specifically, planning is a study-type function. It implies gathering information and identifying decision-alternatives at a level that does not impact current status, but may impact future doing and planning activities. The magnitude of a planning activity should probably be roughly proportioned to the risk or exposure associated with the individual project [22]. The larger the risk, the greater the time, investment, and detail that should be devoted to planning. But even this is not an iron-clad rule.

The scope of planning should include such things as work flow, project organization, project priorities, responsibility flow, resource management, configuration management, quality assurance, and the mechanics of program development, especially the mechanical aspects of installing, integrating, and testing the software. Good contingency planning can avert many work stoppages due to unforeseen circumstances.

Some of the planning will be design-dependent. In these cases, a portion of the design must be done to assign programming responsibilities or to determine the resource requirements.

The documentation of planning information will probably be scrutinized by upper management and criticized by subordinates more than any other documentation in the project. It is sometimes, thus, very advantageous to have the implementation planning documentation include excerptable material directly suitable for summary presentation to management (for example, in the form of overhead projector slides). In this way, separate material for the plan and for management review need not be generated.

10.5.2 Resources

The development resources include manpower, budget, hardware environment, software environment, system loading and schedule, and the program deadline. *Doing* the management of these resources is different than *planning* for their management. Doing requires being able to come up with dollar-amounts and man-months of effort. It requires the preparation of reports and documents as spelled out in the plan, and the phased allocation of resources among the team and within the development environment.

Hopefully, resource management proceeds according to the plan. Work-arounds (exceptions to the established plan) should be discouraged; rather, any unplanned arrangements should be incorporated into the plan, so that, in the end, the final plan agrees with the final methods actually used. In future projects, similar plans are apt to be developed from policies gathered across many projects. As long as work-arounds are permitted without eventually producing a corresponding change in policy, there will be little improvement in the development policies, and no way of assessing whether the established policies will actually work or will always require *ad hoc* exceptions to bail a project out of difficulties.

10.5.3 Scheduling and Cost-Estimation

Developing an accurate initial schedule or cost estimate in the early stages of a project is very difficult. It requires an *a priori* knowledge of the size of the task, the productivity of the team, the phasing of activities in interfacing projects, and a myriad of intangible other premature estimations. Probably software tasks are intrinsically no harder to schedule or cost out than hardware tasks are, when approached using the top-down discipline. Perhaps the greatest unknown in accurate planning is the amount of rework that will be attributable to human inability to cope with program complexity or mid-stream redirections of effort. But a history of such development factors and statistics should be recorded, maintained, and summarized for each project to promote accuracy in future project estimates.

Optimization of a team's productivity, the ability to produce software according to a given schedule, and the accuracy of a pre-estimated budget can only come about when all the contributory factors are modelled with sufficient fidelity to permit mathematical methods to produce them. Until such models can be developed, we are stuck with more subjective, less-accurate estimating techniques.

One method with some merit is performing a preliminary design study prior to beginning the formal top-down, concurrently documented and coded program development discussed earlier. This study consists of a look-ahead, say as hand-drawn flowcharts and tables (with little, if any supporting narrative), through the complete design. The purpose of this preliminary architectural design is to size the entire coming effort and to identify work tasks in order that a work breakdown structure, schedule, and cost estimate can be generated.

The preliminary design need not be detailed nor reflect a microscopically correct program, as long as the architecture is sound and as long as it sizes the program to be written within, say, an accuracy goal of 10%. The work breakdown structure should typically be detailed to tasks no longer than 2–3 manweeks each.

Figure 10-10 shows the skeleton of a software development schedule. The inverted deltas indicate milestones to be estimated; they also are probably the dates of reviews. The figure shows that work on the architectural design does not begin until the program justification (in the SRD) is complete and has been approved. The detailed functional requirements (FRD) and the program specification effort (incorporated in the SSD) have been shown to begin a little later, with the view that work can begin on top-level functional definitions, data-flow diagrams,

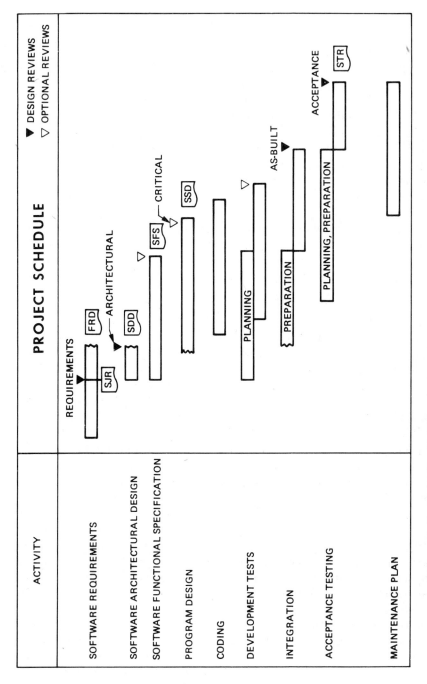

Figure 10-10. Project schedule showing phased concurrency in development activities

flowcharts, and data structures before the full functional detail is put into the SFS. Coding, testing, and so forth, follow as I have previously described.

I have indicated in the schedule that software development begins when the Software Justification Report has been approved. That need not necessarily be the case. I am assuming here that the approving authority for committing manpower, funding, and other development resources does not need as rigorous a set of technical requirements to allocate resources as the oncoming development activity does. The SRD activity may thus extend beyond the first approval stage, may perhaps be written in concert with development personnel and during other developmental activities, and may result in a detailed set of functional requirements, analyses, tradeoffs, and plans.

The development of a maintenance plan and documentation for maintenance is shown on the schedule, and may be part of the development project. Its presence on the schedule signifies that there will probably be activity in the operations area concurrent with the final phases of the software development.

In scheduling a project it is useful to remember that more software projects have gone awry for lack of calendar time than for all other causes combined [86]. The reasons for this effect are primarily related to our poorly developed techniques for estimating; all programmers seem to be optimists and estimate on the unvoiced assumption that "all will go well." The truth is that, whatever can go wrong, will, unless serious precautions are taken.

Furthermore, most estimating practices confuse effort with progress, tacitly assuming that men and months are interchangeable; whereas I showed in Section 10.1 that this interchangeability is clearly not the case. Intercommunication among individuals and other non-production activities must be inserted into the equation.

Because large projects extend sometimes over a few (or many) years, one must anticipate and account for manpower turnover, and a corresponding lengthening of development time for training of new personnel and integrating them into the team structure.

Estimating later milestones during the SRD preparation period may thus require a lot of insight and padded judgement. Once the project proper has begun, however, incremental schedules and costs are more easily estimated. Once the architecture and work breakdown structure are established, each development phase consists of a precise, known number of modules and dummy stubs to be designed, coded, tested, and documented. The program tier diagram (the module hierarchy tree) is a very useful aid in defining, scheduling, and monitoring the project phases. Section 10.5.6 gives more details on the use of the program tier chart as a progress management tool.

Some standard techniques are also available for more detailed schedule planning, such as critical-path-methods, PERT, PERT/time, PERT/cost, and machine-processed scheduling programs. I refer the reader interested in such topics to the DOD/NASA guide [87] for further details.

10.5.4 Reporting System

Regular reporting in the form of activity and progress reports has long been the practice of a good engineering discipline. Good software engineering is no different in this respect. Channels must be available for problem and discrepancy reporting, engineering change requests, engineering change authorization, test reports, progress and status reports, new technology reports, management reports, and so on.

During development, reporting is primarily oriented toward providing accurate and worthwhile media for developing effective management visibility, for communicating the results of technical decisions, for recording the development history, and for displaying the current level of program completion.

10.5.5 Documentation

Job specialization, increasing hardware complexity, the proliferation of programming languages, and the wider range of programming applications has created a crucial communication problem; a greater volume of information of higher complexity passes among growing numbers of people of dissimilar backgrounds. In such an environment, some attempt must be made to rationalize the information flow in the form of documentation. A state of anarchy (or near anarchy) would result if each individual were allowed to decide what, if anything, would be recorded, and when. Standardized documentation, in conjunction with an established system of checkpoints, is a major aid to project control. Standards for documentation must include provisions for workability, accuracy, legibility, and completeness. Work should not be allowed to proceed to subsequent tasks until a review of the documentation is satisfactory.

If documentation is in serious default, my recommendation is simple: stop all activities not related to documentation, and bring documentation up to acceptable standards. Management of software is virtually impossible without quality documentation.

Even if standards have been set, a big question is "What documents are to be produced, and what is the level of detail in each?" I have principally addressed in this work only that documentation actually needed to develop a program. But other documents in a project are obviously required, such as a management plan, operations manuals, standards manuals, test procedures, user guides, SDL procedures, etc.

The only guideline I can give is simply to eliminate repetitive, high-cost, low-use program documentation. In the development process, this strategy provides, as final program documentation, only the Software Functional Specification (SFS), the Programming Specification (PS), and program listings. For the strategy to work, these must constantly be kept current through change control. As for the other forms of documentation in support of this minimum and for the users of the programs, I leave such decisions as prerogatives of the individual organization, project, or customer requirements.

One reason I have stressed documentation requirements for program development is that I believe such documentation provides the primary means for cost-effective program maintenance. I vigorously oppose the practice wherein software is maintained only at the code and operator manual level, without keeping the supporting design-level documents up-to-date. Such practices trace their origins to earlier days of preparing research programs for testing purposes. It is not acceptable today in the development of operational programs having reasonable lifetimes of more than a few months. Continuing the practice of maintaining code and operating manuals only will result in continuing high costs for both development and maintenance [88].

Insofar as is practical, all documentation and data bases used for report generation and subject to change control or frequent modification should be kept in computer files. Correlated data bases should be cross referenced so that all side effects are visible and can be checked out at each update.

The appendices provide suggested topical outlines for many documents possibly produced during the development process. Other guidelines for format and preparation of the material to be included appear in subsequent chapters of this monograph.

10.5.6 Monitoring Progress

Monitoring a development team's progress is based on visibility; visibility is keyed to reporting, documentation, design review, and supervision. Competent monitoring of the technical aspects of a development is an absolute necessity. When not monitored, a team may produce inefficient code or program parts that interface improperly or inefficiently with each other. Fortunately, the top-down, hierarchic, modular approach puts technical visibility within the grasp of the Project Manager, as well as each of the other members of the team.

I gave certain technical monitoring procedures earlier in this chapter as a means for promoting program correctness. These had to do with concurring opinions and audits of the design, coding, and testing activities. Another means of technical monitoring is provided by regular development reviews. I will give guidelines for such reviews in a later section of this chapter.

In Section 5.1.4, I have referred to the use of tier charts as a management tool for monitoring team progress. Figure 10-11 shows a typical partial tier chart for a program, in this case, the MBASIC language processor. the chart lists the various modules, the tier to which they belong, and their state of completion; "S" stands for "stub", "P" for "preliminary", and "*" stands for "completed". An asterisk in the "Page of Next Tier" column indicates that there is no further expansion of that module. Eventually, all entries in the final column contain either a page link or asterisk—no blanks.

A "P" in the "Design" column indicates that a preliminary version was submitted into the project; the asterisk was added later when the design was completed. An "S" in this column indicates that a formal dummy stub was designed to test the module it plugs into; an "S" in the "code" column indicates the stub was actually coded. An "S" in the "Test" column shows that the module was tested using dummy stubs at the next tier, and a "*" in this column shows that the tests were completed using the actual completed code at the next tier.

Other designators may also be useful in these columns to monitor progress. For example, "L" for "look-ahead", "A" for "audited", "C" for "concurred", and "R" for "returned for rework".

The "Phase" column is useful in identifying which modules belong to which scheduled milestones. In the example shown, all of tiers 1 and 2 comprised the first project phase, and all of tier 3, the next phase. The chart shows that design and coding of Phase 1 is complete, but Phase 1 testing awaits the delivery of dummy stubs at tier 3. The main program has been tested using the actual code at tier 2 and dummy stubs at tier 3.

The tier chart helps to identify future phases of development, and relates the state of completion of current phases. It can be used to allocate work,

							Page 1 of 22
							MBASIC/1

TIER CHART

Tier	Module Number	Module Name	Phase	Design	Code	Test	Page of Next Tier
1	1.	MBASIC	1	P*	*	*	1
2	2.	SYSUP	1	P*	*	S	1
	U1.	USWAP	1	P*	*		1
	3.	SYSIZL	1	P*	*		1
	4.	PARSE	1	P*	*		2
	5.	RUNIZL	1	P*	*		2
	6.	RUN	1	P*	*		3
	7.	BATCHC	1	P*	*		3
	8.	BATCHR	1	P*	*		3
	9.	EXIT	1	P*	*		3
2	U2.	IZCORE	2	P*	S		4
	U3.	IPSWRD	2	P*	S		4
	2.5.	NOPWD	2	P*	S*		*
	U4.	FILDIR	2	SP*	S		*
	2.8	BADPWD	2	P*	S*		*
	E1.	SWAP SYSTEM	2	P*	S		*
	U1.7	SAVE RUN	2	P*	S		
	U1.8	SET PARSE	2	P*	S		
	U1.9.	SET RUNIZL	2	P*	S		
	U1.10.	SET RUN	2	P*	S		
	U5.	ADJSEG	2	P	S		
	U6.	IZIO	2	P	S		
	3.3.	NTINIT	2	P	S		
	3.4.	IZTBL	2	P	S		
	•	•	•	•	•	•	•
	•	•	•	•	•	•	•
	•	•	•	•	•	•	•

Figure 10-11. A tier chart for the MBASIC Program

and it can serve as an aid in estimating schedules and production costs. If errors are found in modules at a given tier, the extent of rework can often be sized by looking at the chart.

The figure shows the chart as if it were a page of documentation; in actuality the tiered data base best resides within the computer, which then accesses the information at regular intervals for update and status reporting.

10.5.7 Project Supervision

The methodology described in preceding pages of this monograph provides a basic level of technical control over software development and testing. The Project Manager has visibility into current status by way of the project notebook and the Software Development Library, and thereby, has efficient tools to balance resources and schedule throughout the project.

My first rule for supervising a software development is ruthless enforcement of project standards, especially those relating to documentation requirements. Deviations from standards should be permitted on a case-by-case basis only, and written waivers should be entered into the project notebook or other suitable archive.

My second rule for software development supervision is close technical leadership in the program development. Proper project supervision lies in technical and managerial proficiency, as well as the tools, methods, and development environment provided for the team. There is no substitute for competent leadership, sound judgement, and decisive action.

There may be vagueness in a software development plan for example, concerning how conflicting requirements are to be resolved when they are not specifically spelled out in a list of competing characteristics. There also may be no statement defining what freedom the development team has in interpreting requirements. It is the prerogative, then, of supervision either to solicit such judgements from proper authority, or to analyze and decide on the basis of its own sound technical judgement, the proper course of action.

As I indicated earlier in this chapter, the place for the highest levels of skills is at the top. A supervisor with less technical skill than his subordinates not only fails to give responsible leadership, but risks the quality of the software by making incompetent decisions. Subordinates soon tend to become demoralized and non-productive.

Fortunately, supervisorial skills can be taught to technically adept personnel, perhaps more readily than supervisors seem to find time to learn new technical skills. In either case, it seems to me that organizations need to pursue training programs and encourage continued education for persons in supervisory roles, as well as in the more junior positions.

10.6 DESIGN AND PROGRESS REVIEWS

A series of reviews and audits must be scheduled at meaningful points during the development of a piece of software to permit assessment and concurrence with its progress and status. Adequate evaluation of the development process generally takes place if these reviews focus on functional requirements and design during early development, and on performance and configuration verification during later development.

Informal reviews may be held on an *ad hoc* basis as an effective method for monitoring progress and supervising development. Formal reviews are principally system, configuration, and management oriented, although some level of technical detail needs to be present. Each such review should not be considered complete until all action items assigned by the reviewing board have been closed. It may be proper to suspend certain future phases of activity until all review criteria can be met.

I must assume that some authority empanels the formal review board, appoints its chairman, and dictates to what level their recommendations and action items are obligatory. The review board chairman then is responsible for scheduling the reviews, notifying attendees, and for the generation and distribution of the review minutes. The chairman reports to the convening authority the review board findings and notifies him when all assigned action items have been cleared. If certain phases of the project had been suspended, the convening authority may then direct their reactivation.

In what follows, I shall address the conduct and content of the four reviews shown in Figure 10-10. The discussion of each contains a set of criteria to be met by the presentors, the action solicited from the board, and the procedures to follow. I presume, in all cases, that the board has areas of competence matching the presentation review criteria.

10.6.1 The Requirements Review

The first review I have shown is that acting on the software justification. In Chapter 3, I defined the software justification as that collection of information created to obtain management approval to proceed with the software development. An embryo Software Requirements Document (SRD) containing this justification should be prepared and available to the review panel; it should fulfill the criteria given in Section 3.3.

The presentors are asked to perform the following:

a. Establish the need or "market potential" for the program and identify the objectives of the program, its user and system environment, the configuration needed for its operation, the resources required for its support, and the advantages and disadvantages in the service it provides.

b. Demonstrate that the remaining developmental activities may proceed under a reasonable assurance that major revision of technical and management objectives will not be necessary.

c. Present evidence that the program and its use are feasible with respect to technical considerations, manpower, schedule, and developmental costs.

d. Provide variance estimates or bounds for all planned resources to be expended.

e. Demonstrate that the SRD has been documented in accordance with the content adequacy criteria given in Section 3.3 (and Chapter 11).

The review board action solicited by the presentation is authorization to proceed with the software development plan- and with the software functional definition and design definition activities. If these activities are to be accomplished in-house, formal work directives will need to be issued and project teams established. If these activities are to be accommodated via an external contract, then procurement procedures will need to be initiated.

10.6.2 Architectural Design Review

The second review shown is the Architectural Design Review, and occurs after the architectural design, but before the completion of the detailed software functional specification, although some projects may well elect not to begin program design until the complete detail of the program technical functional definition has also been reviewed and approved.

The architectural review can take place at the completion of the complete look-ahead design and the detailed work breakdown structure (see Section 10.5.3). The review thus scrutinizes the embryonic program Software Design Definition and Functional Specification Documents at a point where they vividly describe the basic structure of the software and the framework for the remaining software implementation. This review also probes the reasoning that went into that material.

The presentors are asked to perform the following tasks:

a. Present the software development plan, which contains updated and detailed project manpower, schedule, and development cost estimates, along with refined variance estimates for these quantities (10% goal). Include an implementation plan, which indicates work priorities and how the implementation process accommodates this priority ranking, including time phasing, if appropriate. Demonstrate that the work breakdown has tasks small enough to facilitate supervision and review by management to determine progress relative to the plan.

b. Present a summary of project standards.

c. Present the program hierarchic functional definition and design architecture, using data-flow diagrams, flowcharts, and explanatory narrative. Show that the program definition and design architecture are technically feasible and compatible and responsive to the software functional requirements. Provide sufficient information so that the end user may assess the appropriateness of user interactions and I/O formats. Identify all amendments to the original SRD, and summarize their impact on the development.

d. Identify satisfactory progress status monitors to be in effect during the final detailed design phase.

e. Provide evidence that the architectural design and documentation are adequate for the later detailed design and implementation, without significant conflicts being likely.

f. Provide the Software Design Definition (SDD) and perhaps the preliminary current version of the embryonic Software Specification Document (SSD) to the review board, and show that these adhere to project standards and are adequate by the criteria given in Sections 3.4 and 4.2.3.

g. Present implementation testing criteria, plans, and procedures, and show that these will fulfill requirements to establish program correctness.

h. Present the preliminary software integration plan if the software is being developed in an environment other than that to be used in operations.

i. Identify required software support and external program interfaces, and evaluate their impact on software delivery.

j. Identify the degree to which the architectural design activity necessitated backup coding and checkout. If minimum levels had been established, state whether this minimum level was exceeded.

The actions sought from the review board are concurrence in the adequacy of the software development in principle and authorization to pursue the development according to the costs and resources and schedule presented. Acceptance by the board signals the initiation of installation and acceptance planning, and authorizes the continuation of definition, design, coding, and checkout under the standards presented.

10.6.3 Critical or "As-Built Design" Software Review

The Critical Review concludes the specification phase of the software development. Obviously, the entire set of detailed flowcharts, or their equivalent, cannot be reviewed in a formal way by the board in any reasonable time. Besides, concurring opinions and audits have taken place for each module, so this level of technical detail is not warranted in the review. Instead, the presentors are asked to provide to the review board the following:

a. Evidence that the design is complete. All internal modules are present. All external modules that currently exist satisfy stub interfaces. All external modules yet to be developed have specific and definitive interfaces. (An audit, plus a randomly chosen sample walk-through of the tier chart and sample examinations of final stubs of the three above type should suffice.)

b. Evidence that all technical requirements have been satisfied. Identify all exceptions or remaining problems, and the disposition of such items relative to liens on delivery.

c. A management report that portrays the team performance in relation to the software development plan. All deviations from the previously presented plan and updated costs, schedules, and manpower should be compared with the initial plan. The software development plan for remaining tasks should also be presented.

d. A summary of all waivers from project standards and any new standards adopted, or old ones amended or deleted, since the last review.

e. A status report on the concurrent coding and checkout efforts, along with a report on the extent to which the design has been verified. Preliminary performance measures and projections for the completed program are in order.

f. The completed SSD, with a QA audit that attests to its completeness and adherence to standards. The presentors should then redemonstrate that these documents conform to the criteria given in Sections 3.4 and 4.2.3.

g. Status reports on integration, acceptance testing, and QA activities.

The action solicited from the board is concurrence that the design meets project objectives and fulfills the SRD, that the development plan is adequate for the tasks remaining, and that exceptions and liens are either acceptable as presented or will be disposed of before delivery. Acceptance by the board constitutes an approval to continue the project in the way presented.

10.6.4 Acceptance Review

The final review shown in Figure 10-10 is the Acceptance Review, which normally signals the end of the development project. This review is primarily held to certify that the program performs within acceptable limits of specified behavior.

The presentors are asked to provide the following for review-board approval:

a. An analysis of the program performance requirements, a set of acceptance criteria relative to these requirements, and the means used to validate the measured performance relative to the given acceptance criteria (the Acceptance Test Plan).

b. Evidence that measured performance satisfies acceptance criteria (the Software Test Report).

c. Final SSD, Software Test Report, and annotated code listings, all approved by a QA audit for completeness and conformity with project standards.

d. A final project management report, delineating total manpower, schedule, and development cost figures. These should be broken down into detailed resources expended in definition, design, coding, checkout, testing, integration, and documentation areas.

Approval by the board is the authority to initiate delivery procedures by which the program will be put into operation.

10.7 EVALUATION OF THE SOFTWARE AND DEVELOPMENT TEAM

The review boards and upper management are charged with responsible evaluations of tangible quantities having sometimes intangible measures of quality. For example, a working program, even if it meets its acceptance criteria, may perhaps not be judged a "good" design. Whether the design is "good" or "bad" is rather subjective, sometimes only a matter of broad personal judgement on the part of a reviewer. The top-down, structured, modular, hierarchic approach has provided the reviewer with some visibility into the product allowing him to make a more conscientious judgement. But still, in the end, the judgement may not be rigorously defensible, only a matter of professional, hopefully expert, opinion.

To make a responsible evaluation, the reviewers need to agree on a set of criteria for judging program quality and for evaluating the performance of its developers. Then they may rate the software and the development team against these, based on evidence supplied at the review. The reviewers also need to agree on how their individual scores are to be combined into final scores and the significance attached to such scores.

To be fair to the developers, these criteria should stem from, or be stated in, the SRD, or established at the outset of the project, or reflect an accepted organizational or professional standard. That way, the developers and the program are being graded relative to stated objectives, rather than on *ex post facto* judgements: "the way things should have been done".

I spoke in Chapter 4 to the subject of defining, and then ranking competing characteristics in a program development in order of first- and second-order dominances. The same technique can be used to aid in defining and ranking criteria for the development team effort. These rankings can lead to weights for combining scores relative to each of the written-down criteria linearly into overall grades. An interactive dominance-ranking program and a project- grading program to aid in making these processes more automatic and more standardized appears in [89].

10.8 SUMMARY

Software development team productivity depends on many intangible aspects of the programming art. A survey [83] made among "programming managers and experts in programming management" indicated, in the consensus of its participants, that the greatest positive correlative effect on productivity was quality external documentation (documentation generated prior to programmer task assignment), the availability of programmer tools, and programmer experience. The use of structured programming and the complexity of application were judged not to affect productivity very much at all. Whether or not program size affects productivity was shown to be a very controversial issue, and no consensus appeared at all relative to programming management experience on the part of a Project Manager.

Why, then, has the present chapter been so concerned with organizational and managerial procedures, and why has the whole work pushed structured methodology so hard? Because I believe that, while treated as individual factors, the organizational, managerial, and technical disciplines may not contribute to productivity as significantly as do some other single factors, nevertheless, when these are merged into a solid, unified discipline, the potential contribution is as great as any of the variables surveyed.

The organizational approach I have discussed places interfaces along lines of required project documentation and expounds the use of corroborative collaboration among team members as a method to find errors, improve program quality, train junior team members, and test the adequacy of the documentation produced. I have given outlines for material to be presented in reviews to further these goals.

The remainder of this monograph consists of material that details the methods presented (or indicated) in these first ten chapters as "rules", or standards to be applied during a software development.

Good programming does not result from preaching generalities, as I have been doing up to this point. Good programming comes from seeing, over and over, how real programs can be improved by the application of sound principles of good practice and a little common sense.

Problems for Chapter 10

10-1 Replot Figure 10-1 to depict team production rate R as a function of the number of workers. Compare with Figure 10-2, and discuss the differences.

10-2 Develop a formula for team productivity in terms of lines delivered per dollar (wages and salary only) for the software development team in Section 10.2. Use individual salaries and productivity indices, and determine a way to find the highest team productivity.

10-3 Assume that a coder coding a correct design from a specification produces L lines of code, in which a certain fraction, f, are faulty. Some of these, a factor of q of the faulty lines, are caught by a peer checking the code. These Lfq lines are returned to the coder for recoding, whereupon the cycle repeats. Assume errors uncaught in one cycle will not be caught in the next cycle. Prove that the total number of lines generated code is

$$L_{total} = \frac{L}{1 - fq}$$

$$\approx \frac{L}{1 - f} \qquad \text{if } q \approx 1$$

(only L of which are retained). Prove the number of remaining errors in the code is

$$\# \text{ errors} = \frac{Lf(1 - q)}{1 - fq}$$

Next, suppose that the program is run, and tests find a fraction Q of these errors. These lines are returned to the coder for correction, whereupon the coding cycle starts all over. Show that the grand total number of lines coded and the number of remaining undetected errors are

$$L_{gr. tot.} = \frac{L}{1 - fq - Qf(1 - q)}$$

$$\approx \frac{L}{1 - f} \qquad \text{if } q \approx 1$$

$$\# \text{ errors} = \frac{Lf(1 - q)(1 - Q)}{1 - fq - Qf(1 - q)}$$

$$\approx \frac{Lf(1 - q)(1 - Q)}{1 - f} \qquad \text{if } q \approx 1$$

10-4 Design and flowchart a structured program to maintain the tier chart of a program as outlined in Section 10.5.6. Include the capability to update and query the data base for number of modules identified, designed, coded, tested, completed, by phase, etc.

REFERENCES

1. NASA Guide, *Computer Program Documentation Guidelines*, NHB 2411.1, National Aeronautics and Space Administration, Washington, DC, July 1971.

2. *Computer Program Systems for ADP Management: Documentation Standards*, NASA X-502-70-157, Goddard Space Flight Center, Greenbelt, MD, Dec. 1969.

3. Comella, P. A., *Computer Software Documentation*, NASA TM X-66161, Goddard Space Flight Center, Greenbelt, MD, Jan. 1973.

4. Boehm, B. W., "Software and Its Impact: A Quantitative Assessment," *Datamation*, Vol. 19, No. 5, May 1973.

5. Baker, F. T., "Structured Programming in a Production Programming Environment," in *IEEE Trans. on Software Engr.*, Vol. SE-1, No. 2, pp. 241–252, June 1975.

6. Dijkstra, E. W., "The Structure of the THE Multiprogramming System," *Commun. ACM*, pp. 341–356, May 1968.

7. *American National Standard Vocabulary for Information Processing*, ANSI-X3.12-1970, American National Standards Institute, Inc., NY, Feb. 18, 1970.

8. *American National Standard Flowchart Symbols and Their Usage in Information Processing*, ANSI-X3.5-1970, American National Standards Institute, Inc., NY, Sept. 1, 1970.

9. Robert, D. C., "File Organization Techniques," *Advances in Computers*, Vol. 12, Academic Press, NY, 1972.

10. Hoare, C. A. R., "Notes on Data Structuring," *Structured Programming*, Academic Press, NY, pp. 83–174, 1972.

11. *Webster's New Collegiate Dictionary*, G. and C. Merriam Co., Publishers, Springfield, MA, 1961 Edition.

12. Mills, H. D., "Mathematical Foundations for Structured Programming," IBM Document FSC72-6012, Federal Systems Div., IBM Corp., Gaithersburg, MD, Feb. 1972.

13. Royce, W. W., "Managing the Development of Large Software Systems: Concepts and Techniques," Western Electronics Conference (Westcon), Hollywood Park, CA, Aug. 1970.

14. Strunk, W., and White, E. B., *The Elements of Style*, MacMillan Co., NY, 1959.

15. *Preparation of Software Requirements Documents*, DSN Standard Practice 810-16, Jet Propulsion Laboratory, Pasadena, CA, Dec. 15, 1975.

16. Einhorn, M., "Programming, Documentation, and Scheduling," Class project, West Coast University (otherwise unpublished).

17. Wynne, D., "Writing Specifications for Programs," *Inst. and Contr.*, pp. 62–63, Oct. 1973.

18. Parnas, D. L., "A Technique for Software Module Specification with Examples," *Commun. ACM*, Vol. 15, No. 5, pp. 330–336, May 1972.

19. Walsh, D., *A Guide for Software Documentation*, Advanced Computer Techniques Corp., 437 Madison Ave., NY 10022, 1969.

20. Gray, M., and Landon, K., *Documentation Standards*, Brandon/ Systems Press, Inc., NY, 1969.

21. Buxton, J. N., Randell, B., *et al.*, *Software Engineering Techniques*, Report on a Conference sponsored by the NATO Science Committee, Rome, Italy, p. 12, Oct. 27–31, 1969 (available through Scientific Affairs Division, NATO, Brussels 39, Belgium).

22. Shaw, J. C., and Atkins, W., *Managing Computer System Projects*, McGraw-Hill Book Co., NY, 1970.

23. Meyers, G. J., *Composite Design: The Design of Modular Programs*, Technical Report TR00.2406, IBM, Poughkeepsie, NY, Jan. 29, 1973.

24. Dijkstra, E. W., "Notes on Structured Programming," in *Structured Programming*, Academic Press, NY, 1972.

25. Wirth, N., "On Multiprogramming, Machine Coding, and Computer Organization", *Commun. ACM*, Vol. 12, No. 9, pp. 489–498, Sept. 1969.

26. Donovan, J. J., *Systems Programming*, McGraw Hill Book Co., NY, pp. 265–348, 1972.

27. Knuth, D. E., *The Art of Computer Programming, Fundamental Algorithms*, Vol. I, Addison-Wesley Publishing Co., Reading, MA, pp. 258–268, 1969.

28. Constantine, L. L., *Fundamentals of Program Design*, Prentice-Hall, Inc., Edgewood Cliffs, NJ, 1976.

29. Stevens, W. P., *et al.*, "Structured Design," *IBM Systems Journal*, No. 2., pp. 115–139, 1974.

30. Aho, A. V., and Ullman, J. D., *The Theory of Parsing, Translation, and Compiling*, Vol. II, Prentice-Hall, Inc., Edgewood Cliffs, NJ, pp. 791–807, 1973.

31. Rich, R. P., *Internal Sorting Methods Illustrated with PL/1 Programs*, Prentice-Hall Inc., Edgewood Cliffs, NJ, 1972.

32. Knuth, D. E., *The Art of Computer Programming, Fundamental Algorithms*, Vol. I, Addison-Wesley Publishing Co., Reading, MA, pp. 315–328, 1969.

33. Aho, A. V., and Ullman, J. D., *The Theory of Parsing, Translation, and Compiling*, Vol. I, Prentice-Hall Inc., Edgewood Cliffs, NJ, 1973.

34. Dijkstra, E. W., "A Constructive Approach to the Problem of Program Correctness," *BIT*, Vol. 8, No. 3, pp. 174–186, 1968.

35. Dijkstra, E. W., "Structured Programming," *Software Engineering Techniques*, NATO Science Committee, Edited by J. N. Burton, and B. Randall, pp. 88–93, 1969.

36. Böhm, C., and Jacopini, G., "Flow Diagrams, Turing Machines, and Languages With Only Two Formation Rules," *Commun. ACM*, Vol. 9, pp. 366–371, 1966.

37. Hoare, C. A. R., "An Axiomatic Approach to Computer Programming", *Commun. ACM*, Vol. 12, No. 10, pp. 576–583, Oct. 1969.

38. Elspas, B., *et al.*, "An Assessment of Techniques for Proving Program Correctness," *Computing Surveys*, Vol. 4, No. 2, pp. 142–145, June 1972.

39. Manna, Z., "The Correctness of Programs," *J. Comput. Sys. Sci.*, No. 3, pp. 119–127, 1969.

40. Landon, R. L., "Bibliography on Proving the Correctness of Computer Programs," *Machine Intelligence*, Vol. 5, American Elsevier Publishing Co., NY, pp. 569–579, 1970.

41. Ashcroft, E., and Manna, Z., "The Translation of 'GOTO' Programs to 'WHILE' Programs," in Proceedings of 1971 IFIP Congress, Ljubljana, Yugoslavia, August 23–28, 1971. American Elsevier Publishing Co., NY, 1972.

42. Brinch Hansen, P., *Operating System Principles*, Prentice-Hall, Inc., Edgewood Cliffs, NJ, 1973.

43. Dijkstra, E. W., "Cooperating Sequential Processes," *Technische Hogschule, Eindhoven*, 1965. Reprinted in *Programming Languages*, Edited by F. Genuys, Academic Press, NY, 1968.

44. Hoare, C. A. R., "Towards a Theory of Parallel Programming," *International Seminar on Operating System Techniques*, Belfast, Northern Ireland, Aug–Sept. 1971.

45. Brinch Hansen, P., "The Programming Language Concurrent PASCAL," in *IEEE Trans. on Software Engr.*, Vol. SE-1, No. 2, pp. 199–206, June 1975.

46. Coffman, E. G., *et al.*, "System Deadlocks," *Computing Surveys*, Vol. 3, No. 2, pp. 67–68, June 1971.

47. Perlis, A. J., "The Synthesis of Algorithmic Systems," *J. ACM*, Vol. 14, No. 1, pp. 1–9, Jan. 1967.

48. Sammet, J., "Roster of Programming Languages," *Comput. Automat.*, June 30, 1971.

49. Dahl., O. J., and Hoare, C. A. R., "Hierarchical Program Structures," *Structured Programming*, Academic Press, NY, 1972.

50. Wulf, W. A., *et al.*, *Bliss Reference Manual*, Dept. of Computer Science, Carnegie-Mellon University, Jan. 15, 1970 (Rev. Oct. 25, 1971).

51. Miller, E. F., Jr., "A Compendium of Language Extensions to Support Structured Programming," RN-42, General Research Corp., Santa Barbara, CA, Jan. 1973.

52. Basili, V. R., "SIMPL-X, A Language for Writing Structured Programs," Nat. Tech. Info. Service Report AD755-703, U. S. Dept. of Commerce, Springfield, VA, Jan. 1973.

53. Flynn, J., "SFTRAN User's Guide," Comput. Memo. 914-337, Jet Propulsion Laboratory, Pasadena, CA, July 1973.

54. Waite, W., "The Mobile Programming System STAGE2," *Commun. ACM*, Vol. 13, No. 7, pp. 415–421, July 1970. (Also in Appendix A of *Implementing Software for Non-Numeric Applications*, Prentice-Hall, Inc., 1973.)

55. *Fundamentals of MBASIC*, Vols. 1 and 2, Jet Propulsion Laboratory, Pasadena, CA, Feb. 1974.

56. *Fundamentals of MBASIC*, Vol. 1, Jet Propulsion Laboratory, Pasadena, CA, pp. 18–21, Feb. 1974.

57. Mills, H. D., "Top-Down Programming in Large Systems," *Debugging Techniques in Large Systems*, Edited by R. Rustin, Prentice-Hall, Inc., pp. 43–45, 1971.

58. Tennent, R. D., "PASQUAL: A Proposed Generalization of PASCAL," Dept. of Computing and Information Science, Queens University, Kingston, Ont., Feb. 1975.

59. Katzan, H., Jr., *Advanced Programming*, D. Van Nostrand Reinhold Co., NJ, pp. 153–163, 1970.

60. McDaniel, H., *An Introduction to Decision Logic Tables*, John Wiley and Sons, Inc., NY, 1968.

61. Pollack, S. L., *Decision Tables: Theory and Practice*, Wiley-Interscience, John Wiley and Sons, Inc., NY, 1971.

62. Chapin, N., "Parsing of Decision Tables," *Commun. ACM*, Vol. 10, No. 8, Aug. 1967.

63. *Proceedings of the Decision Table Symposium*, CODASYL System Group and Joint Users Groups of the ACM, Sept. 1962.

64. Reinwald, L. T., and Soland, R. M., "Conversion of Limited-Entry Decision Tables to Optimal Computer Programs I: Minimum Average Processing Time," *J. ACM*, Vol. 13, No. 3, July 1966, and "Conversion of Limited-Entry Decision Tables to Optimal Computer Programs II: Minimum Storage Requirement," *J. ACM*, Vol. 14, No. 4, pp. 724–755, Oct. 1967.

65. Veinott, C. G., "Programming Decision Tables in FORTRAN, COBOL, or ALGOL," *Commun. ACM*, Vol. 9, No. 1, Jan. 1966.

66. Press, L. I., "Conversion of Decision Tables to Computer Programs," *Commun. ACM*, Vol. 8, No. 6, June 1965.

67. Kirk, H. W., "Use of Decision Tables in Computer Programming," *Commun. ACM*, Vol. 8, No. 1, Jan. 1965.

68. Pollack, S. L., "Conversion of LEDT's to Computer Programs," *Commun. ACM*, Vol. 8, No. 11, pp. 677–682, Nov. 1965.

69. Shwayder, K., "Conversion of Limited Entry Decision Tables to Computer Programs—A Proposed Modification to Pollack's Algorithm," *Commun. ACM*, Vol. 14, No. 2, pp. 69–73, Feb. 1971.

70. Ganapathy, S., and Rajaraman, V., "Information Theory Applied to the Conversion of Decision Tables to Computer Programs," *Commun. ACM*, Vol. 16, No. 9, pp. 532–539, Sept. 1973.

71. Knuth, D. E., *The Art of Computer Programming, Fundamental Algorithms*, Vol. I, Addison-Wesley Publishing Co., Reading, MA, pp. 187–189, 1969.

72. King, J., "A Verifying Compiler," *Debugging Techniques in Large Systems*, Edited by R. Rustin, Prentice-Hall, Inc., Edgewood Cliffs, NJ, pp. 17–40, 1971.

73. Brown, J. R., "Practical Applications of Automated Software Tools," Paper No. 21/3 of Automatic Software Verification, *Wescon Record*, Sept. 19–22, 1972.

74. Krause, K. W., and Smith, R. W., "Optional Test Planning Through Automated Network Analysis," *IEEE Symposium on Software Reliability*, Apr. 30, 1973.

75. Brinch Hansen, P., "Testing a Multiprogramming System," Information Science Dept., California Institute of Technology, Pasadena, CA, Nov., 1972.

76. McCornock, M. D., "Midnight Musings on Real-Time Systems Development," MKM Computing, Inc., 3436 Verdugo Road, Glendale, CA 91208, Apr. 1974.

77. Mills, H. D., "On the Statistical Validation of Computer Programs," IBM Report FSC72-6015, Federal Systems Div., IBM Corp., Gaithersburg, MD, 1972.

78. Feller, W., *An Introduction to Probability Theory and Its Applications*, Vol. I, John Wiley and Sons, Inc. NY, pp. 43–45, 1950.

79. Tausworthe, R. C., "Random Numbers Generated by Linear Recurrence, Modulo 2," *Mathematics of Computation*, Vol. XIX, No. 90, pp. 201–208, April. 1965.

80. Baker, F. T., "Chief Programmer Teams: Principles and Procedures," IBM Report FSC71-5108, Federal Systems Div., Gaithersburg, MD, June 1971.

81. Boehm, B. W., *et al.*, *Software Development and Configuration Management Manual*, TRW Systems Group, Santa Monica, CA, Dec. 17, 1973.

82. Baker, F. T., and Mills, H. D., "Chief Programmer Teams," *Datamation*, Vol. 19, No. 12, pp. 58–61, Dec. 1973.

83. Scott, R. F., and Simmons, D. B., "Programmer Productivity and the Delphi Principle," *Datamation*, Vol. 20, No. 5, pp. 71–77, May 1974.

84. Luppino, F. B., and Smith, R. L., "Programming Support Library Functional Requirements," Vol. V of *Structured Programming Series*, RADC-TR-74-300, U. S. Air Force, July 25, 1974.

85. Foster, R. A., *An Introduction to Software Quality Assurance*, Space Systems Division, Lockheed Missiles and Space Co., Sunnyvale, CA, 1973.

86. Brooks, F. P., "The Mythical Man-Month," *Datamation*, Vol. 20, No. 12, pp. 45–52, Dec. 1974.

87. DOD and NASA Guide, *PERT COST*, Office of the Secretary of Defense and NASA, Washington, DC, June 1962.

88. "Improvement Needed in Documenting Computer Programs," *Report to the Congress*, B-115369, by the Comptroller General of The United States, Washington, DC, Oct. 8, 1974.

89. *Fundamentals of MBASIC, Appendices*, Vol. 2, Jet Propulsion Laboratory, Pasadena, CA, pp. A-35–49, Feb. 1974.

INDEX

*NOTE: Page numbers that appear in **boldface** type indicate the reference for the primary discussion or definition of an item.*

Examples

Diagrams